ELECTORAL POLITICS

David Edgeworth Butler

ELECTORAL POLITICS

Edited by

DENNIS KAVANAGH

CLARENDON PRESS · OXFORD
1992

Oxford University Press, Walton Street, Oxford OX2 6DP

Oxford New York Toronto
Delhi Bombay Calcutta Madras Karachi
Petaling Jaya Singapore Hong Kong Tokyo
Nairobi Dar es Salaam Cape Town
Melbourne Auckland
and associated companies in
Berlin Ibadan

Oxford is a trade mark of Oxford University Press

Published in the United States
by Oxford University Press, New York

British Library Cataloguing in Publication Data
Data available

Library of Congress Cataloging in Publication Data
Electoral politics / edited by Dennis Kavanagh.
[Includes bibliographical references and index.]
1. Elections. I. Kavanagh, Dennis
JF1001.E42 1992 324—dc20 92-15700
ISBN 0-19-827381-9

Typeset by Cambridge Composing (UK) Ltd
Printed and bound in
Great Britain by Bookcraft (Bath Ltd)
Midsomer Norton, Avon

Preface

THIS volume of essays is presented to David Butler on the occasion of his retirement as a Fellow of Nuffield College, Oxford, in September 1992. It is a recognition by former students, colleagues, and collaborators of his outstanding achievements in the study of elections and related topics. The contributors are drawn from Europe, the United Kingdom, and the United States. Although the chapters reflect David's different interests, the focus on issues of the electoral process provide a thematic unity. They include chapters on: electoral behaviour (Donald Stokes, and Richard Rose and Ian McAllister); the functions of elections (Hugh Berrington and Anthony King); the media and elections (David McKie and Colin Seymour-Ure); and electoral arrangements and their political consequences (Vernon Bogdanor, John Curtice, Arend Lijphart, Cornelius O'Leary, and Austin Ranney).

Thanks are due to April Pidgeon in the Department of Politics at Nottingham University for helping to put the book together under the constraints of such tight deadlines.

Dennis Kavanagh

University of Nottingham   *November 1991*

Contents

David Edgeworth Butler: A Biography

Born October 1924. Married 1962 Marilyn Evans (a Fellow of St
Hugh's College, Oxford, 1973–86; since 1986 King Edward VII
Professor of English Literature, Cambridge). Three sons.

St Paul's School, 1938–42
Lieutenant Staffs. Yeomanry 1943–5)
New College, 1943, 1945–7
BA 1947 MA 1950
Princeton University, 1947–8 (Proctor Visiting Fellow)
Nuffield College, 1949–51 (D. Phil. 1951)

Research Fellow, Nuffield College, 1951–4
Fellow 1954 (Dean and Senior Tutor, 1956–64, Domestic Bursar,
    1976–7)
Emeritus Fellow, 1992
Counsellor, Personal Assistant to H. M. Ambassador, British
    Embassy, Washington, 1955–6
Visiting Fellow or Professor
    Cornell University, 1952 and 1958
    University of California at Berkeley, 1954
    University of Illinois, 1960
    University of Michigan, 1965
    Australian National University, 1967, 1972 (also briefly in
        1969), 1974, 1975, 1977, 1980, 1983, 1984, 1986, 1987, and
        1990)
    California Institute of Technology, 1985
    University of Virginia, 1989
    Johns Hopkins University, 1992
Adjunct Scholar, American Enterprise Institute for Public Policy,
    Washington, 1978–

Honorary Doctorate, University of Paris II, 1978
Honorary Doctorate of Social Sciences, Queen's University, Belfast,
    1985
Member of the American Academy of Arts and Sciences, 1987
CBE, 1991

PUBLICATIONS

The British General Election of 1951 (1952)

The Electoral System in Britain, 1918–1951 (1953; 2nd edn., *The Electoral System in Britain since 1918* (1963))

The British General Election of 1955 (1955)

The Study of Political Behaviour (1958)

Elections Abroad (ed.) (1959)

The British General Election of 1959 (with R. Rose) (1960)

British Political Facts, 1900–1960 (with J. Freeman) (1963); 5th edn. (with A. Sloman) *1900–1979* (1980); 6th edn. (with G. Butler) *1900–1985)* (1986)

The British General Election of 1964 (with A. S. King) (1965)

The British General Election of 1966 (with A. S. King) (1966)

Political Change in Britain (with D. Stokes) (1969; 2nd edn. 1977) (awarded the Woodrow Wilson Prize by the American Political Science Association for the best work in political science published in 1969–70)

The British General Election of 1970 (with M. Pinto-Duschinsky) (1971)

The Canberra Model (1973)

The British General Election of February 1974 (with D. Kavanagh) (1974)

The British General Election of October 1974 (with D. Kavanagh) (1975)

The 1975 Referendum (with U. W. Kitzinger) (1976)

Policy and Politics (ed. with A. H. Halsey) (1978)

Coalitions in British Politics (ed.) (1978)

Referendums (ed. with A. Ranney) (1979)

The British General Election of 1979 (with D. Kavanagh) (1980)

Democracy at the Polls (ed. with A. Ranney and H. Penniman) (1981)

European Elections and British Politics (with D. Marquand) (1981)

Governing without a Majority: Dilemmas of Hung Parliaments (1983; 2nd edn., 1987)

Democracy and Elections (with V. Bogdanor) (1983)

The British General Election of 1983 (with D. Kavanagh) (1984)

A Compendium of Indian Elections (with A. Lahiri and P. Roy) (1984)

Party Strategies in Britain (with P. Jowett) (1985)

The British General Election of 1987 (with D. Kavanagh) (1988)
British Elections since 1945 (1989)
Sovereigns and Surrogates: Constitutional Heads of State in the Commonwealth (ed. D. Butler and D. A. Low) (Cambridge Commonwealth Series, 1991)
Congressional Redistricting (with B. Cain) (1991)
India Decides, 1952–1989 (with A. Lahiri and P. Roy) (1989, 2nd edn. 1991)
Electioneering (ed. with A. Ranney) (1992)
The British General Election of 1992 (with D. Kavanagh) (1992)

OTHER ACTIVITIES

Served on Council of Hansard Society in 1960s
On Open University Social Studies Board, 1964–8 and 1978–84
Elected to Executive of Political Studies Association 1983 (with responsibility for relations with Government and Parliament)
President of the Politics Association, 1984–7
Institute of Contemporary British History (Chairman of the Advisory Committee), 1985
The Constitutional Reform Centre (Member of the Advisory Committee), 1985
Vice-Chairman of Chataway (Hansard) Commission on Fair Play in Elections
Joint editor of *Electoral Studies*, 1982

1

David Butler and the
Study of Elections

David Butler's contribution to the study of elections is such that his name and the subject have become almost inseparable. He is associated with the popularization of two words—*psephology* and *swing*—although he hastens to add that he invented neither. Psephology (the study of elections) appeared in the first sentence of his first book. It was meant as a joke but developed a life of its own, and he has become the best-known practitioner of the subject. David was still an undergraduate when he developed the notion of swing as a measure of change in the fortunes of parties from one election to another. This chapter attempts an assessment of his work and presents a necessarily partial and incomplete portrait of the man.

EARLY YEARS

David Butler was born on October 1924, the youngest of four children. He was brought up in the heart of Bloomsbury and now no walk around the Euston Station area is undertaken without his reminiscing about his youthful escapades. The family history is steeped in academe, in Oxbridge, and in the humanities. His great grandfather, George, became a Fellow at Sidney Sussex College in 1794 and his grandfather, Arthur, was awarded a Fellowship at Oriel in 1853. His father, Harold Edgeworth Butler, had been a student at New College, Oxford, in 1896, and then became a New College don in 1900 before moving in 1911 to the chair in Latin at University College, London. He held the post until retirement in 1943. A grandfather on his mother's side was the distinguished London University historian, Professor A. F. Pollard. A second cousin was R. A. Butler, and another relation was the notable Professor of Economics at Oxford, Francis Ysidro Edgeworth. His aunts included Ruth Butler, a Fellow at St Anne's College, Oxford, and Violet Butler, a tutor in Economics and then head of Barnett House in Oxford, which trained social workers. The Butler family is firmly rooted in the genealogical soil of Lord Annan's intellectual aristocracy.

An interest in public affairs was weaker in David's father, the classical scholar, than his mother. Her father, A. F. Pollard, stood as a Liberal candidate for the London University seat and she rather deplored Professor Butler's indifference to the political scene. David's first memory of an election, perhaps appropriately, is waiting for his mother outside a polling booth at St Pancras in the 1931 general election.

David was educated at St Paul's School, in Hammersmith. His father and grandfather had both attended Rugby School, and David and his brother Michael (two years his senior) were both entered for the school. But Professor Butler, as a London University appointed governor at St Pauls, became convinced of the merits of day education and decided to send the boys to the school. David has fond memories of the school, not least of its failure to typecast most of its pupils. At school his interest in elections and statistics was a foretaste of what was to come. Although he had no aptitude for sport, he acquired a fascination for the Wisden Cricketers' Almanac and was scorer for the school cricket team. A middle-ranking student until the age of 12, he then developed rapidly, and entered the classics eighth form largely because, with a classics don father, he was expected to. But his real love was history—political history—and he soon moved to that. Two masters left an impression on him: the High Master, Walter Oakeshott, later Headmaster of Winchester and then Rector of Lincoln College, who was a man of great wisdom and integrity, and Eynon Smith, who taught ideas by a Socratic method, encouraging his students to question and argue.

David went to New College, Oxford, in January 1943 to read Politics, Philosophy, and Economics (PPE), and took most of his papers in Economics. After two terms he entered the army and, following Sandhurst, served as a Lieutenant in the Staffordshire Yeomans, crossing the Rhine in an amphibious tank. He was demobilized in September 1945, a year earlier than usual, 'by a clerical mistake', as he describes it. He resumed his studies and took his finals in 1947. At New College he was a contemporary of Tony Benn and Peter Blaker, now a Conservative MP. All three still remain good friends.

The Politics component in the PPE degree in the immediate post-war Oxford would now be regarded as rather old-fashioned. The study of political institutions went little beyond descriptive and historical treatment of institutions, and the range was narrow in terms both of countries (Britain, the United States, France, the Soviet Union, and the Commonwealth) and of political phenomena. At Oxford, Modern Greats was part of a 'civilizing' rather than a social science education, and was taught more in the languages of history, constitutional law, and philosophy. The American influence of behaviouralist approaches to the study of politics had little impact outside the new departments at Manchester, under W. J. M. Mackenzie, and at Keele, under S. E. Finer, and politics was just emerging as a university subject outside the LSE and Oxford. Ironically David was to play a major role in spearheading the move for more behavioural and quantitative studies in Britain. David's chosen subjects as an undergraduate took in more economics than politics and included very little philosophy. He is quick, commonsensical, and intuitive, but he does not have a theoretical cast of mind. At an Oxford University seminar in the late 1980s he recalled his hopelessness in philosophy in tutorials forty years earlier with Sir Isaiah Berlin. At his fifth philosophy tutorial in December 1945 he told an astonished Berlin, 'I can't remember which is deductive and which is inductive for more than ten minutes.' Because Butler was an ex-serviceman, Berlin was able to arrange for him to take an abbreviated course in PPE, which avoided any philosophy. Berlin boasts that he 'emancipated David from philosophy!', testimony to the failure of the tripartite PPE.

THE NUFFIELD ELECTION STUDIES

David Butler will forever be associated with the Nuffield election studies of post-war British general elections. His academic career, stretching from undergraduate study to his final years as an Oxford don, has involved him in the study of every general election

campaign from 1945 to 1992. By 1987 the Nuffield election studies
had run to thirteen volumes and nearly five thousand pages. The
first study of the 1945 election was written by the history don, R.
B. McCallum, later Master of Pembroke College, Oxford, and
Alison Readman, a research student at Nuffield College. The
origins of the series and David Butler's involvement are accidental.

McCallum was on his way to a meeting of the Nuffield College
committee in March 1945 which was to discuss proposals for
research in politics when the war ended. He was trying to think of
a proposal which would justify his membership of the committee
and had the idea of studying the forthcoming general election (after
all, the new College was supposed to study contemporary events).
The committee welcomed the idea and persuaded him to do it.
Only the previous year he had published a study of the 1918
general election, a contest which, he believed, had been widely
misunderstood for the previous twenty-five years by the superficial
though influential ('hard-faced men') account of J. M. Keynes in
his *The Economic Consequences of the Peace*. McCallum wanted
to kill at birth such myths, which quickly grew up about elections
and which could have harmful effects for public policy.

In 1966, looking back on his flash of inspiration, McCallum
wrote in a personal letter: 'I thought that when there was an
election, after the war it must be photographed *in flight*, studied
and analysed [emphasis added]. The original object was to provide
a convenient and dispassionate account of an election for future
historians, a guide to how contemporaries saw the election.' The
first authors saw the 1945 election as a historical event and wanted
to provide a document for use by future historians. Obviously,
historians of an earlier period would regard such an account of,
say, a nineteenth-century election as a priceless source. David
Butler has often quoted McCallum's hope that his work would
achieve 'the immortality of other men's footnotes'. In fact, perusal
of works on British politics will show that the Nuffield election
studies are among the most heavily cited of books.

David's New College tutor in economics, Philip Andrews, aware
of his interest in election statistics, advised him to visit R. B.
McCallum, who was preparing a study of the 1945 general
election, McCallum wanted 'some statistics for my book' and
commissioned Butler to provide them. In fact, it was Andrew Ensor
(son of R. C. K. Ensor, the historian), a junior lecturer at New

College, who gave him the idea of calculating swing at general elections. This was, he later admitted, 'the basis of everything that I subsequently did'. David wrote some tables for McCallum, who encouraged him to develop the ideas into a statistical appendix for the 1945 volume. The anthropologist Professor Mary Douglas (née Tew), then a student lodging with David's aunt—Violet Butler—remembers Miss Butler, in 1947, saying, 'You must meet my brilliant young nephew, who has devised a method of forecasting the result of general elections based on bowling averages.' The appendix not only launched his academic career but gained him the Proctor Fellowship to spend 1948 at Princeton University and study the presidential election. He still regards his visit to the United States as the most educative year of his life. He attended the party conventions, observed Truman's upset victory in the election, hitchhiked for six thousand miles around the Continent, and made many life-long friends.

He returned to England in December 1948 and was awarded a studentship at Nuffield College. He again wrote a statistical appendix for the 1950 election study, which was authored by Herbert Nicholas, a Fellow of New College. Nicholas could, in his own words, 'only lisp statistics'. McCallum often paid tribute to the assistance of 'a young man with a wonderful head for statistics' and recommended him to Nicholas. Butler then took over the 1951 and 1955 volumes and since then has co-authored every subsequent volume until the study of the 1992 election. Over time, he handed the statistical appendices to Michael Steed and John Curtice, and the chapters have grown in length, refinement, and sophistication.

McCallum and Nicholas were contemporary historians: they showed that an event could be studied objectively and systematically, close to its occurrence. David added something else, the study of election results, trends, and patterns. In the process he invented a subject. In a recent letter to the present writer, Nicholas recalled his young collaborator:

I soon discovered that I had secured the services, not merely of an electoral statistician, but of someone who whole-heartedly shared my interest in the political infrastructure of the whole electoral process. To a degree now barely credible, the operations of the party organizations, at local as well as at national level, and the formulation and application of media policy, both of press and broadcasting, to the electoral contest were areas hidden from academic scrutiny, breeding grounds of dubious historical analogies and unverified generalizations. His approach was, first, to be precise about the statistics, and squeeze out of them every last drop of information that they can offer, and then go on to fieldwork and personal enquiry, recognizing the hazards but seeking always to bring the same objectivity to bear upon the intangible as upon the quantifiable. Here each of his talents reinforced the other: interviewees, the practitioners of the political arts, were much more predisposed to reveal the secrets of the trade to someone who, with an electoral Wisden at his command, could provide them with precise and useful information—on who scored how much against whom, in what circumstances, and at what time. Without losing his political detachment—no one has ever been able convincingly to pin a party label on him—David won acceptance by politicians, their technicians, and their reporters, as one who spoke their language, entered fully into their problems, and made allowances for their limitations.

In November 1949 David had his greatest intellectual excitement. Sitting in the Radcliffe Library, reading the 1908–10 Royal Commission on the electoral system, he came across the testimony of James Parker Smith about the 'cube law' on the relation of votes and seats. The law stated that, if votes are divided between parties in the ratio a : b, then the seats will divide in a ratio $a^3 : b^3$, so exaggerating the majority in seats for the winning party. David used a primitive calculating machine for the 1931, 1935, and 1945 general elections and found that it worked each time. He was even more excited to discover that the Parker Smith formula had been anticipated in earlier work by F. Y. Edgeworth.

Over Christmas in 1949 he wrote an anonymous piece on his findings for *The Economist*. The article was read by Winston Churchill, holidaying in Madeira. As a result, during the general election campaign in February 1950, young Butler was abruptly summoned to dine with Churchill at Chartwell. He spent over four hours periodically trying to explain his findings to the great man, but for most of the time listening to digressions on the vast sweep of history. He was summoned again by Churchill on the eve of the 1951 election, and at one point Churchill asked, 'You don't think I'm a handicap to my party do you?' David tried to dodge the question but was forced to say, 'I don't think you're quite the asset you once were, sir.'

There has been much change in the conduct of post-war British elections. In 1950 Mr Attlee was driven by his wife, Violet, in the pre-war family saloon, with a large detective sitting in the back but with no other entourage. Night after night he travelled around the major cities making major hour-long speeches at mass rallies. Churchill, more grandly, journeyed by special train and again spoke on most nights during the election. The speeches were delivered largely to the converted and were given extensive press coverage the following morning. This was a very different world from that of Peter Mandelson and Saatchi and Saatchi. Now there is much more sophisticated planning and 'pacing' of election campaigning by party headquarters. Forty years ago there were no early morning press conferences aimed at capturing the midday news headlines, few houses had televisions, and radio hardly covered the election at all. Forty years ago there were no opinion polls, public or private, but in the 1987 general election there were seventy-three published nation-wide opinion polls during the four-week campaign. The major political parties now use communications agencies which link design, the themes of the leaders' speeches, research, copy-writing, advertising, and election broadcasts. In real terms the parties are spending ten times as much as they did on campaigns forty years ago.

Not only has David Butler lived through these changes, but his series of election studies has documented and assessed them.

ÉLITE INTERVIEWS

In writing his election studies until 1959, David drew heavily on the public record, limited as it was. He also interviewed a few party officials. But much of the information was necessarily gleaned from the newspapers, for it was not until 1959 that television and radio provided coverage of the election campaigns. Compared to later Nuffield election studies, the early books were sketchy on élite thinking about campaign strategy. Indeed, as the 27-year-old author of the 1951 Nuffield election study, he lamented in the preface:

One does not know—and if one knew one could not reveal—the arguments (about campaign strategy). Years will elapse before such information is available. It depends on the presentation of the memoirs of those concerned, or perhaps, more reliable but certainly more distant, the opening of their papers to the research students. (Butler 1952: 9–10)

A decade later he had changed his mind that our ignorance of *haute politique* was inevitable. For the 1959 study he and Richard Rose, his co-author, started to interview politicians, a practice that was extended when collaborating with Tony King in 1964 and 1966, and which has been maintained ever since. James Douglas recalls John Wyndham, then head of the economics section in the Conservative Research Department (and later Macmillan's private secretary), warning him about an anticipated visit from David in 1951 or 1952: 'There is an Oxford don coming in to see us. You had better talk to him but not say too much.'

One of David Butler's most reliable interviewees was Michael Fraser (now Lord Fraser of Kilmorack), the Chairman of the Conservative Research Department from 1951 to 1974, and Executive Deputy Chairman of the party from 1964 to 1975. Michael had been a key confidant of successive Conservative post-war party leaders down to Edward Heath and was on close terms with many other prominent party figures. His attitude to David, and the election studies, was divided between his perennial concern for security (which may have arisen from his wartime experience) and his commitment to accurate history. He was torn between preserving confidentiality about his masters' affairs and ensuring that David, as Clio's acolyte and agent, got his facts right. On the whole David resolved the dilemma by developing his own version of the lobby system and probably ensured for the Nuffield election studies both a higher standard of accuracy and a fuller range of sources than most other studies of contemporary political history.

Given his quick-fire conversation, David is a remarkably good interviewer of politicians. He has a knack of asking the right questions and getting people to confide in him. He is straightforward about his approach. As he once said to me: 'I've never believed in aggro-interviewing. The politicians are doing us a favour, and the least we can do is to show interest in and sympathy for their problems.' In other words, rapport is essential, or 'they need a little love'. I was amused to read an entry in Dick Crossman's diaries for February 1970, that David 'was more careful than ever to maintain his neutral position and for once he didn't bully me or try to get information out of me in any way' (1977: 298). The idea of Butler bullying Crossman or of the latter either trying or managing to be discreet are both mind-boggling. For Sunday, 18 April 1965, Crossman wrote that Butler paid 'one of his routine visitations. I suppose he has a diary which says "See Crossman every four months". As usual he puts his questions to me and puts down his answers in his little book' (1975: 198).

David's name frequently occurs in the published diaries of Tony Benn. In the first volume, covering the period to 1967, he is often quoted expressing optimism about Labour's electoral prospects (which David would regard as a classic case of the listener hearing only what he wanted to). One chastening entry for 14 May, 1964 reads: 'David Butler and Marilyn came to lunch today and he said he thinks we shall win Devizes quite comfortably.' This is followed for 15 May by: 'We have lost Devizes by over 1,000 votes' (Benn 1987: 114).

David's concern about quoting or being quoted out of context has made him guarded about the status of the rich store of accumulated notes of interviews (running into thousands of pages) with key figures, dating back to Hugh Gaitskell in 1955. He regards the interviews as working or background notes, not as historical documents. They repeat gossip—which may be quite untrue—they may have been transcribed inaccurately, and his memory is fallible.

Of politicians he has interviewed for the election studies he found Mrs Thatcher 'formidable', genuinely liked Tony Benn, though in recent years he often thought his views nonsensical, and found Enoch Powell 'mesmeric'. (In 1969 and 1970 he and Michael Pinto-Duschinsky, his collaborator on the 1970 study, had a number of interviews with Enoch Powell. Before one interview in July 1970 they had learnt that the new Tory MP John Davies had been appointed Minister of Technology in the Heath government. At first Mr Powell refused to believe the report, but, when convinced, he said, menacingly, 'You will remember this occasion. It brings nemesis three months early.') Like Mrs Thatcher, Mr Powell liked to analyse a question, suggesting all sorts of embellishments and interpretations never envisaged by the questioner. As Leader of the Opposition, Mr Heath was tense and uneasy, answering questions like a *viva voce*. Interviewing Harold Wilson varied in usefulness. A less happy interview was in 1969 when he appeared more interested in performing for the benefit of an aide, Gerald Kaufman. R. A. Butler was always helpful. In early 1964, not long after Lord Home had beaten him for the leadership of the Conservative party and premiership, RAB pointed to a newspaper cartoon which showed him literally saving Sir Alec's bacon and complained: 'All this praise does me no good with the colleagues.' David would describe to me Douglas Hurd, Chris Patten, and Shirley Williams as 'pure gold', but of others to whom he had listened politely he would mutter afterwards, 'a lot of guff there'.

His nerve was most impressive when we interviewed Mrs Thatcher in her room in the House of Commons in August 1978. She was then Leader of the Opposition and was anticipating Mr Callaghan calling an autumn general election. She was finishing tidying up her office (and had even defrosted the fridge early that morning), before going on holiday the next day. She was remarkably attentive and charming during the opening exchanges. My notes refer to her as 'soignée'. A few minutes into the interview David mentioned that Mrs Thatcher was outside the prevailing consensus. The atmosphere changed immediately and she unleashed a barrage of hostile questions. 'What do you mean by consensus?' After a three-second pause she offered five different definitions of the term and challenged him to say which one he referred to. I knew that he was floundering. After further exchanges, in which he may have been using well-worn phrases about the need for compromise and the politics of the possible— with an implicit rebuke for her style—she returned to the attack: 'Do you realize what you are saying?' and 'Do you consider yourself fit to hold an academic appointment?' All this was said with deliberate Thatcher emphasis and hostility on the key words. The lady was on the warpath and the atmosphere was extremely uncomfortable. A by-now shaken collaborator looked to me for support, perhaps to begin a new line of questioning. I am afraid to report that I was no use to him; I simply looked the other way. Some ninety minutes later she escorted us out of the office and said, 'You do understand me, don't you?'

Politicians and party officials agree to be interviewed for a variety of reasons. Some genuinely want to help to get the story right—or at least their part of it; some want 'a mention', as one Labour official said dismissively of other informants whose statements were at variance with his; some want to use the authors to put a favourable gloss on their activities; and some see David out of habit. As Robert Worcester, the MORI opinion pollster, says, 'David *is* part of the general election furniture.' Tony Benn, who has been interviewed by David at every campaign since 1955, comments, 'His visits to me rank with an inspection by a Field Marshal and his forecasts are treated with respect.'

I can recollect some key participants in the Conservative campaign in the 1987 general election actually seeking us out. They claimed to be aggrieved by a hurriedly written 'inside' account of that election, serialized in the *Sunday Times*. One person close to Mrs Thatcher remarked, 'It would be awful if in thirty years' time people turned to that for a history of the election.'

In the October 1974 election we were able to learn more about the pressures on Mr Heath to make what his entourage called 'the supreme sacrifice' (the offer to surrender the party leadership if the Conservatives were to lead a coalition government). In a review of 'The British General Election of October 1974' on 6 November 1975 David Wood, the Political Editor of *The Times*, praised David as 'one of the best political reporters of his time ... He is the perfect complement to political reporting of elections in newspapers and broadcasting, because he begins where everybody else leaves off to turn to the new Government and all it portends'. Wood wrote that the Nuffield authors revisited the battlefield and talked to the generals who won or lost—'the political journalism of hindsight with a value all of its own'.

Key participants in the Alliance campaign in the 1983 election had resolved that they would present us with a laundered version of David Steel's brutal attempt to replace Roy Jenkins as leader during the election campaign. We gradually managed to piece together a full account.

PROBLEMS IN STUDYING CONTEMPORARY HISTORY

The Nuffield election studies have been praised for the immense amount of hard information about the social backgrounds of candidates, statistics of numerous aspects of the constituency results, numbers of postal votes, constituency expenses, media reports, and accuracy about what actually happened during the election campaign. And, because much of it is in a series format, it is possible to compare the material over time.

But what of the criticisms? One problem is that the books address different audiences and are subject to different expectations (see Ranney 1976: 224). The books to some extent fall between two schools, not being scholarly enough for the academics and yet too scholarly for the non-academic. Indeed, as political science has become more rigorous and quantitative, so some academics have become dismissive of the series. They look in vain for the hypotheses which the authors are testing, models, evidence in the form of documents and interview sources, and analysis of independent and dependent variables. I can say only that this approach would be grossly unrealistic in describing such events and I suspect that David would invite such critics to have a go at writing their own election studies. The books have also been criticized for not being more like the best-selling accounts of the US presidential elections by T. H. White. In fact Nuffield authors have not possessed White's journalistic talents and a US presidential election is very different from a British general election.

The Nuffield authors have often been suspected of learning secrets which politicians would not tell to journalists. Participants have, it was claimed, been prepared to speak for the record of history, safe in the knowledge that their revelations would not be trumpeted or their confidences betrayed. As part of the implied bargain, the Nuffield authors have been accused of being excessively discreet in print; they pulled their punches and even informed observers have had to read between the lines. Hugo Young, reviewing the study of the 1983 election, commented: 'If the 1983 book has a fault, it lies, as it has before, in the very refusal of the authors to play up the quality of the information to which they have access. One knows from experience how good their [the authors'] contacts are . . . and how freely their sources will speak to them, relieved, no doubt, not to be confronted by menacing and unreliable journalists' (1984). Indeed, the authors have made a practice of showing relevant passages to key participants beforehand, not to give the reader the power of veto, but to give him or her the opportunity to suggest corrections. There have been a few occasions when I have been aware of pressures, principally from opinion pollsters and Labour party officials, who wished to advance either their own ambitions or those of the leader.

There are, of course, more fundamental objections to contemporary history *per se*. Critics argue that to write a 'true history' one would have to wait for more documents to become available and for the passage of time that produces a more informed perspective.

A good deal of material is already available for a contemporary event, in the form of richer and more detailed press reports and analyses, broadcasting coverage, and interviews with key decision-makers, and many participants are prepared to be interviewed off the record. These are all important sources and are available at the time of the election. Some of the sources, notably the immediate memories of key actors, become fallible over time and will not be available in years to come. (It is worth adding that T. H. White's study of the 1960 US presidential election, *The Making of the President*, provided a challenge in its use of élite interviews to discuss campaign strategies.) David often defends his studies of the general elections in the 1950s and 1960s by noting that later accounts and memoirs have forced only minor corrections to what the Nuffield studies reported close to the time. There is, moreover, a case for writing a dispassionate account of events close to their occurrence, without leaving the field entirely to journalists, who operate to extremely tight deadlines, or to the often self-serving accounts of politicians (see Seldon 1988).

Some campaign participants object that the academic study of elections takes the poetry out of politics. Often this is a euphemism for defending the prejudices and interests of politicians. The Prime Minister, Harold Macmillan, speaking at the Oxford Union on 3 December 1959, gave Nuffield and David Butler a back-handed compliment.

One of the latest so-called sciences is one called psephology—flourishing in one of those new Colleges—the study of how the people voted last time, how they will vote next time; all apparently capable of mathematical calculation, irrespective of the election campaign or the issue at stake. The source of political Calvinism (of which Dr Gallup is the founder) is only redeemed by the recent discovery that their predetermined anticipations are generally proved wrong. The electors do show, from time to time, a regrettable outbreak of political Free Will.

Yet at this time Harold Macmillan, in a visit to the economics section of his party's Research Department, commented to James Douglas, a researcher with an interest in survey research, 'These polls and things are all nonsense aren't they? But I think we ought to keep track of them. James, you have a slide-rule; you had better do it.'[1]

I have often been present in interviews when prominent politicians and officials accused David of undermining voluntary party activity, a consequence of his pointing to the modest impact constituency campaigning or the personality of the candidate has on the outcome. Barbara Castle, reviewing the 1970 election book in *New Society*, commented: 'Dedication in politics was at a discount. All that mattered was THE SWING—almost Calvinistic in its fatalistic overtones. The key to the swing lay in the statistical analysis, of which the psephologists were the high priests' (Castle 1971: 641). Noting the larger number of interviews conducted by the authors, she complained that they had not talked to her! Sometimes the election studies, and David Butler, have been dismissed by people who largely objected to public relations, opinion polls, advertising, and other features of modern election-eering. The books, in other words, are part of the election hype. Or the critics may have felt that he, and other election pundits, were getting too much space and time in the mass media. Why should the commentators get more attention than the players? The young David Butler shared some of these fears. The preface to the 1951 Nuffield election study, already quoted, contained another interesting passage. Warning about the dangers of research into elections, it said:

If some popular ideas about it are illusions, they may at least be healthy illusions. It is a good thing that people should believe that the vigour of the local campaign, the quality of the candidate, and the efficiency of the party organisation will have a decisive influence on the result. If one destroys the mystery of democracy, or fosters the idea that the actions which make up the democratic process are unimportant, one may breed cynicism; one may discourage party organisations from seeking the best candidates; one may dissuade candidates from waging the most energetic campaign; and one may deter voters from voting. There are grave dangers in increasing knowledge about the nature of elections, for the more completely politicians understand how the ideas of the electorate can be manipulated, the more mechanistic politics may become; increasing indifference may develop on the part of the public, and a wider opportunity may be opened for the unscrupulous charlatan to achieve success . . . But the pursuit of knowledge cannot be abandoned because of the hazards of discovery. (Butler 1952: 9–10)

A remarkable outburst came from Iain Macleod when he reviewed *Political Change in Britain* in *The Times* in 1969. Macleod was usually both fair-minded and perceptive, and one wonders if his advancing illness (he was in constant pain) played a part. He was, one gathered, angry at what he regarded as an excessively even-handed newpaper article of David's about the Labour government's decision to overrule the Boundary Commission's report in 1969. More crucial, I suspect, was his conviction that at the end of the day there was no substitute for the politician's instinct. Like many politicians he resented the academic pundit who pontificated on television and radio about politics without being subject to any of the pressures or disciplines under which politicians had to operate. As the mathematician G. H. Hardy commented, 'there is no scorn more profound, or on the whole more justifiable, than that of men who make, for men who explain. Exposition, criticism, appreciation is work for second rate minds' (Little 1957: 1).

Macleod may also have objected to the study's claim that, because most people voted in line with their social class and inherited party loyalties from their parents, Labour, as the party of the working class, was steadily becoming the 'natural' majority party in the last third of the twentieth century. Conservatives could still win elections occasionally, but only by dint of outstanding performances by themselves and/or ineptitude by the Labour party. A gloomy internal Conservative memorandum at the time acknowledged that the older voters dying off were disproportionately Tory and that new voters were more pro-Labour. It said: 'Our three main weaknesses can be summarised as Death, Youth and Working Class.' But no sooner was *Political Change* off the presses than the Conservatives won the 1970 general election and have been in office for much of the time since.

It is relevant to acknowledge that the mass media have presented an even more public face of David Butler since BBC television provided its first all-night coverage of a general election in 1950. Grace Wyndham Goldie, then a producer and later head of current affairs, invited McCallum to act as the programme's election analyst. He accepted, on condition that he had David at his side. The latter's card-index mind enabled him to offer instantaneous comments on each constituency result. In 1951 he accompanied Herbert Nicholas in the television studio. In these years of BBC monopoly of television, he was the nation's foremost ('because the only one', he would say) psephologist. In the 1960s and 1970s he and Robert McKenzie, another tele-academic, were household names. No BBC coverage of by-elections, local elections, and general elections took place without the analytical contributions of the two men. The contrast between the two was marked. David's serious, Oxford manner and his severely factual and even statistical contributions offset McKenzie's avuncular personality, cheery countenance, warm Canadian voice, and general commentary.

It was McKenzie's role to provide the 'grand-think' interpretations of the results and conduct interviews with leading politicians. He could be jealous of David's exposure and I suspect that his academic side realized that David's brief contributions on the significance of each constituency result and the regional and social trends in the results were more solid. On the whole, McKenzie's knowledge of constituencies was thin and his familiarity with statistics rudimentary. In the 1959 general election programme David correctly forecast an increased Conservative majority after the first handful of constituency results had been announced on television, showing swings to the Conservatives. He noted that swings were pretty uniform across most seats and knew that he could, therefore, calculate the likely number of seats which would change hands. McKenzie, barely understanding the notion of uniform swing, thought that the outcome was still in doubt until many more results had been declared.

Yet McKenzie always respected David Butler's knowledge, integrity, and indifference to what fee the BBC was paying. 'The key to David is that he was a boy scout,' McKenzie said to me in 1979. More relevant was that David found the broadcasts 'so much fun' and he would have been doing such an analysis had he not been on the air. After the 1979 general election, in search of more colour, BBC television dispensed with his expertise and he took to analysing the results for BBC Radio Four on election night. For some years after 1962 he wrote regular features on elections and opinion polls for the *Sunday Times*, and then for the *Times*. These provided an enormous amount of solid information for the public and probably contributed substantially to the popular understanding of elections and the analysis of the results.

BUTLER AND POLITICAL SCIENCE

As a political scientist, David Butler has been squarely in the British empirical tradition. He has never shown much interest in political philosophy or classic texts, international relations, or the study of policy-making. And his interest in political institutions is largely of how people behave in those institutions. The Isaiah Berlin story was an early indication of the atheoretical side of David. He learns more by conversation than by keeping up with the literature of a subject. If forced to choose, he would prefer to learn about his subject by talking to politicians than reading books: 'You learn a language by speaking it, not from books.' He is sceptical about grand theories, generalizations, and doubts that there is a science of politics, in the sense that there are laws of political behaviour. In a recent lecture, he commented:

I do not believe that there is anything worthwhile that we can say about politics which is an eternal truth. Every interesting proposition about the ways in which Britain is governed seems to me to be just a probability statement, an assertion about norms, a guess at the rule of the game prevailing at one particular period of time and in this particular part of the world. It is not and can never be an eternal verity. (Butler 1992: 129)

He would support his scepticism about laws of politics with the history of his 'cube law'. With adjustment, it had fitted British elections during the 1950s and 1960s: 1 per cent movement in votes produced a switch of seats in Parliament of roughly 3 per cent. But in the 1970s the law, in his own words, 'went sour', degenerating into a square law and then into one of about the power of 1.5. By 1987 only eight, rather than eighteen, seats were changing hands for each 1 per cent swing of votes. There were no eternal laws. In contributions to conferences and seminars he will answer questions with 'I don't know' or 'We don't know'. In a review of a book on the complex nature of political science he wrote that it might be a splendid book but it was all beyond him.

Hence the study of politics is best understood as accurate description of events. In studying events one has to get the story right about what happened. And, for contemporary events, one can do this by talking to the key actors. It is fair to say that studies of elections have been largely one-sided. Voting behaviour and elections have been abstracted from the political context and rarely connected with the working of the political system, and David Butler has some responsibility for this. But in the 1980s he was quick to spot the problems for many established constitutional practices and thinking, from changes in voting behaviour and in the party system. As the two-party system declined and the prospects for a deadlocked Parliament and minority or coalition government increased, so there were new constitutional uncertainties. For example, in the event of a deadlock, who would the monarch invite to form a government and would she automatically assent to a minority Prime Minister's request for a dissolution? In 1983 he analysed these issues in *Governing without a Majority: Dilemmas of Hung Parliaments*, in anticipation of the 1983 election. This was republished in 1987, for the next general election. The volumes were ill-timed, although in both years the Alliance attracted considerable support and a number of commentators discussed the likelihood of a hung Parliament. He could note ironically that both editions were followed by landslides for the Conservatives. His interest in constitutional questions is that of a commentator, rather than an advocate. But perhaps he is now weakening in his former hostility to a Bill of Rights, if not to a written constitution, of which he used to say: 'we should keep things away from the bloody lawyers.'

David Butler has encouraged interest in many new areas—not only psephology, but also electoral systems, hung parliaments, coalitions, redistributions, and referendums. If Britain is his main interest, his work is not narrowly British; witness *The Canberra Model* (1973), a book of essays on Australian politics; *India Decides 1952–1989* (1991), a compendium of election results in India; and *Congressional Redistricting* (1991), a study of constituency boundary-drawing in the United States. His comparative work on constitutions, elections, and voting behaviour has often taken the form of transplanting his knowledge to another country, using his experience of Britain to understand that country. He found the approach more successful for India and Australia than for the United States. In middle age he has grown to like Australia and India enormously. In India he plays a backroom role, helping Indian psephologists interpret constituency results on television. Australia's open society and climate appeal to him. But intellectually he was struck by what he regarded as virgin territory and the neglect of Australian politics by the country's political scientists. His scepticism about the value of political comparisons has also weakened. His co-edited volumes of essays, *Democracy at the Polls* (1981), *Sovereigns and Surrogates: Constitutional Heads of State in the Commonwealth* (1991), and *Electioneering* (1992) are attempts to explore the common elements in political institutions in different countries.

It is striking that so many of David Butler's books have been the result of collaboration. Does he like to feel pressures from a co-author, somebody to prick his conscience, and force him to meet a deadline? He has co-authored (with Donald Stokes) *Political Change in Britain* (1969) and (with Bruce Cain) *Congressional Redistricting* (1991). In these books the US mastery of social science techniques was added to David's knowledge of British politics. But in many other cases it was a means of sharing the work. Apart from the Nuffield election studies, all co-authored since 1955, he has written books on British elections for European Parliament, with David Marquand and then with Paul Jowett, on the 1975 referendum with Uwe Kitzinger, on Indian elections with Ashok Lahiri and Prannoy Roy, on the role of governors-general (*Sovereigns and Surrogates*) with Tony Low, and successive editions of *British Political Facts* with Jenny Freeman, then Anne Sloman, and, more recently, with his son Gareth. He has also co-edited books on election campaigning with Austin Ranney and Howard Penniman, and on the consequences of electoral systems with Vernon Bogdanor. And in 1978, together with another Nuffield Research Fellow, A. H. Halsey, he edited a volume of essays in honour of Sir Norman Chester, Warden of Nuffield College.

David Butler has produced over thirty books, either singly or jointly. His D. Phil. thesis was published by Oxford University Press in 1953 as *The Electoral System in Britain, 1918–1951* and a second edition was brought out in 1963. The publishers have often asked him to update this classic text, but he thought that things had changed too much for him to keep to the original plan of the book. The cube law, as noted, effectively broke down in the 1970s, with the decline of the two-party system. Another so-called Butler law—about the very modest impact on the vote of local election campaigns and the personalities of candidates—was qualified in the 1980s. Hard-working incumbents and some of the Liberal and Alliance MPs showed the impact that a good local campaign could have. The notion of election swing goes back a long way, but it fell to David, while still an undergraduate, to provide the first precise measure and to develop it as a measure of electoral change. Recently scholars have developed different measures—more suited to multi-party politics. His book on Australian politics, which has attracted much favourable comment, *The Canberra Model* (1973), is an eloquent statement of the case for studying a neglected political system.

His most notable book has been the first nation-wide study of British voting behaviour, which he wrote with Donald Stokes, a distinguished American political scientist. In the preface to the 1951 election book he regretted the lack of knowledge of élite thinking and of mass voting behaviour. He blazed a trail for both. *Political Change in Britain* (first published in 1969, with a revised version in 1974) was based on interviews in 1963, 1964, and 1966 with panels of voters. The book won the prestigious Woodrow Wilson Prize from the American Political Science Association and was a pioneering piece of research. His concern for the facts— factual accuracy—has borne fruit in his *British Political Facts*, a reference book that had gone into six editions by 1988. This is an indispensable work of reference and will effectively settle many arguments about British politics in the twentieth century. After all, David recalls that his father 'brought us up never to argue about a question of verifiable fact'.

In addition to his writings David Butler has been active within his academic profession. He is Chairman of the Advisory Committee of the Institute of Contemporary British History, a key member of the Hansard Society Commission on Fair Play in Elections, and has President (1984–7) of the Politics Association, an association of school teachers of the subject. He has also been joint editor of the journal of *Electoral Studies* since it was first published in 1982. But perhaps one should not make too much of this. He did not do a great deal of undergraduate teaching or lecturing in Oxford and took little part in administration outside Nuffield or in the affairs of the University. He advanced the frontiers of his research by narrowing his front, focusing firmly on what he regarded as the essentials.

As a person David has many remarkable qualities. Two of the most prominent are his optimism and his sheer busyness. Having so many activities in hand has meant that, if he was disappointed in one task, he could proceed to the next. Also remarkable is his energy, indeed hyperactivity. He always seems to be bustling and rushing somewhere. In recent years, since his wife Marilyn was appointed to the Edward VII chair in English at Cambridge in 1986, he has commuted between Oxford and Cambridge. I have known him arrive at Heathrow at 9 in the morning from a flight from Australia (having written an article for the *Spectator* on the flight) and a few hours later give a promised talk to students in Oxford. This illustrates both his concern about punctuality and his determination to carry out commitments, regardless of personal inconvenience.

David talks and lectures at high speed. In conversation, he sometimes seems to be thinking of his next question before you have answered his last one. His welcome for deadlines and apparent relish for working in a breathless hurry were, of course, additional reasons why some academics, for ever sniffing out superficiality, held him in suspicion. His desire for haste has sometimes got the better of him. It is not just a question of car crashes, losing his tank down the Rhine in 1945, or keeping up with the academic literature on his subject. He has tended to think on his feet, requiring the stimulus of argument and conversation. In discussion he could always rely on his formidable memory and he can be splendidly direct in getting to the point. Like a good teacher he loves explaining himself. I have marvelled at the patience and interest with which he explained some intricate problems to the very young. His gift as a teacher and supervisor has been for firing students with his own enthusiasm.

As a co-author nothing irritated me more than his weakness for the telephone. It is likely that, if he were a subject on *Desert Island Discs* and was asked for one object to take to the island, it would be a telephone or, better still, a number of them. With deadlines fast approaching for submission of a manuscript, David would willingly put aside his pen to answer the ringing telephone. He also has a love of gadgets—he is a do-it-yourself fanatic. Although he is at ease with himself, it is difficult to imagine him taking a leisurely walk or lying on a beach.

THE NUFFIELD COLLEGE CONNECTION

No account of David Butler is complete without an acknowledge-ment of his love-affair with Oxford University and Nuffield College (for further discussion see Chester 1986). He would like to be remembered above all as a Fellow of the College where he played a major part in its formative years and served it with distinction for over forty years. The College was created by a large gift from Lord Nuffield, as a graduate centre for the social sciences. He was one of the College's first postgraduates and did his D. Phil. between 1949 and 1951. In 1951–4 he was a Research Fellow at the College and was then elected to a Fellowship, which he held for nearly forty years. Over the years he has visited many universities abroad and turned down numerous offers of university chairs elsewhere. From September 1955 he spent a year outside academic life as a personal assistant to the British Ambassador in Washington DC, Roger Makins, later Lord Sherfield. He is quick to acknowledge the support and encouragement which Norman Chester, the College Warden from 1954 to 1978, provided. As an Official Fellow at the College, it was Chester who had encouraged David to work on his thesis topic. Nuffield provided him with the intellectual company of economists and sociologists, as well as political scientists. He also loved talking shop, which one could do more easily in Nuffield than elsewhere in Oxford. The College itself was for some years the object of suspicion in Oxford, suspicion not only of the social sciences but also because of the involvement of many College Fellows in public affairs, particularly in advising decision-makers and in writing for the media about topical issues. Because the College had no undergraduates, dons at other colleges regarded some of the Fellows as pampered.

At Oxford he supervised scores of graduate students who subsequently went into the world of politics (the Liberal MP Alan Beith, the Conservative Euro-MP Caroline Jackson), administration, the media (Robert Taylor and Brian Walden), and academe. Past Nuffield students who have gone on to gain chairs in politics include Hugh Berrington, Milton Cummings, Martin Harrison, Tony King, Cornelius O'Leary, Richard Rose, and Colin Seymour-Ure. His Friday afternoon seminars, to which he invited prominent figures from public life, were memorable occasions. He has organized countless study or discussion groups on topical constitutional issues, attended by leading politicians and civil servants. Because these were held under so-called Chatham House rules, participants could speak freely, on the understanding that they would not be quoted. It was the mix of the academic and the 'real' political world at Nuffield that so suited his temperament. Also inseparable from David Butler has been a splendid secretary, employed by the College, Audrey Skeats (née Carruthers). Audrey was first thanked in the preface to the 1951 election study. Forty years later she is being thanked yet again in a forthcoming Study of the 1992 General Election.

Politicians and commentators often wondered about David Butler's politics. In fact he is a cross-bencher. He has views on issues and likes and dislikes about politicians, but he does not fit into any party package. Above all, he has never been happy with the true believer on any side. In the 1950s he claimed impartiality to the extent of abstaining in elections, but has voted in all general elections since 1959. He has never been wistful about not pursuing a career in politics, not out of any distaste or sense of superiority but because he was happy in what he was doing. His energy, interest, and good memory have allowed him to lead a full and contented life.

Note

1. Letter from Herbert Nicholas, 3 Apr. 1991. Macmillan was not only publisher of the Nuffield election books starting in 1950. He also took a close interest in the books and Herbert Nicholas received several letters from him.

References

Benn, T. (1987), *Out of the Wilderness Diaries, 1963–67* (London: Hutchinson).

Butler, D. E. (1952), *The British General Election of 1951* (London: Macmillan).

—— (1992), 'Voting Behaviour and the Party System', in B. Jones and L. Robins (eds.), *Two Decades in British Politics* (Manchester: Manchester University Press), 129–38.

—— and Ranney, A. (1992) (eds.), *Electioneering* (Oxford: Oxford University Press).

Castle, B. (1971), 'Fallacies of Psephology', *New Society*, 15 Apr.

Chester, D. N. (1986), *Economics, Politics and Social Studies in Oxford, 1900–85* (London: Macmillan).

Crossman, R. H. S. (1975), *Diaries of a Cabinet Minister*, i (London: Hamilton).

—— (1977), *Diaries of a Cabinet Minister*, iii (London: Hamilton).

Little, A. (1957), *A Critique of Welfare Economics* (2nd edn., Oxford: Clarendon Press).

Ranney, A. (1976), 'Thirty Years of Psephology', *British Journal of Political Science*, 6: 217–30.

Seldon, A. (1988) (ed.), *Contemporary History* (Oxford: Blackwell).

Wood, D. (1975), 'Review of *The British General Election of October 1974*', *The Times*, 6 Nov.

Young, H. (1984), 'Into the Valley of Death', *Times Literary Supplement*, 24 Jan.

2

Political Change in Britain

ANTHONY KING

David Butler and Donald Stokes entitled their pioneering study of the British electorate of the 1960s and early 1970s *Political Change in Britain*. Their subject was the influences that bear upon individual voters as they decide how to cast their ballots and the ways in which individuals' voting decisions are summed across the whole mass of voters to produce the outcomes of general elections. Butler and Stokes's focus was on the electorate and not on the various other forms that political change can take, but they were well aware that 'the ebbs and flows of popular favour affect, often in quite unexpected ways, the whole conduct of British government' (1974: 3).

This chapter also is concerned with political change in Britain. It is not primarily concerned, however, with change in the electorate. Its focus, rather, is on the actions of British governments in introducing radical changes in public policy, not just in one field of policy (say, the introduction of immigration controls or floating exchange rates) but across a broad range of policies. Specifically, it is concerned with the three great discontinuities in the gross pattern of public policy that have been brought about by British governments in the twentieth century: the three that are associated with the Asquith government before the First World War, the Attlee government after the Second World War and the Thatcher government between 1979 and 1990. What were the sources of change in each of these cases? What, if anything, do the three cases have in common?

THE GREAT DISCONTINUITIES

Before we proceed, a brief reminder may be in order of the breadth and scale of the changes brought about by the Asquith, Attlee, and

Thatcher administrations. All three administrations were described in their day as radical. They more than deserved the description.

The Asquith government, together with its immediate predecessor under Sir Henry Campbell-Bannerman, inaugurated the British welfare state. Asquith, in one of his last acts as Chancellor of the Exchequer before he succeeded Campbell-Bannerman as Prime Minister in 1908, introduced a scheme of non-contributory old age pensions. A few months later Winston Churchill, the President of the Board of Trade, created 'trade boards' to fix minimum wages in low-paid industries and what were called 'employment exchanges' (now Jobcentres) to improve the workings of the labour market and combat unemployment. In 1911 David Lloyd George, Asquith's successor as Chancellor, introduced for the first time a scheme of contributory 'national insurance', covering both health care and unemployment. Had the First World War not broken out and had the Liberals won the 1914 or 1915 general election, the Asquith government would almost certainly have initiated large-scale public housing schemes and might well have taken the first steps towards nationalizing the railways. The Asquith administration's radical impetus had by no means been dissipated when the war intervened.

The Attlee government between 1945 and 1951 moved on three major fronts. First, it radically extended the social welfare system that Asquith and Lloyd George had inaugurated and which had been built upon between the wars. In particular, it made national insurance comprehensive and established the National Health Service. Secondly, it endorsed the wartime Coalition government's commitment to full employment and pursued policies, including Keynesian counter-cyclical policies, towards that end. Thirdly, it undertook a massive nationalization programme, taking the nation's railways, coal mines, gas and electricity industries, central bank and road haulage and steel industries into public ownership. By 1951 the British state's peacetime responsibilities had been transformed, compared with what they had been in, say, 1931 or 1921.

The Thatcher government was equally radical, if in a somewhat different direction. It jettisoned the Attlee administration's commitment, endorsed by all subsequent administrations, to full employment. It shifted the emphasis of economic policy away from Keynesianism towards monetarism. It abandoned the language (and practice) of economic planning in favour of the language (and practice) of the free market. It introduced successive pieces of legislation aimed at curbing trade union power in a way that it had not been curbed since the beginning of the twentieth century. Not least, it totally reversed the long-established tendency in Britain for more and more industries and firms to find their way into the public sector, 'privatizing' (the word itself was new) the gas and electricity industries, the steel industry, British Telecom, British Leyland, Cable and Wireless, the Rolls-Royce aeroengine company, and many other previously state-owned firms. The Thatcher government also abolished the rates and introduced a poll tax. Towards the end of Margaret Thatcher's period in office, someone wrote a book entitled *Mrs Thatcher's Revolution* (Jenkins 1987). No one thought that the use of the word 'revolution' was in any way excessive.

All three of these episodes did constitute discontinuities. Certainly, what the three governments did was not wholly without precedent (the beginnings of the modern welfare state can be traced back into the nineteenth century, and the Churchill government after 1951 had denationalized part of the steel industry), and policy was not equally discontinuous in every field (Asquith and Attlee pursued conservative foreign policies, and Thatcher largely preserved the welfare state while questioning its philosophical foundations). Nevertheless, the breaks with the past were substantial and wide-ranging. Moreover, no other governments in the twentieth century have attempted change on anything like such a scale. What set these powerful forces for change in motion?

Let us consider a number of possibilities.

VOTERS' DEMANDS

One view of policy change that appears to be widely held, though it is seldom clearly articulated, assigns a crucial initiating role to the electorate.[1] Voters make demands on parties and politicians. Parties and politicians in turn are aware of these demands and are inclined to accede to them. If they do, there is a good chance they will be rewarded at the polls. If they do not, there is a good chance they will be punished. This theory of the democratic process underlay many of the early objections to the extension of the franchise. There was a fear that politics would become a 'Dutch auction'.

Voters' demands appear to have played little role in the policy innovations of the Asquith era. No survey evidence of the kind that Butler and Stokes collected for the 1960s exists for the 1900s. If it did, it would probably (though by no means certainly) show that majorities of voters were in favour of old age pensions, trade boards, and labour exchanges but that opinion was much more evenly divided over (and quite possibly hostile to) national insurance. Be that as it may, social policy as an issue figured only in very general terms in the 1906 general election campaign and likewise played only a small part in the two campaigns of 1910. The three contests were dominated, at least in politicians' and political observers' eyes, by free trade, Welsh disestablishment, Nonconformist grievances over Church schools, 'Chinese slavery', the 1909 'people's budget', Home Rule for Ireland, and the power of the House of Lords.

In 1906 nearly two-thirds of Liberal candidates, 59 per cent, referred to the desirability of old age pensions in their local election addresses (Russell 1973: 71), but in his keynote speech of the campaign at the Albert Hall—the equivalent of a latter-day party manifesto—Sir Henry Campbell-Bannerman, the Prime Minister, conspicuously failed to promise pensions. The passage in his speech on social reform came towards the end and was studiously vague. In 1910 the Liberals took credit for having introduced old age pensions, but otherwise social reform was no more than a subtext in the two election campaigns of that year. The specific proposal of national insurance, which had already been mooted, caused the government some difficulties in December 1910, because of successful lobbying by existing industrial insurance interests.

The available evidence, such as it is, suggests that the Liberals before 1914 probably gained a modest electoral advantage from their espousal of pensions and national insurance but that the advantage was indeed modest. Certainly Liberal ministers, in their private letters as well as in their public speeches, seldom if ever referred to social reform in vote-maximizing terms, that is, as a potential election-winner for the Liberal party. The only partial exception was Lloyd George himself. Lloyd George does not seem to have supposed that his 'welfare state' schemes would win his party large numbers of votes in the short term; but he was uneasily aware that, unless the Liberals took up the cause of social reform, they were in danger of being outflanked in the long term by the Labour party, especially after (as seemed inevitable) the franchise was extended to include all adults and not merely the 60-odd per cent of adult males who possessed the vote in 1910. Lloyd George feared that British Liberalism could become 'what Continental Liberalism now is—a respectable middle-class affair—futile and impotent' (Grigg 1978; 293).

The situation after 1945 was in some ways more straight-forward. Every contemporary observer agreed that the 1945 election was fought over 'food, work, and homes' and that a majority of voters did, in some meaningful sense, 'demand' full employment, public housing, the full Beveridge national insurance scheme, and the introduction of a comprehensive national health service. Certainly the leaders of the main parties behaved as though they were under considerable electoral pressure. The Conservatives as well as Labour promised to aim at improved housing and full employment; the Conservatives as well as Labour promised to implement the Beveridge reforms and to bring in a national health service. Indeed, on these issues the 1945 election seems to have been fought in largely 'valence' rather than 'position' terms: the debate was not over the two parties' policies as such but rather over which of them could be more trusted to carry out policies on which both of them were agreed. The scattered Gallup polls of the time support the view that there was a substantial degree of national consensus on these issues and that the consensus was highly positive.

The exception was nationalization. The Gallup data suggest that majorities of voters in the 1940s favoured the nationalization of some industries (for example, gas and electricity) but not others (notably steel and road haulage). The Gallup data also suggest that most voters were not desperately exercised about nationalization one way or the other. Asked their main reason for voting for the party that they had in 1945, roughly one in ten of Conservative supporters mentioned hostility to state control and nationalization as a reason for voting Conservative; but almost no Labour supporters volunteered nationalization as a reason for voting Labour (Gallup 1976). Most voters' attitudes seem to have been ones of faintly benign, or faintly malign, indifference. The authors of the 1945 Nuffield election study remarked, with gentle irony, that

'Nationalization proved not nearly as engrossing as had been expected' (McCallum and Readman 1947: 150).

The relationship between the great Thatcher discontinuity and the wishes of the voters is easily the most intriguing of the three (as well as being the best documented). Whereas the Asquith government proceeded to a considerable degree independently of public opinion and the Attlee government's policy changes had either the electorate's positive support or its passive indifference, the Thatcher government was not only not spurred on by the hope of electoral gain in many of the major changes it made: it actually ran—and, so far as one can tell, knew it was running—considerable electoral risks. Thatcher was a revolutionary. The British people were not (Crewe 1988).

In only one field, trade union reform, did Thatcher and her colleagues have the electorate's unequivocal backing. Most voters had wanted the power of the unions curbed since at least the late 1960s. The Wilson government's proposal to legislate against the unions in 1969 was in part a response to electoral demands, and its loss of the 1970 election probably owed something to its having withdrawn its proposals under pressure from the unions. Labour suffered throughout the 1970s and 1980s from its close association with the unions and from voters' (largely correct) belief that a Labour government, while it might stand up to the unions on occasion, would never really try to put them in their place. By contrast, the Heath government's Industrial Relations Act of 1971 was widely welcomed among voters, and so, by very large majorities, were the Thatcher government's reforms of the 1980s. The fact that by the end of that decade the Labour party had substantially retreated from its original pledge to repeal the Thatcher changes is a measure of voters' strength of feeling, and their near-unanimity of feeling, on the issue.

Voters knew that a Thatcher government would take some action against the unions when they cast their ballots in the 1979 election: the Conservatives' manifesto referred explicitly to the subject, which was also a central theme in the Conservatives' campaign. Voters did not know, however, that a Thatcher government would embark on a major programme of privatizing hitherto state-owned industries. They did not know for the good reason that Thatcher and her colleagues did not know either; the privatization programme became a programme, and developed its own momentum, only after the 1979 election. In the event, voters' responses to privatization in the 1980s resembled their predecessors' response to the Attlee government's programme of nationalization a generation earlier. A few individual acts of privatization were approved of; more were disapproved of. But most voters remained largely agnostic on the issue. Few politicians believed that there were many votes in it either way. They were probably right. One of the Thatcher government's major breaks with the past was thus neither voter-led nor in any significant way voter-resisted.[2]

The same cannot be said of the Thatcher administration's abandonment of the commitment to full employment, its espousal of free-market economics, and its replacement of the old domestic rating system by the poll tax. These lines of policy, and a number of others, including the government's alleged 'cuts' in the National Health Service and other welfare services, met with the disapproval, often the strong disapproval, of substantial majorities of voters, and the Conservative party won the 1983 and 1987 elections despite its changes of policy in these fields rather than because of them. The Thatcher government represents one of the clearest cases since Britain became a democracy of a government frequently and in a number of different fields acting contrary to its own best electoral interests. Thatcher prided herself on 'going with the grain' of public sentiment, but in fact she and her colleagues often did the opposite. The Prime Minister's personal insistence on sticking to the poll tax when it seemed likely that it would cost her party the next election was one of the reasons for her fall. She defied the electorate; the electorate, albeit indirectly, got its revenge.

What is one to make of all this? It seems that, in connection with all three of the great discontinuities, voters and their wishes played a crucial role, but seldom in the specific way—voters' demands followed by parties' and politicians' responses—that was outlined briefly above. Only in connection with the post-1945 extensions of the welfare state and the post-1979 trade union reforms does the electorate seem to have played a genuinely activating role, in the sense that the victorious party won, and the losing party lost, in large part because of voters' beliefs about which party would be likely to perform best on the issue in question. There is no evidence in any of the three cases that majorities of voters actively sought (as distinct from expecting, in the post-war Labour case) the radical, across-the-board policy changes that then ensued.

The voters' role in the three cases was crucial, but it was also, in a sense, 'primitive'. It consisted simply of returning to office a government that then proceeded to behave in the radical ways just described. The voters' role in each case was more enabling than mandating. Voters for the most part did not tell the governments what to do; they merely installed them in office, and the governments then (as the British say) 'got on with it'. This being so, one is still left with the problem of explaining why these three administrations came to be radical and why they came to be radical in the ways that they did. If the voters were crucial only in a limited and largely permissive sense, who or what *was* crucial?

INTEREST GROUPS

One possibility that needs to be considered, if only briefly, is that the Asquith, Attlee, and Thatcher governments acted as they did in response to pressure from interest groups. Powerful and organized interests in the society, it might be thought, brought pressure to bear on the governments, and this pressure induced them—or played a large part in inducing them—to engage in radical, across-the-board policy innovation.

This possibility needs to be considered, because the view is widely held (and not always erroneously) that interest groups play a large and often determining part in political life. Some accounts have assigned such groups a central role in the governmental process (Truman 1953). This possibility can, however, largely be dismissed, because there is no reason to think that interest groups were important, let alone crucial, in any of the three cases. Indeed, there is every reason to think that they were neither important nor crucial.

At the turn of the twentieth century, interest groups, as they have subsequently developed, were in their infancy. There was no Age Concern to press for the introduction of old age pensions, no Child Poverty Action Group to press for national insurance, no Shelter to press for an extension of public housing. Interest groups were, as we have seen, actively involved in the public debate over national insurance, and they were also deeply involved in the private discussions that preceded the introduction of the 1911 National Insurance Bill and accompanied its passage through the

House of Commons; Lloyd George had to make substantial concessions to doctors' organizations as well as to the private insurance interests. But neither these nor any other organized interest groups provided the impetus behind the Asquith government's reforms.

Interest groups likewise did not provide the Attlee government's reforms with any of their impetus. The 1945 government's welfare state reforms were a response to electoral pressure and also, more important, to the Labour party's own convictions. The welfare lobby had still not come into being and, even if it had, would probably have had little political clout. For its part, nationalization had been a feature of Labour party policy since the party had adopted, in 1918, a constitution calling for 'the common ownership of the means of production, distribution and exchange'. Nationalization was a central part of Labour doctrine. Interest groups figured in the policy process in the 1940s only to the extent that a number of trade unions that were powerful in the party, notably the various transport unions and the National Union of Mineworkers, pressed at Labour party conferences for public ownership to be extended to their industries.

The role of interest groups in initiating the Thatcher government's policy changes was wholly negligible. The abandonment of the commitment to full employment, the partial abandonment of Keynesian demand management, the taking-up of the cause of free-market economics, the assault on trade union power, privatization, and the poll tax—none of these owed anything to interest-group activity. Bodies like the Institute of Directors and the Confederation of British Industry might applaud from the sidelines, but they were not prime or even secondary movers. On the contrary, one of the aims of the Thatcher reforms was not to respond to old 'interests' but to create new ones—for example, in efficient local government and in the ownership of shares in previously nationalized industries. Thatcher's relationship with interest groups was altogether more proactive than reactive.

CIVIL SERVANTS

Many writers on policy initiation have stressed the role of senior civil servants (or, as the Americans say, 'bureaucrats') in bringing about policy change, and it is therefore worth asking what their role was in connection with the three cases being reviewed here. As in the case of interest groups, the short answer is, or seems to be, 'negligible'.

Senior public officials like Sir Herbert Llewellyn Smith at the Board of Trade and W. J. Braithwaite, who worked closely with Lloyd George at the Treasury in developing the national insurance scheme, undoubtedly contributed substantially to the Asquith government's pre-1914 reform measures; and the great French historian of Victorian and Edwardian Britain, Elie Halévy, went so far as to say that 'in the background of political life [men like these] played a part probably more important than the great political figures who occupied the stage while they worked in the wings' (1952: 265). But this is clearly an exaggeration, at least as regards the Liberal government's welfare state reforms. Llewellyn Smith may have been the principal architect of labour exchanges, but the impetus behind old age pensions and, in particular, national insurance was overwhelmingly ministerial and political. Lloyd George, in reality as well as in public perceptions, was the central figure.

In the case of the post-war Attlee government, the policy-initiating role of the Civil Service was, if anything, still further diminished. Certainly, most senior Treasury officials viewed with favour the new Keynesian ideas and were inclined to take it for granted that the British economy would be planned to some degree during the post-war period as it had been during the war; but neither the Beveridge reforms nor the National Health Service was gestated within the womb of the Civil Service, and the Labour government's nationalization proposals certainly were not. Emanuel Shinwell was not the only minister to claim that, while officials were not in any way obstructive, they had done lamentably little to prepare the details of Labour's nationalization bills. Civil servants between 1945 and 1951 co-operated with ministers; they did not take the lead.

The role of the Civil Service was the smallest of all in the case of the great Thatcher discontinuity. It is probably fair to say that in 1979 most senior officials were broadly in favour of the mildly corporatist, somewhat interventionist governmental regime that Britain had had ever since the war and, perhaps more to the point, did not think that Britain could be governed in any other way. In particular, they believed that any government would have to co-operate with the trade unions and were very sceptical that there was any effective way in which trade union power could be curbed. In 1979 most civil servants did not look forward to having to educate Thatcher in the facts of power. For her part, Thatcher detected the Civil Service's scepticism and resented it. In the event, she and her ministers got their way; but it was *their* way that they got. Civil servants did not by and large initiate, and ministers came to realize that they could gain prime ministerial approval by thinking up new ideas which reluctant officials were then forced to accept. By 1990 the original irony in the phrase 'Yes, minister' had been largely expunged. With regard to the Civil Service, as well as with regard to interest groups, the Thatcher government was a proactive rather than a reactive force.

PARTY DOCTRINE

The role of political parties in the three episodes of radical policy change is considerably more varied. One well-known and coherent model of party government holds that political parties develop bodies of doctrine, and then develop policies in terms of such doctrine. If they are elected to power, they are then in a position to translate their policies, developed in opposition, into governmental action, and this they do. How far is this model consistent with, how well does it explain, the experiences of the Asquith, Attlee, and Thatcher governments?

The model is not at all applicable to the politics of Edwardian England. The Liberal party in its heyday was not an 'institutional-ized' party by subsequent standards. It had few formally consti-tuted structures; it had few offices and few elections to fill those offices; the party in the country was only loosely connected with the party in the House of Commons. In particular, the party had no formal structures, and few informal ones, for 'making policy'. The party's policy was what the leader and other leading figures in the party said it was. It emerged consensually or not at all. It was no accident that the party did not issue an election manifesto in 1906. No one expected it to; it had no mechanisms for doing so. Campbell-Bannerman's Albert Hall speech did duty instead; and

on most subjects apart from free trade Campbell-Bannerman took
care not to make any firm commitments.

It was thus left up to the Prime Minister, individual Cabinet
ministers, and the Cabinet as a whole to develop policy. The fruit
of their deliberations was Liberal policy by virtue of being the
policy of a Liberal government, not by virtue of having emanated
from Liberal party organs—which it had not. The pre-1914 Liberal
government was a party government only in the narrow sense of
being a government consisting entirely of members of one party.

The Attlee administration was quite different. It was undoubtedly a party government in the sense of the model. During the
1930s successive Labour party conferences and a series of party
policy documents committed a future Labour government to
nationalizing a range of basic industries, and during the war the
party drew on the Beveridge Report in preparing its plans for a
national health service and a comprehensive social security system.
Labour's policies were brought together and set out in some detail
in the party's manifesto for the 1945 election, *Let Us Face the
Future*. *Let Us Face the Future* was as specific as Campbell-
Bannerman's Albert Hall address had been vague, and the post-
war Labour government proceeded to implement almost the whole
of it. Little in the programme that had not been contained in the
manifesto was omitted from the government's legislative programme; little was included in the programme that had not been
contained in the manifesto. Apart from steps taken to deal with
unforeseen circumstances, *Let Us Face the Future* constituted, in
an almost uncanny way, a prospective history of the Attlee
administration. The experience of the immediate post-war years
did much to encourage the development in people's minds of the
party government model just referred to.

The Thatcher government after 1979 represented a partial
reversion to the policy-making practices of the pre-First World
War era. Certainly, the Conservative party in opposition in the late
1970s was institutionalized and had machinery, quite elaborate
machinery, for making policy; Butler and Kavanagh (1980) have
described how some sixty working parties on Conservative policy
were set up under Thatcher's leadership between 1975 and 1979,
and the Conservatives fought the 1979 election on the basis of
three documents that had been adopted in opposition: *The Right
Approach*, published in 1976; *The Right Approach to the Econ-*

omy, published a year later; and the 1979 election manifesto itself, *Time for a Change*. But in fact all this policy-making in opposition counted for very little when the Conservatives came to power. It certainly counted for less than Labour's policies had done after 1945. It counted for less in two senses.

In the first place, much of the policy set out in the two *Right Approach* documents (and, to a lesser extent, in the manifesto) was not actually implemented. For example, *The Right Approach to the Economy* had said that 'in forming its monetary and other policies the [new Conservative] government must come to some conclusions about the likely scope for pay increases ... and this estimate cannot be concealed from the representatives of the employers and the unions whom it is consulting' (Butler and Kavanagh 1980: 154); but this statement, with its suggestion of tripartite consultations among government, employers, and unions and its hint that a pay 'norm' might be adopted, found no echo in the Thatcher government's actual practice. The Conservative documents were thus altogether less good predictors of subsequent government policy than *Let Us Face the Future* had been in Labour's case.

In the second place, the Thatcher government, like the Campbell-Bannerman and Asquith governments before it, was in no way constrained by the limits of the party policies that had been adopted in opposition. Not only did it *not* implement several of these policies, but it also, and more significantly, went far beyond its original policy declarations. Like the pre-1914 Liberal governments, the post-1979 Thatcher government was unusually creative. It invented new policy—it invented whole new lines of policy—as it went along. It took existing policy and drove it further and harder than anyone had expected, and it developed entirely new policy. Jim Prior (1986) has described the consternation that he and several of the other Cabinet 'wets' felt when they realized after 1979 that Thatcher and those around her had 'cut loose' and were determined not to be bound by their pre-1979 understandings and commitments.

The Thatcher government went further than anyone had imagined it would in imposing tight fiscal and monetary policies (there were two revolts in the Cabinet on the issue in 1981), and it also pressed ahead in an unexpectedly determined manner with its policies for reforming the laws relating to industrial relations and trade unions. But its sharpest break with the past came in the field of privatization. *Time for a Change* contained strictly limited commitments to privatization; the party promised only 'to sell back to private ownership the recently nationalised aerospace and shipbuilding concerns' and to sell shares in the National Freight Corporation (Craig 1990: 273). But in the event privatization became a central element in the Thatcher revolution, and between 1979 and 1983 alone the government sold off to the private sector not just British Aerospace but Cable and Wireless, Amersham International (a biotechnology company), Britoil and Associated British Ports, along with substantial blocks of shares in other government-owned companies.

This process of government policy running well ahead of party policy persisted throughout Thatcher's period in office. For example, a substantial section of the 1987 Conservative manifesto, *The Next Moves Forward*, was devoted to the National Health Service, but the document contained no premonitory hint whatsoever of the radical changes that were to be introduced within three years: the internal market in the NHS, the creation of NHS hospital trusts, the introduction of budget-holding by the larger general practices. Official party policy plodded; the Prime Minister raced forward.

Party doctrine and party policies thus played only a small part in inspiring the Campbell-Bannerman–Asquith 'great discontinuity'. They were more important in bringing about the great changes of the Attlee era, but they were again of only peripheral significance in connection with the Thatcher changes. The party government model referred to earlier holds well in the Attlee case (which helped to inspire it), but it holds either not at all or much less well in the Asquith and Thatcher cases. Since we have already dismissed voters' demands, the activities of interest groups, and initiative-taking by civil servants as more than partial explanations of the three cases, it is clear that we still have a good deal of explaining to do.

And the simplest explanation remaining to be considered seems also to be the best: that politicians usually innovate, not because the voters tell them to (though sometimes they do), not because they are pressed to by interest groups (though sometimes they are), and not because they are persuaded to by civil servants (though that sometimes happens too), but because they get it into their heads that they want to innovate and, more precisely, that they want to innovate along particular lines. The intellectual life of politicians is crucial. Big policy changes come about, more often than not, because powerful politicians have big ideas. And party doctrines and policies are also, of course, to a considerable extent intellectual in their origins.

THOUGHTS IN POLITICIANS' HEADS

It is striking that historians writing about the 1906–14 reforms, and modern commentators writing about those of Thatcher, are almost unanimous in attributing the changes to a few key individuals and also to the influence on those same individuals of ideas and 'intellectual currents' that were known to be running at the time.

The moving force in the Asquith administration was Lloyd George, who often took the initiative personally, especially in connection with the health provisions of the National Insurance Act. Lloyd George picked up ideas from civil servants and other acquaintances and also on his frequent foreign visits. He was influenced by the circumstances of his own childhood, and he was also influenced—who could not have been?—by the almost universal view among Edwardian intellectuals that poverty and squalor were social phenomena (rather than being the fault of individuals) and that it was society's duty, via the state, to take remedial action.

Historians of Edwardian England are eloquent on the point:

The explanation is probably superficial which looks wholly either to Parliamentary developments or to industrial organization to account for the marked turning away from Victorian economic and social ideas in the years just before the First World War. The trend of opinion in the upper classes is perhaps best seen in the literature of the time, for example, in the plays of George Bernard Shaw and John Galsworthy and the novels of H. G. Wells rather than in the specific doctrines of the Fabians or the legislation of a Liberal Parliament. This literature was increasingly critical of conventional purposes and arrangements; so much so that one might say the thought of the age had stumbled against the injustice which lies at the root of all organized society. (Court 1954: 288)

This reform programme . . . reflected a deep change in public opinion. A new attitude towards social problems was arising. In Victorian times widespread poverty and distress were accepted as inevitable. Now it was coming to be believed that the nation ought to take steps to guard its members ... against the extremes of hardship in sickness, old age or unemployment. (Hill 1961: 301)

How far opinion had come in little more than a decade from the hopeless demand for State intervention put forward in the 1894 Minority Report of the Labour Commission ... is suggested in Lloyd George's own vigorous assertion of the State's responsibility, as in a speech at Swansea ... in 1908: 'In so far as poverty is due to circumstances over which the man has no control, then the State should step in to the very utmost limit of its resources.' 'Very utmost limit' could hardly have been intended to be taken too literally, but that it could be said at all was evidence of a change in spirit and emphasis ... (Bruce 1968: 163)

In view of this intellectual climate, it would have been surprising if the Asquith government had *not* acted.

The Asquith government's reforms were thus broadly consensual. Specific provisions of the National Insurance Act aroused the hostility of adversely affected interest groups and voters; but the principle that the state should actively seek to alleviate poverty went largely uncontested among the political classes. There was certainly nothing approaching a clash of ideologies. On the day Lloyd George introduced the National Insurance Bill, Austen Chamberlain, a serious contender for the Conservative leadership, wrote in his diary: 'Confound L. G. He has strengthened the government again. His sickness scheme is a good one, and he is on the right lines' (quoted in King 1973: 309).

The same was true of the political–intellectual climate in which the Attlee government's reforms were put in place. A minority of Conservative back-benchers vocally championed the cause of rugged individualism and private enterprise, but the great majority of Conservative leaders, like the whole of the Labour party, accepted the validity of the post-war full-employment commitment, accepted the need for a substantial expansion of the welfare state, and also accepted, if without any great enthusiasm, the pragmatic case for the nationalization of basic public services.

Again, historians of that time are almost unanimous in identifying a *Zeitgeist*—a spirit of the age—that both contributed to and helped to legitimate Labour's policy revolution:

There existed, so to speak, an implied contract between Government and people; the people refused none of the sacrifices that the Government demanded of them for the winning of the war; in return, they expected that the Government should show imagination and seriousness in preparing for the restoration and improvement of the nation's well-being when the war had been won. (Hancock and Gowing 1949: 541)

The war, it could be argued, was won by 'planning'. Through careful analysis of the present and mortgaging of the future, shortages were made good, raw materials allocated and effective use made of manpower. Where necessary, powers of government were enlarged and used, and with scarcely any ideological justification or apology ... During the war all parties and nearly all elements in public opinion ... accepted the notion that reforms of education, health, housing and social insurance should be legislated according to plan. (Havighurst 1962: 378–9)

It was noticeable at the time, and has since been emphasised by historians, that no serious objections were raised, and no anti-nationalisation campaigns organised, before 1949, by which time all the measures except that relating to steel had been completed. (Barry 1965: 374–5)

Like Campbell-Bannerman and Asquith before them, Attlee and his colleagues were 'going with the grain'. They were the bearers of an ideology, but they encountered few ideological resistances.

The history of the post-1979 Thatcher government is also largely a history of ideas—thoughts in politicians' heads—being worked out in practice; contemporary observers almost at once drew attention to the fact by inventing the term 'Thatcher*ism*'. There was, however, a major difference between the Thatcher period on the one hand and the Asquith and Attlee periods on the other. It lay not in the role of ideas—they were important in all three cases—but in the fact that, in the Thatcher years, unlike the others, there was no consensual *Zeitgeist*. On the contrary, Thatcher's ideas drew attention to themselves and to their own importance by being hotly contested within the Conservative party and also by the Opposition. There developed a debate about Thatcherism in a way that there never developed a debate about 'Asquithism' or 'Attleeism'.

Thatcher's ideas were multifold: about the central place to be accorded monetary policy in the making of economic policy; about the superiority of the free market over any conceivable form of state planning; about the superiority of private enterprise over any conceivable form of state-owned enterprise (the latter being seen as a contradiction in terms); about the need to contract the frontiers of the state; but at the same time about the desirability of asserting the authority of the central British state over both local government at home and foreign governments abroad. None of these ideas was particularly original; each could be challenged. But they were *her* ideas in the sense that she and those around her were their political carriers. And it is quite clear that without her and her ideas the Thatcher revolution would never have taken place. Whereas Attlee was a man of his time who led a party with an agreed policy, Thatcher imposed her will on her time and also, for more than a decade, on her party. She was the prime mover. A Conservative government in the 1980s presided over by any of the other politicians who competed with her for the Conservative leadership in 1975 would have been a very different government.

And yet again almost all the contemporary commentators laid stress on the intellectual origins of the Thatcher discontinuity. Stuart Hall referred to the remarkable 'ideological transformation' wrought by the Thatcherites and to their success in 'providing a philosophy in the broader sense—an alternative ethic' (1983: 28). Andrew Gamble noted that from the mid-1970s onwards

the refurbished doctrines of liberal political economy made rapid progress. Keynesianism was in considerable disarray; the monetarist doctrines on the control of inflation became increasingly influential; and state expenditure, state intervention and state enterprise all came under considerable attack (1990: 139).

Peter Jenkins at the same time drew attention to the similarities between Thatcher herself and the contemporary ideologue-in-politics of the far Left, Tony Benn:

Fundamentalism would seem to flourish in the rubble of collapsed belief. Thatcherite and Bennite enthusiasm coincided with the revival elsewhere of Christian and Islamic fundamentalism. Everywhere people were groping for new certainties in an uncertain world. The consensus which Benn and Thatcher so despised had been founded in rationality: the age of Social Democracy had been the age also of the social scientist as the age of Keynes had been the age of the economist. The Keynesian notion of 'managing the economy' suggested that government was a technocratic business, comparable to the science of management. But now, in the 1970s, as things went badly and as economies declined to be managed and the governed to be governed, the priesthood of the expert fell into disrepute and the magic men were deserted by their skills. There now took place a retreat from rationality. Monetarism was a mystical creed at the heart of which lay the search for some Holy Grail of authority which would serve as surrogate for God or gold. Marxism, reviving at the same time, answered a similar need for a project which, unlike Keynesianism or Social Democracy, was capable of transforming the human condition. It was amid this intellectual and spiritual ferment, born of a dawning social pessimism, that Margaret Thatcher and Tony Benn arose as peddlers of new and simple faiths. Between them they changed the political vocabulary of the times. She placed herself at the head of an intellectual offensive against 'a generation and more of collectivist theory' which she blamed largely on Keynesianism, in Nigel Lawson's words, 'that great engine of creeping socialism'. For Benn, Keynesianism was the creed of declining capitalism, devoid of remedy for ailing manufacturing industry. They were the first political leaders to face squarely the issue of decline. (1987: 54)

Where they differed was that, in the fervent debates that followed, Thatcher won and Benn lost.

All three discontinuities thus bear witness to the importance of ideas and to practising politicians in their role as bearers of ideas. Put crudely, especially in the Asquith and Thatcher cases: no new ideas, no politicians to pick them up, no great policy transformations. Ideas are certainly not a sufficient condition for great policy transformations (parties still have to win elections); but they do appear to have constituted necessary conditions in the Britain of the twentieth century. Keynes was broadly right when he wrote, in *The General Theory of Employment, Interest and Money*, 'I am sure that the power of vested interests is vastly exaggerated compared with the gradual encroachment of ideas' (quoted in Kavanagh 1990: 18).[3] The power of electorates, political parties, and bureaucracies can also, as this chapter has tried to show, be vastly exaggerated.

If this view is broadly correct, or even if the role of ideas is assigned a smaller but still significant place in inspiring and directing political action, questions arise. Where do politicians get their ideas from? How are policy ideas in fact propagated among the political classes?

HOW THOUGHTS GET INTO POLITICIANS' HEADS

Most politicians are not original thinkers. Given their temperaments and motivations and the demands made on their time, it would be amazing if they were. Rather, they are typically pickers-up of other people's ideas. There appear to be moments when politicians are 'in the market' for new ideas, perhaps because existing policies have failed, perhaps because a new problem has presented itself, perhaps because the end in view is clear but the means for achieving it are not. At such moments the more creative politicians read selectively and listen selectively.

They do not by and large read books and learned journals (though those who do, like Sir Keith Joseph in the 1970s, may exercise a disproportionate influence). Rather, their reading consists largely (apart from government papers when they are in office) of ephemera: newspapers, weekly magazines, pamphlets, transcripts of lectures, occasionally the more accessible articles in specialist publications. Their reading will consist partly of the newspapers and magazines that they see regularly; but its content will be influenced, too, by what friends and advisers draw to their attention ('Have you seen this?' 'I thought the attached might be of interest').

Politicians' oral worlds are similarly constructed. A politician in the market for new ideas will seek out civil servants, journalists, businessmen, economists, social researchers—anyone who seems to have expertise to offer. Lunches, seminars, private meetings, visits to foreign universities will follow. It does not matter much whether the ideas thus transmitted are firsthand or secondhand: politicians are interested in the utility of ideas, not in their provenance. Some politicians acquire, usually for relatively short periods of time, individual mentors or groups of mentors, people who form part of their intellectual network and who help extend that network.

In the years after 1900 there was no shortage of new thinking, and it was widely disseminated:

The Liberal press [at the turn of the century] were devoting a great deal of space to these . . . ideas. When Massingham left *The Daily Chronicle* for *The Daily News* in 1899 (Harold Spender and Vaughan Nash accompanying him), he formed a team of advanced writers and reformers, which, with the backing of George Cadbury, campaigned continually for social politics, for social justice and for unity amongst the Progressive ranks. (Emy 1973: 132–3)

The whole Liberal press, including the *Speaker* and the *Nation*, was permeated with new thinking about 'social politics', and many of the more intellectual Liberal MPs who were elected in 1906 functioned in a dual capacity as both politicians and propagandists.

Lloyd George looked constantly for advice and advisers, especially as he worked out his national insurance scheme. In late 1910 he recruited an *ad hoc* advisory group, comprising the Attorney-General, a young Liberal whip, a junior Treasury minister, and three Treasury civil servants, chosen not because of their official duties but because Lloyd George trusted and valued them. One of the latter, W. J. Braithwaite, was dispatched to Germany to make a rapid study of the state insurance system there. When Braithwaite got back, he was almost immediately summoned to the south of France, where Lloyd George was on holiday. The young civil servant recorded in his diary the informal conference that then took place on the pier at Nice:

It was crowded. [Lloyd George] found a quiet and sheltered corner where he could not hear the band too clearly. He arranged a circle of chairs or got others to arrange it, fussing about over it all ... ordered drinks all round, put me on a chair in the middle—a straight stiff one I remember with a table against it on which I spread out a wallet—full of notes and papers—and when everyone was settled down in their lounge chairs—L. G. just opposite to me—with their drinks, he said: 'Now then, tell us all about it'. (quoted in Grigg 1978: 322)

The gestation period of the Asquith government's reforms was thus relatively short. Scarcely anyone had thought of national insurance at the turn of the century; by 1911 it had become law. The gestation period of the Attlee government's reforms was much longer, and, as we have seen, they were the result less of individual political entrepreneurship than of the Labour party's collective policy-making processes. The Attlee reforms did have intellectual roots, but they went deeper than Asquith's and Lloyd George's. The one exception was the wartime Beveridge Report, which was eagerly seized upon by Labour party leaders who were on the lookout for a well-researched and well-thought-out scheme that would enable the party to achieve its social objectives. In the climate of 1942–5 the fact that the report was the work of a Liberal and had widespread Conservative backing was an added advantage.

In the mid- and late 1970s Margaret Thatcher and Sir Keith Joseph were veritable archetypes of politicians who are actively, almost desperately, in the market for new thinking. Britain's influence in the world was declining. The British economy was failing. The Heath government, which had started with such promise, had also culminated in failure. Joseph and Thatcher wanted to know why it had done so and how a future government might do better. They established the Centre for Policy Studies. They listened to the Institute for Economic Affairs. They read the more accessible works of economists like Friedman and von Hayek. They also read the writings of economic journalists like Samuel Brittan and Peter Jay. It was of considerable assistance to them in their search for ideas that large sections of the economics profession were coincidentally challenging the received Keynesian wisdom and rediscovering classical economic theory. Like Lloyd George, Thatcher was a constant seeker-out of people who could provide her with intellectual ammunition with which to fight her political wars.

Stuart Hall, writing in 1983, described part of the process, noting that intellectual transformations 'do not take place by magic':

For years bodies like the Institute for Economic Affairs have been plugging away in the margins of the Conservative Party and the informed public debate on economic policy, refurbishing the gospel of Adam Smith and the free market, undermining the assumptions of neo-Keynesianism, planning and projecting how the 'competitive stimulus' could be applied again to one area after another of those sectors which, as they see it, have fallen into the corporatist abyss.

Gradually, in the more hospitable climate of the 1970s, these seeds began to bear fruit. First in the learned journals, then in the senior common rooms, finally in informal exchanges between the 'new academics' and the more 'sensitive' senior civil servants, a monetarist version of neo-classical economics came to provide the accepted frame of reference for economic debate. The economic journalists helped to make this revolution in ideas acceptable in the media and the serious financial press—and thus, not long after, in the boardrooms of enterprises which everyone imagined had long since abandoned open competition for the safer waters of state capitalism. (1983: 28)

Not the least of the beneficiaries of this process of intellectual propagation was Thatcher herself.

IMPLICATIONS FOR POLITICAL SCIENCE

The reasons for telling the story told in this chapter, some of it quite familiar already, are straightforward. Political scientists typically take as their units of analysis such 'hard' (or at any rate 'hard'-seeming) phenomena as voting behaviour, party competition, the activities of interest groups, and the politics of bureaucracies. In the past, with notable exceptions like Samuel Beer (1982*a*, 1982*b*), W. H. Greenleaf (1983*a*, 1983*b*), Dennis Kavanagh (1990), John Kingdon (1984), and Peter Hall (1989), they have not shown much interest in such a 'soft' phenomenon as the thoughts in politicians' heads,[4] nor in tracing the development of political *opinion*—meaning politicians' opinions—as distinct from more formal political *thought*.

Yet, as this chapter has sought to show, at least two, and probably all three, of the three great policy discontinuities in the Britain of the twentieth century cannot be understood without an understanding of the movements of ideas that helped to give rise to them and subsequently shaped them. The Asquith changes cannot be understood except in terms of the new Liberalism; the Attlee changes cannot be understood unless the development of British socialist ideas is taken into account; the Thatcher changes are unintelligible except in the light of the decline of Keynesianism, the rise of neo-liberalism, and Thatcher's personal yearning for ideas that would help her draw the right lessons from the failure of the Heath administration.

A second reason for telling the story is that political science seems to have a built-in tendency to focus on the 'demand' side of the political process: on the political demands of voters, interest groups, and others. Even the structure and content of party competition are often explained, as in the work of Downs (1957), largely in terms of parties' responses to voters' preferences. Yet an analysis like the one just presented suggests that political scientists should also give heed to the 'supply' side of democratic politics: to the alternatives that the parties present to the voters and to the innovations and the other actions of governments that are important in themselves and that voters respond to. It is one of the strengths of the Nuffield election studies that they deal wth British elections 'in the round', looking at both sides of the politician–voter relationship.

If political scientists do take a greater interest in the supply side of politics in future, and if, specifically, they do take an interest in political opinion, then they face a considerable challenge. The work of historians in this field tends to be not only *post hoc* but also totally unsystematic. Little effort is made to track in detail—perhaps by means of content analysis—the rise (or indeed the non-rise) of specific policy ideas, and there appears to be no body of theory specifying in any degree of detail when a market for new ideas may be said to exist and which ideas might be expected to be saleable in this market and which might not. The rise of Thatcherism in the 1970s and 1980s thus came as a surprise—as well as (for many) a shock. In fact, it probably should have been anticipated. With better tools of analysis, it might well have been anticipated. If such shifts in political opinion could be foreseen, the changes brought about by the ebbs and flows of popular favour might affect the whole conduct of British government in ways that were somewhat less unexpected.

Notes

1. The use of the word *demands* is widespread in political science, and is also rather strange. *Demands* is a strong word, much stronger than, say, *requests*. More than that, it implies that, if the demands are not met, sanctions will follow, as in the phrase 'demanding with menaces'. But voters and interest groups make demands in this sense only very rarely. In the first place, voters, in particular, seldom articulate their preferences in a sufficiently clear and unambiguous way for them to be identifiable as demands. In the second place, voters and interest groups are only very seldom in a position to impose effective sanctions. A more subtle vocabulary seems in order.
2. There was another field in which the Thatcher government had broad electoral support, though it was a line of policy that began to be developed under Heath rather than under Thatcher: the sale of council houses.
3. The theme of this chapter—the importance of ideas and intellectual developments to the making of public policy—is also the theme of King

(1973). Kavanagh (1990), in an analysis consistent with that presented here, devotes a whole chapter to the intellectual origins of Thatcherism.

4. Writers who have commented on the role of ideas in politics frequently use the word *agenda* in this context, as in the title of Kingdon (1984) *Agendas, Alternatives, and Public Policies*. The choice of word is understandable, but it may be somewhat misleading. The agenda of a meeting lists the items to be discussed—the items that are 'on the agenda'—but may reveal little or nothing about the specific content of the discussions that are to take place. One can ask that an item be put on the agenda without necessarily having specific proposals to make. Equally, one can develop specific proposals and only then, as a separate operation, try to get them put on the agenda. Saddam Hussein of Iraq put Kuwait on the British and American political agendas in 1990 without anyone at first having any specific proposals for dealing with him. Likewise, proposals for privatization were developed in Britain long before they appeared on any major politician's personal agenda, let alone the agenda of the whole political community. As in the case of *demands*, a more subtle vocabulary seems to be needed.

References

Barry, E. E. (1965), *Nationalisation in British Politics: The Historical Background* (London: Jonathan Cape).

Beer, S. H. (1982*a*), *Modern British Politics: Parties and Pressure Groups in the Collectivist Age* (2nd edn., London: Faber and Faber).

—— (1982*b*), *Britain against Itself: The Political Contradictions of Collectivism* (London: Faber and Faber).

Bruce, M. (1968), *The Coming of the Welfare State* (4th edn., London: B. T. Batsford).

Butler, D., and Kavanagh, D. (1980), *The British General Election of 1979* (London: Macmillan).

—— and Stokes, D. (1974), *Political Change in Britain* (2nd edn., London: Macmillan).

Court, W. H. B. (1954), *A Concise Economic History of Britain: From 1750 to Recent Times* (Cambridge: Cambridge University Press).

Craig, F. W. S. (1990) (ed.), *British General Election Manifestos, 1959–1987* (3rd edn., Chichester, West Sussex: Parliamentary Research Services).

Crewe, I. (1988), 'Has the Electorate Become Thatcherite?', in R. Skidelsky (ed.), *Thatcherism* (London: Chatto and Windus), 25–50.

Downs, A. (1957), *An Economic Theory of Democracy* (New York: Harper and Row).

Emy, H. V. (1973), *Liberals, Radicals and Social Politics* (Cambridge: Cambridge University Press).

Gallup, G. H. (1976), (ed.), *The Gallup International Public Opinion Polls: Great Britain, 1937–1975* (New York: Random House).

Gamble, A. (1990), *Britain in Decline: Economic Policy, Political Strategy and the British State* (3rd edn., London: Macmillan).

Greenleaf, W. H. (1983*a*), *The British Political Tradition: The Rise of Collectivism* (London: Methuen).

—— (1983*b*), *The British Political Tradition: The Ideological Heritage* (London: Methuen).

Grigg, J. (1978), *Lloyd George: The People's Champion, 1902–1911* (London: Eyre Methuen).

Halévy, E. (1952), *The Rule of Democracy, 1905–1914 (Book I)* (London: Ernest Benn).

Hall, P. A. (1989), (ed.), *The Political Power of Economic Ideas: Keynesianism across Nations* (Princeton, NJ: Princeton University Press).

Hall, S. (1983), 'The Great Moving Right Show', in S. Hall and M. Jacques (eds.), *The Politics of Thatcherism* (London: Lawrence and Wishart), 19–39.

Hancock, W. K., and Gowing, M. M. (1949), *British War Economy* (London: HMSO).

Havighurst, A. F. (1962), *Twentieth-Century Britain* (Evanston, Ill.: Row, Peterson).

Hill, C. P. (1961), *British Economic and Social History, 1700–1939* (2nd edn., London: Edward Arnold).

Jenkins, P. (1987), *Mrs Thatcher's Revolution: The Ending of the Socialist Era* (London: Jonathan Cape).

Kavanagh, D. (1990), *Thatcherism and British Politics: The End of Consensus?* (2nd edn., Oxford: Oxford University Press).

King, A. (1973), 'Ideas, Institutions and the Policies of Governments: A Comparative Analysis', *British Journal of Political Science*, 3: 291–313, 409–23.

Kingdon, J. W. (1984), *Agendas, Alternatives, and Public Policies* (Boston, Mass: Little, Brown).

McCallum, R. B., and Readman, A. (1947), *The British General Election of 1945* (Oxford: Oxford University Press).

Prior, J. (1986), *A Balance of Power* (London: Hamish Hamilton).

Russell, A. K. (1973), *Liberal Landslide: The General Election of 1906* (Newton Abbot, Devon: David and Charles).

Truman, D. B. (1953), *The Governmental Process* (New York: Alfred A. Knopf).

3

Press Partisanship: Into the 1990s

COLIN SEYMOUR-URE

PARTISANSHIP NEWLY IN QUESTION?

'The daily newspapers have ceased to be retailers of news—they are merely mammoth political pamphlets of the most violent partisan type': not a grumble in 1992, nor even a comment in one of David Butler's early election studies, but a contemporary comment on electioneering in 1910 (quoted in Blewett 1972: 309). The press never has been a neutral observer of parties and elections. On the contrary, papers have been an engine of party growth. *Militant*, strictly, is just a newspaper. Similarly, as the old Liberal party declined, so did the Liberal press. Parties and newspapers, politics and journalism, are historically entwined, and their connections have been tracked during election campaigns since 1945 in the Nuffield election studies with which David Butler's name has been so closely associated. Press partisanship typically has not been excused: it has been justified, rather, by reference to the partisanship of competitors. This chapter considers how far, as we move further into the 1990s, the patterns of content and readership still give credence to that justification. Or is press bias, possibly stronger now than at any time for fifty years, a problem not only for one or another party but for the press itself?

The enduring assumption of politicians and journalists alike that most newspapers will both report an election campaign and campaign themselves is in sharp contrast to the history of election television. Television has progressively insinuated itself, to the point where such sweeping claims as that 'TV *is* the campaign' seem mere truisms. This development, too, provides good grounds for exploring the trend of newspaper partisanship. Broadcasters were so fearful of changing the nature of elections in the process of reporting them—and falling foul of the law by favouring one candidate over another when doing so—that they stayed largely silent until the

1959 campaign. The whole thrust since then has had the effect of making broadcasters participants, shaping the campaign as much as newspapers ever did. The nearest they have come to avoiding this is in their judgements about, say, the important issues of the campaign and about the questions to put to party leaders. Here, they have adopted a tribune role, arguing, not as one partisan with another, like the press, but with each party indifferently on behalf of the elector/viewer. They have legitimated their behaviour by resorting to opinion polls, which provide useful backing for awkward questions. More than ever before, however, television may have partisan consequences even if it has no partisan intentions. With more channels and fewer effective rules about 'balance', such as have governed for years the party election broadcasts, television is likely to be seen by politicians in the future much less than in the past as a counter to the bias of the press. Therefore the press itself may be subject in the future to less tolerant scrutiny.

Among newspapers, the notable change, in the context of partisanship, has been the shift to tabloid format. The scale is easily dramatized. At the 1959 election 5.7 million people bought two tabloid papers and 10.4 million bought seven broadsheets. In 1987 12.2 million bought six tabloids and 2.6 million bought five broadsheets. Gone were the middle-ground broadsheet *News Chronicle* (1960) and *Daily Herald* (1964), while the *Daily Mail* and the *Daily Express* changed to tabloid format in 1971 and 1977. In approach, the change is epitomized in the comments of the Nuffield election study of 1979: 'The written text merely served to reinforce the "images" the headline writers wished to suggest to the readers, so much so that the medium of the headline was often more useful in propaganda terms than the accompanying article' (Butler and Kavanagh 1980: 238). The dominance of tabloid newspapers has accompanied, and arguably facilitated, a strong resurgence of press partisanship since 1979.

Regardless of style and format, there are reasons also for supposing partisanship may have more significant electoral consequences because the influence of the press may be growing. Harrop, for example, bases such a claim partly on the very fact of stronger press partisanship. But he argues the case by reference also to the declining circulation of Labour newspapers and the consequent increase in voters reading the 'wrong' paper; the increasing recognition by readers of their paper's partisanship; the growing readership of the more influential broadsheet papers; the backdrop of greater electoral volatility; and the increasingly important indirect role of the press in shaping the agenda of television news (Harrop 1987: 58).

Harrop's judgement is that, on balance, the electoral impact of the press remains small. He argues elsewhere (Crewe and Harrop 1986: 146–8) that press partisanship may have accounted in the period 1964–79 for a swing to the Conservatives of about 1 per cent (ten seats) between one election and another. More recent analysis by Miller, however, suggests a stronger effect. For instance, after reinterviewing in March 1987 a national sample interviewed one year earlier, he concludes that the more tabloid the paper, the more likely were its readers to swing to the Conservatives, independently of their initial party preferences. *Sun* and *Star* readers in particular, especially those not strongly partisan, swung to the Conservatives heavily (Miller *et al.* 1990; Miller 1991).

Papers' ideas about the nature of news and of elections probably help some parties more than others too, irrespective of the papers' intended partisanship. Papers like splits and rows: parties try to avoid them. Papers dislike a 'quiet campaign': the government party quite often wants one. Papers like clear-cut issues that differentiate the parties tidily and are discussed by lively personalities: issues are not always like that, nor do parties wish to talk about the same ones. Some issues (housing?) seem to fit the graphic style of tabloid papers better than others (European unity?). Non-election events sometimes intrude unexpectedly (for the parties) into press coverage. Slips and chance remarks (Pym on over-large majorities (1983); Kinnock on enemy occupation (1987)) haunt their perpetrators. Papers emphasize individual leaders (for example, in the choice of photographs); parties may prefer to emphasize their 'team'.

Even if papers apply news values impartially, just like television, their judgements tend to favour one or another party implicitly— and sometimes randomly. The electoral impact may be just as great or as small as that of deliberate partisanship.

THE SCALE OF ELECTION COVERAGE

The examination of partisan trends can start with a brief look at the scale of election coverage. The press does still regard a general

election as a very important event: that much at least can be taken
for granted. In 1983 election news ranged from 27 per cent of total
news (*Star, Mail*) to 45 per cent (*Express*) (Table 3.1). Total
election coverage ranged from an average 142 column inches a day
(*Star*) to 653 (*Guardian*). The 1987 news percentages are not
available. The average *total* daily column inches of election coverage ranged from 216 in the *Star* to 671 in the *Guardian*. Table 3.1
also includes column inches for February 1974. Allowing for some
differences in the number of pages, the absolute levels were not
substantially different.

A more selective measure is the number of lead stories on the
election and the number of editorials (Table 3.1 again). These
reflect qualitative judgements, implicit in the former and explicit in
the latter, about the election's importance. Lead stories are easiest
to compare, because each paper has only one a day. On this
measure, 1987 was a less noteworthy election than 1983, except in
the *Sun* (which led with the election twice as often). The broadsheet
papers led with the election about four days out of five, the middle-
market tabloids slightly less, and the other tabloids one day (or
less) out of two. In 1983 the broadsheets and the *Express* had an
election lead nearly every day. Editorials were fewer in 1987 too,
but the percentages are confusing because papers often had several
each day. Only the *Mirror* and the *Star* averaged fewer than one
per day about the election. The *Guardian* had thirty-one altogether,
but this was a lower percentage of its total than were the fourteen
of the *Mirror*.

On this basis, we could expect the 1992 election to dominate the
news—to lead it most days in the broadsheets and perhaps in the
middle-market tabloids, but to take second place possibly more
often than not in the mass-market tabloids. Papers vary from one
election to another, and not always in the same direction as each
other.

THE GENERAL QUALITY OF COVERAGE

Qualitative measures of coverage are more difficult to apply.
Surveying post-war elections from the vantage-point of 1984,
Harrop writes that, with the development of political television,
the broadsheet papers have placed 'increasing emphasis on back-

TABLE 3.1. *National daily papers, election coverage, February 1974, 1983, 1987*

Coverage	Daily Mirror	Daily Express	Daily Mail	Star	Sun	Daily Telegraph	Guardian	The Times	Today	Independent
Election news (as % of all news)										
1983	29	45	27	27	28	38	36	32	—	—
Election coverage: (av. col. ins. per day)										
1974 (Feb.)	293	244	260	—	246	321	739	555	—	—
1983	177	291	225	142	169	463	653	562	—	—
1987	266	363	336	216	226	429	671	653	296	586
Lead stories (no.)										
1983 (23 days)	14	20	19	7	5	23	22	23	—	—
1987 (22 days)	9	18	15	3	11	23	18	16	13	19
Editorials: (no. and max. possible)										
1983	22/23	34/54	28/48	14/26	31/53	37/61	31/56	23/59	—	—
1987	14/22	27/31	29/39	14/42	27/54	24/43	31/55	22/55	21/29	25/40

Source: Derived from Butler and Kavanagh (1974, 1984, 1988).

ground information such as poll analyses, expert commentaries, opinion columns and so on'. In tabloids, by contrast, 'background is still squeezed out between isolated snippets of information and larger doses of propaganda' (Crewe and Harrop 1986: 143). The broadsheet/tabloid contrast was much less marked before television: 'all newspapers gave greater weight to news, most especially to reports of speeches' (ibid.). To Craik, in a comparable survey, this tendency suggests that 'the press has largely abandoned its own distinction between news ("objective reporting") and comment (in editorials and by commentators)'. She sees 1979 as the turning-point, 'as straight news virtually vanished from the press to be replaced by accounts that explicitly contained impressions and opinions' (Craik 1987: 77).

Harrop's analyses of the 1983 and 1987 campaigns for the Nuffield election studies are full of such judgements and refer to the traditional range of partisan techniques. First, there were inequalities of space. The broadsheet papers were generally scrupulous: in 1987 'the quality dailies gave no more coverage to Labour than to the Conservatives'—with the exception of the *Daily Telegraph*, which 'concentrated on Labour's defects.' (Butler and Kavanagh 1988: 168). 'Labour's defects' were the central focus of the campaign. But, as Table 3.2 shows, all the tabloids except the *Mirror* gave more space to Labour. The *Mirror* gave more to the Conservatives.

This practice of giving more space to your opponents had shown up almost as strongly in 1983. It is the best simple indicator of the revival of full-blooded, no-holds-barred press partisanship since 1974. An analysis of the elections of 1966 to October 1974 was able to conclude (in 1975) that 'papers have consistently given more space to the party they support editorially' (Seymour-Ure 1977: 181) (see Table 3.2). Since the 1980s, in contrast, *knocking copy* rules. In 1987 the practice was most extreme in the *Sun* and the *Mirror*. The techniques of knocking copy are nothing new, but they have regained popularity. For example, the most distinctive feature of press coverage in 1987, according to Harrop, was 'well-prepared smears against individual politicians'—a new trend (Butler and Kavanagh 1988: 180). The *Sun* 'not only made hay with any scandal it could find about Labour politicians, but also linked the party as a whole with sexual minorities' (ibid.: 168–9). In 1983, similarly, 'The *Sun*'s leader columns displayed a talent for

TABLE 3.2   *National daily papers, distribution of space between parties in general elections, 1966–74, 1983, 1987*

Paper	Party support	Con. (%)	Lab. (%)	Lib. (%)
Daily Mirror				
1966	Lab.	33	59	8
1970	Lab.	35	58	7
1974(1)	Lab.	41	49	10
1974(2)	Lab.	34	59	7
1983	Lab.	59	30	9
1987	Lab.	48	44	6
Daily Express				
1966	Con.	59	33	7
1970	Con.	49	42	9
1974(1)	Con.	43	42	15
1974(2)	Con.	43	54	12
1983	Con.	37	41	16
1987	Con.	40	44	15
Daily Mail				
1966	Con.	61	33	6
1970	Con.	50	38	12
1974(1)	Con.	49	33	18
1974(2)	Con.–Lib. coalition	39	54	8
1983	Con.	43	35	18
1987	Con.	35	54	10
Sun				
1966	Lab.	44	42	13
1970	Lab.	37	47	16
1974(1)	Con.	49	36	14
1974(2)	all-party coalition	39	53	8
1983	Con.	44	41	13
1987	Con.	22	73	5
Daily Sketch				
1966	Con.	51	38	11
1970	Con.	51	40	9

TABLE 3.2 (*Cont.*)

Paper	Party support	Con. (%)	Lab. (%)	Lib. (%)
Daily Telegraph				
1966	Con.	52	31	18
1970	Con.	53	36	11
1974(1)	Con.	54	34	12
1974(2)	Con.	49	40	11
1983	Con.	44	37	15
1987	Con.	31	39	26
Guardian				
1966	Lab./Lib.	29	43	28
1970	Lab./Lib.	45	40	15
1974(1)	Con.–Lab.–Lib. balance	40	40	19
1974(2)	More Lib.	35	45	20
1983	no Con. landslide	37	34	19
1987	Lab.	36	32	17
The Times				
1966	Lib.?	40	47	13
1970	Con./Lib.	42	51	6
1974(1)	Con./Lib.	43	39	18
1974(2)	Con./Lib.	40	46	14
1983	Con.	35	40	16
1987	Con.	34	34	28
Daily Star				
1983	Con.	35	40	16
1987	Con.	34	46	17
Today				
1987	coalition	32	36	25
Independent				
1987	uncommitted	35	35	24

Note: Minor parties excluded. The period covered is the three weeks of each campaign, i.e. 18 weekdays. In 1970 a strike reduced coverage to 16 days. No data were collected for the 1979 election.

Source: Data collected for Nuffield election studies.

political invective but not for sustained argument' (Butler and Kavanagh 1984: 188). There was also a revival of stunts. As Harrop puts it, 'If in doubt, run a red scare. This traditional maxim of the Tory press was followed by the *Daily Mail* and the *Daily Express*' (Butler and Kavanagh 1988: 171). Campaigning series have proved popular too. The *Mirror*'s final-week coverage in 1983 was dominated by a 'Waste of a Nation series', with selective statistics and graphic pictures illustrating 'the human consequences of Conservative policies' (Butler and Kavanagh 1984: 189). The *Express* ran 'Spot the Trot' and 'Labour's Guilty Men' series.

Polls, finally, can make good knocking copy. Butler and Kavanagh noted in 1987 that, while pollsters and client papers honoured an agreed code of conduct, 'other papers, as they reported their rivals' poll findings, often in summary form, were less scrupulous, and a number of their reports had decidedly misleading headlines' (Butler and Kavanagh 1988: 126). With polls so numerous (seventy-three in 1987, between 11 May and 11 June, up from fewer than ten in 1955), the potential for a more substantial partisan misuse must inevitably be high—if only through decisions about how prominently and where in the paper to feature them, and which of one's rivals' (including the broadcasters') to take up. The strongest test will come if and when the Conservative press is again faced, as it was in 1966, with persistently unfavourable polls.

Most of these observations obviously refer to the tabloid press. The broadsheet papers, by comparison, have consistently been models of non-partisan rectitude in their news columns: 'The quality dailies provided a depth and range of election coverage sufficient to satisfy the most demanding enthusiast,' remarks Harrop of the 1987 election (Butler and Kavanagh 1988: 172). Their coverage was also 'more balanced'. Such comments could have been made after any post-war election. But in 1987, as Harrop confirms, the contrast with the tabloids could never have been more sharp.

THE PATTERN OF SUPPORT: PAPERS, PARTIES, AND READERS

Much of the significance of press partisanship depends on the pattern of newspaper readership. The number of papers supporting

TABLE 3.3. *National daily papers, partisanship at general elections, 1945–1987: Summary*

Press partisanship	1945	1950	1951	1955	1959	1964	1966	1970	Feb. 1974	Oct. 1974	1979	1983	1987
No. of papers supporting													
Con.	4	5	5	5	5	6	4	4	5	4	5	7	7
Lab.	2	2	2	2	2	3	2	2	1	1	2	1	2
Lib.	2	2	1	1	1	—	1	—	—	—	—	—	—
Mixed	—	—	1	1	1	—	1	2	2	3	1	1	1
None	1	—	—	—	—	—	1	—	—	—	1	—	1
Total circulation (mill.)	12.8	16.6	16.6	16.2	16.1	15.8	15.6	15.1	14.7	14.8	14.9	14.8	14.9
Total votes cast (mill.)	24.0	28.8	28.6	26.8	27.9	27.7	27.3	28.3	31.3	29.2	31.2	30.1	32.5
Con.													
circulation (%)	52	50	52	52	54	57	55	57	71	69	67	78	74
votes (%)	40	43	48	50	49	43	42	46	38	36	44	42	42
Lab.													
circulation (%)	35	50	39	40	38	42	42	43	32	50	27	22	26
votes (%)	48	46	49	46	44	44	48	43	37	39	37	28	31
Lib.													
circulation (%)	13	10	10	9	9	—	3	5	5	26	—	—	2
votes (%)	9	9	1	2	6	11	8	7	19	18	14	25	23

Note: Totals include papers with divided support and may sum to more than 100%.

Source: Derived from Seymour-Ure (1991: Table 8.2).

TABLE 3.4 *Parties and national daily papers, 1987 General Election*

Party	Vote (%)	No. of dailies supporting	No. of ownership groups	% Share of circulation	If *Sun* supported Lab.		If *Sun* supported Alliance	
					Papers	Circulation	Papers	Circulation
Con.	42	7.3	6	74	6.3	46	6.3	46
Lab.	31	2.3	2	26	3.3	53	2.3	26
Alliance	23	0.3	*	2	0.3	*	1.3	28

Notes: *Today* supported a coalition and is credited 0.3 to each party. It is omitted from the 'Ownership Groups'. The *Independent* was uncommitted and is excluded.
 * Less than 1 per cent.
Source: Derived from Butler and Kavanagh (1988: 165–6).

each party in the general elections since 1945 is summarized in Table 3.3, with the parties' shares of votes and total circulation. Table 3.4 gives a little more detail for 1987. In that year the Conservatives had 42 per cent of the vote but 74 per cent of national daily circulation. Labour's share was not drastically out of line (31 per cent/26 per cent). But the nearly one-in-four voters supporting the Alliance had no editorial endorsement at all beyond the partial support of *Today*. The extent to which this disadvantage is nothing new for Labour is indicated in Table 3.3. Only in 1950 and October 1974 (when several papers split their loyalty) has Labour had a larger share of circulation than of votes. These totals conceal, however, the fact that it is by no means only non-Conservative voters who read the 'wrong' paper.

The imbalance of voters and circulation depends very largely on the views of the two largest tabloids, the *Sun* and the *Mirror*. It would have taken only a shift by the *Sun* to Labour (see Table 3.4) for the imbalance in 1987 to swing the other way (31 per cent of the vote for Labour, and 53 per cent of circulation). If the *Sun* had decided to support the Alliance, on the other hand, the ratio of party votes to circulation would have come fairly closely in line. Equally, if Murdoch switched his papers away from the post-Thatcher Conservative party in 1992, the impact in these terms would be dramatic. A shift by the *Sun* in 1987 would have made little dent, of course, in the imbalance of *numbers* of party papers. A Labour voter had a choice of one broadsheet and one tabloid in 1987; a Conservative, of three broadsheets and four tabloids.

Simple measures of a fair distribution of circulation do depend, then, very substantially on shifts in the support of just one or two tabloids. That having been said, however, it is worth noting that talk of newspapers changing their party support is *extremely* hypothetical in the post-war era. In the twelve elections after 1945 there was just one straight, Pauline conversion from one major party to the other. This was the *Sun*'s move from Labour in 1970 (when Murdoch had not long owned it) to Conservative in February 1974. All other movements have been glosses, compromises—flirtations with coalition or a centre party. Populars have sometimes gone through a 'First the facts, then the verdict' exercise (the *Mirror*'s tactic in 1966), but the verdict has never been in doubt.

The relation between partisanship and readers looks different again if account is taken of *social class*. Table 3.5 shows readership

TABLE 3.5 *Newspaper readership and social class, 1990* (per cent of each class reading paper)

Paper	AB (18% of pop. 15+)	C1 (24%)	C2 (28%)	DE (30%)
Daily Mirror	8	18	30	31
Daily Express	10	11	8	6
Daily Mail	14	13	8	6
Star	1	3	8	9
Sun	7	17	29	31
Today	3	5	5	3
Daily Telegraph	16	6	2	1
Financial Times	5	2	*	*
Guardian	8	4	1	1
Independent	8	3	1	1
The Times	9	3	1	*

Note:
   * Less than 1 per cent.
Source: Joint Industry Committee for National Readership Surveys (JICNARS), Jan.–Dec. 1990.

of the national dailies by social class for January–December 1990. It is a long familiar pattern. Working-class readership is bunched: about 60 per cent of C2DE readership (three-fifths of the population) is of the *Mirror* or the *Sun*. (But duplication figures suggest overlap of about 30 per cent.) The higher up the class scale you go, the more evenly is readership distributed and the greater is the range of political coverage to which the class collectively is exposed in an election campaign. The same data are shown in Table 3.6 in summary according to papers' political support. The point for a Labour partisan to score is that fewer than one working-class reader in three reads a Labour tabloid—the 'natural paper of the working class'. Labour leaders reach half their natural class constituency through hostile tabloids, and they have only a small chance of reaching the AB classes through a Labour paper at all.

The force of that claim is somewhat weakened—but to an uncertain extent—by readership duplication. A great deal of duplication is claimed by survey respondents. In Table 3.7 the papers are grouped by their party support. Readers of Conservative papers

TABLE 3.6. *Daily newspaper reading, by social grade and newspaper partisanship, 1990*

Social grade	% reading		
	Con. broadsheet	Con tabloid	Lab.
AB	31	32	16
C1	11	44	22
C2	3	53	31
DE	1	52	32

Note: Excludes *Independent*, *Today*.
Source: JICNARS Jan.–Dec. 1990.

claiming also to read a Labour paper range from 15 per cent of *Telegraph* readers to 48 per cent of the *Star*'s. The mode is 20–2 per cent. Almost one in three *Sun* readers say they see the *Mirror* or the *Guardian*. Not surprisingly, readers of the *Mirror* and the *Guardian* are exposed in rather greater proportions (60 per cent in each case) to papers supporting the Conservative party.

Table 3.8 shows the distribution of party support among each national daily paper's readers in late 1990, 1987, and 1975. The distribution obviously varies with the popularity of the parties, so in 1990 the Conservative and Liberal Democrat figures were generally down and Labour's were up. A clear trend is difficult to discern, and there is considerable variation between papers. But the figures confirm, again, how many partisans habitually read the 'wrong' paper—and particularly how many Labour voters read Conservative papers. The tendency is shown in a different form in Table 3.9, where the readers of each paper are expressed as a percentage of each party's vote in 1987. Because of duplicate reading, some voters are counted more than once, so the figures cannot be used at all precisely. Even so, it seems likely that more Labour voters were reading a Conservative daily than a Labour daily, while nearly every Conservative voter read a Conservative daily. Alliance voters read fewer papers than others, and only a handful (8 per cent) saw a paper that was not editorially unfriendly.

A last point about press partisanship and readers is the reminder that in 1987 many readers still did not identify the partisanship of their paper correctly. Fifteen per cent of its readers did not identify the *Daily Telegraph* as Conservative, for example. Twelve per cent

TABLE 3.7 *Readership duplication, 1990*

Paper	% of readers also reading						
	Con. broadsheet	Con. tabloid	Any Con.	None	Mirror*	Guardian	Either Lab.
Con. papers							
Sun	2	28	30	54	31	1	32
Daily Mail	15	37	52	58	16	3	19
Daily Express	11	41	52	56	22	3	25
Daily Star	5	73	78	30	46	2	48
Daily Telegraph	14	38	52	60	10	5	15
The Times	34	35	69	48	11	10	21
Financial Times	52	47	99	24	12	13	25
Lab. papers							
Daily Mirror	4	56	60	57		2	
Guardian	24	35	59	58	11		
Uncommitted/coalition							
Independent	37	30	67	51	11	16	27
Today	10	89	99	37	32	4	36

Note
* *Daily Mirror* includes *Daily Record*.
Source: JICNARS, Jan.–Dec. 1990.

TABLE 3.8. *Party supported by daily newspaper readers, 1990 (1987 and 1975 in brackets)*

Press partisanship	Con. (%)	Lab. (%)	Lib./Alliance (%)
Conservative in 1987			
Daily Express	65 (70; 58)	20 (9; 26)	12 (18; 12)
Daily Mail	67 (60; 55)	19 (13; 26)	13 (19; 16)
Star	22 (28; —)	70 (46; —)	5 (18; —)
Sun	36 (41; 23)	50 (31; 59)	10 (19; 13)
Daily Telegraph	76 (80; 70)	13 (5; 10)	11 (10; 18)
Financial Times	72 (—; 79)	17 (—; ?)	11 (—; 15)
The Times	54 (56; 47)	23 (12; 22)	21 (27; 24)
Labour in 1987			
*Daily Mirror**	18 (20; 27)	73 (55; 57)	7 (21; 12)
Guardian	10 (22; 33)	61 (54; 33)	23 (19; 29)
Uncommitted/coalition in 1987			
Independent	27 (34; —)	48 (34; —)	19 (27; —)
Today	38 (43; —)	42 (17; —)	16 (40; —)

Notes: 1990: Labour lead over Conservative, 6%; 1987: Conservative lead over Labour: 11%; 1975: Labour lead over Conservative, 2%.
   * *Daily Mirror* excludes *Daily Record* in 1990.
Sources: MORI, Oct–Dec. 1990; MORI/*Sunday Times*, 27–8 May 1987 (Butler and Kavanagh 1988: 187); MORI, Sept. 1975.

of *Sun* readers and 16 per cent of *Star* readers thought their papers were Labour, and 13 per cent of *Guardian* readers thought the *Guardian* was Conservative (MORI, quoted in Butler and Kavanagh 1988: 187).

IMPLICATIONS OF PRESS PARTISANSHIP

Looking only at column inches and readership figures does not tell us what people actually read nor how they interpret it. Nevertheless, it is easy enough to make political capital from the kind of simple data presented above. Indeed, the claim of this chapter is that it is easier to do so at the start of the 1990s than at any time in the post-war era. Perhaps the temptation of a future non-Conservative government to 'correct' partisan bias will be quickly stopped by calculations of cost and benefit. If Labour can get office

TABLE 3.9.   *Readers of daily newspapers as a percentage of each party's vote, by party affiliation, 1987 general election*

Paper	% Con. voters who read	% Lab. voters who read	% Alliance voters who read
Conservative papers			
Daily Express	22	4	11
Daily Mail	20	6	12
Star	8	18	10
Sun	34	35	29
Daily Telegraph	16	1	4
The Times	5	1	4
TOTAL	(105)*	(66)*	(70)*
Labour Papers			
Daily Mirror	13	49	26
Guardian	2	8	4
TOTAL	(15)*	(57)*	(30)*
Uncommitted/coalition			
Independent	2	3	4
Today	3	2	5
TOTAL	(5)*	(4)*	(8)*
Total readership as % of party's total vote	126	127	108

Note:
    * Percentages are rounded and totals do not all sum.
Sources: JICNARS readership figures and MORI/*Sunday Times* poll of readers' partisanship, as reported in Butler and Kavanagh (1988: Tables 8.1, 8.7).

despite the press, why bother to try and curb press partisanship—with all the outcry from libertarians (of all colours) about press freedom and with the prospect that a future Conservative government might readily use the precedent to Labour's disadvantage?

Whether or not intervention remains hypothetical, any attempt to correct excessive press partisanship would have to decide what 'fairness' and 'balance' should actually mean. The historical pattern (for example, in the decades before the First World War) suggests a variety of possible criteria, some of which are implicit in the previous pages.

There is a clear distinction, firstly, between the balance in a press-and-party system as a whole and the balance within an individual paper. In a press–party system we might look for a balance between the number of partisan papers and the number of parties, so that each party was represented by a proper number of loyal papers. We might also hope for a balance between total circulation and total votes for each party, and even a balance in the degree of partisanship of the papers (are some more loyal or propagandist than others, and so on?).

Within any individual paper, we might look for fair and balanced coverage. This could mean keeping editorial partisanship strictly in the leader columns and/or giving the major parties 50/50 coverage. Alternatively, it could mean giving the parties coverage proportionate to their respective strengths. This last is the practice of the broadcasters. But how would it be judged for the press? By the polls? By previous electoral votes? By readers' political preferences? Lastly, fairness could mean giving the parties coverage very largely on their own terms: that is, adopting their own judgements of the important issues, personalities, and events, and presenting them generally as their campaign managers would like them to be presented.

A practical problem for the hypothetical policy-maker is that measures of balance within a party–press system do not necessarily coincide with those for individual papers. In the former there might be extremely partisan papers which collectively provide a balanced system because each party had the correct amount of newspaper support. It would be a balance, literally, of opposing weights. Viewed singly, however, each paper would appear hopelessly unfair and unbalanced in relation to the parties it opposed. The system of national dailies in the 1990s contains residual elements of both these alternatives. The broadsheet papers tend, in their reportage, to use 'single-paper' criteria of balance—so that Labour readers of *The Times*, for instance, may feel as well satisfied with the coverage of their party as Conservatives do with theirs. Party endorsement is kept (explicitly) for the leader and opinion columns. The tabloid papers, on the other hand, now make no attempt at 'fairness' to the parties they oppose. The *Sun* (unless having a change of heart for the 1992 election) implicitly tells its Labour readers to go and read the *Mirror* if they want the Labour view of an election campaign. Where Liberal Democrats are supposed to go is an unanswered question.

This could be one quite reasonable way for a policy-maker to treat the present configuration of national dailies: one set of rules for the broadsheets, another for the tabloids. If the two kinds of publication are not really 'newspapers' in the same sense, it may be better not to apply the same criteria to them, just as different criteria have been applied to the broadcasters in an era of public-service broadcasting. Much of the (unread?) reportage and analysis in the broadsheets, in fact, is arguably motivated by comparable 'public-service' values, such that those papers resemble the broadcasters more than they do the tabloids. In 1987, for instance, television and the broadsheet papers gave very similar ratios of coverage to the various parties.

So we return to the mutual affinities of the different media. The broadsheets may have editorial values closer to the broadcasters, but the tabloids resemble television more closely in their emphasis on personalities and graphics and in their limited capacity to report in detail. In general, there is a symbiosis of press and television reportage. Both media set agenda and follow up each other's stories. The press reports politicians' television performances as part of the hustings. Both media rely heavily upon polls. Party election broadcasts have turned into advertisements (such as 'Kinnock the Movie' in 1987), while political advertising in the press grew substantially (and expensively) in 1983 and 1987.

The student of politics can accept that forums and styles of political communication necessarily change in response to changes in the technologies and utility of particular media. When television watching occupies people for twenty-five hours or so every week, it cannot remain isolated from politics. Equally, if tabloid papers are what most people will buy, tabloid politics is to some extent inevitable. But beyond the issue of fairness to particular parties lie larger questions—about the linkages of political leadership to voters and the future of mass parties. The full significance of the kind of data this chapter briefly explores may, therefore, lie in its support for the conclusion that in the 1990s party leaders look as though they have less control than at any other time in this century over whether and how their ideas and activities are presented to the public, and they have fewer opportunities to be sure of presenting them on their own terms. That surely bodes ill both for the future of the mass party as a political institution and, if a party in government loses patience, for the political independence of the press.

References

Blewett, N. (1972), *The Press, the Parties and the People: The General Elections of 1910* (London: Macmillan).

Butler, D., and Kavanagh, D. (1974), *The British General Election of February 1974* (London: Macmillan).

—— —— (1980), *The British General Election of 1979*, (London: Macmillan).

—— —— (1984), *The British General Election of 1983*, (London: Macmillan).

—— —— (1988), *The British General Election of 1987*, (London: Macmillan).

Craik, J. (1987), in J. Seaton and B. Pimlott (eds.), *The Media in British Politics* (London: Avebury), 64–89.

Crewe, I. (1990), *Guardian*, 19 Nov.

—— and Harrop, M. (1986), *Political Communications: The General Election Campaign of 1983*, (Cambridge: Cambridge University Press).

Harrop, M. (1987), 'Voters', J. Seaton and B. Pimlott, (eds.), The Media in British Politics (London: Avebury), 45–63.

Miller, W. (1991), *Media and Voters: The Audience, Content and Influence of Press and Television at the 1987 General Election* (Oxford: Clarendon Press).

—— Clarke, H. D., Le Duc, L., and Whiteley, P. (1990), *How Voters Change* (Oxford: Clarendon Press).

Seymour-Ure, C. (1977), 'National Daily Papers and the Party System', in O. Boyd-Barrett, C. Seymour-Ure, and J. Tunstall, *Studies in the Press* (London: HMSO), 159–202.

—— (1991), *The British Press and Broadcasting since 1945* (Oxford: Blackwell).

4

Dialogue of the Deaf? The Élite and the Electorate in Mid-Century Britain

HUGH BERRINGTON

And we are here as on a darkling plain,
Swept with confused alarms of struggle and flight,
Where ignorant armies clash by night.

(Matthew Arnold, *Dover Beach*)

Politicians, however democratic the mode of their election, how-ever broad the suffrage by which they are chosen, are never representative of those they represent. Such a paradox poses problems both for the conduct of democratic government itself, and for the attempts of politicians to mobilize the electoral coalitions on which their chances of power rest.

Political representatives are unrepresentative in three main ways. They differ from most of their electors by virtue of their social backgrounds and their education, and, above all, because of their deep and continuing involvement in politics. It is an unusual man or woman who stands for election to Parliament.

The contrast between the social-class backgrounds of politicians, and of ordinary voters, requires little discussion. The ground is well-trodden. Decision-makers, throughout the Western world, are drawn in striking disproportion from the well-born, the well-to-do, and the upper-middle and middle classes. The kingdom of heaven may discriminate against the rich, but both the kingdoms and the republics of this world have a bias against the poor. No matter how democratic the electoral procedures may be, national parliaments and political executives rarely, if ever, mirror the class make-up of their electorates. Legislators and Cabinet ministers have usually been insulated from the day-to-day experiences of those who voted for them.

You probably don't realise, Charles [said Clementine Churchill, Winston's wife], that he [Winston] knows nothing of the life of ordinary people. He's

never been in a bus and only once on the Underground ... That was
during the General Strike, when I deposited him at South Kensington. He
went round and round, not knowing where to get out, and had to be
rescued eventually. (Moran 1966: 269)

It is hard indeed for a political leader to gauge grass-roots
opinion if he never overhears the common discourse of his country-
men on the train, in a bus, or in a shop. It seems even harder for
some to apprehend that most people have led lives whose nature
they can hardly begin to understand. 'In the life of an Englishman,'
wrote Duff Cooper, Churchill's contemporary and government
colleague, 'no period is more important than the years that he
spends at public school' (1953: 18), blind to the truth that few
Englishmen have ever shared such an experience.

Class, though, is an easy target, and there is much more to the
insulation of political leaders than their social origins or the size
and sources of their incomes. A more telling difference lies in
education. Political leaders are usually distinguished from ordinary
voters by a longer period of formal schooling, and following that
by university or professional training. It is not simply that politicians are better-informed than their electors, though their stock of
knowledge, both general and political, is likely to be much bigger,
more diverse, and much more detailed than that of the average
voter. More significant is the difference in the style of reasoning
and in the mode of discourse. Above all, the politician's belief-
system is likely to be far more complex, and much more sophisticated than that of most of his or her compatriots.

There is something, though, that outstrips both class and education as a cause of the unrepresentativeness of political leaders. It is
that the politician *is* a politician: no matter how humble his or her
family, no matter how rudimentary his or her formal education,
the politician will be psychologically untypical of the electorate.
For ordinary voters, politics is often peripheral; for the MP it is the
chief, perhaps the only, interest in life. The psychological effort
needed to adapt to the mode of thought of the passive citizen can
be immense. Moreover, most of the politician's everyday routine
serves to reinforce his isolation from the politically uninvolved.
Most of his or her time is spent working with, and talking to,
similar people. Only the local surgery or the canvass brings contact
with the politically inactive. The gap between rich and poor,

between company director and unskilled worker, may seem broad; so, too, may that between a university graduate and a pensioner who left school at fourteen; but neither is as wide as the gap between the politically dormant and the man or woman whose life is dedicated to politics. 'It had been love at first sight . . . with the irresistible canvass-cards and the marked-up registers that could not be denied' (Hattersley 1984: 180).

THE ASSESSMENT OF PUBLIC OPINION

There is nothing novel in itself about the attention that modern politicians pay to the measurement of public opinion. Politicians have always been seeking to appraise public opinion—through guesswork, through anecdote, through personal sampling. Thus, Duff Cooper, describing the appearance after the Munich Agreement of privately circulated newsletters, said:

They thrived on the suspicion that truth was being concealed, and they satisfied the demand for it that was felt by men and women of all parties. I say 'men and women' because I could count at that time, among my own acquaintance, twelve happily married couples, who were divided upon the issue of Munich, and in every case it was the husband who supported and the wife who opposed Chamberlain. Many would have expected that women would have been more ready than men to accept the spurious peace at its face value. But it was not so. (1953: 251)

From a tiny and biased quota sample, Duff Cooper inferred considerable feminine opposition to appeasement. All politicians are pollsters of a sort.

This concern with public opinion dates at least from the introduction of a broad suffrage, if not before. Unfortunately the technical means of identifying public opinion did not keep pace with the expansion of the electorate. After half a century of the systematic study of public opinion it is easy to forget the crudity of the ways in which politicians sought to make their own appraisals.

Such appraisals were based on three main sources: personal contact, public indicators such as by-elections and general elections, and, to use an omnibus term, hunch. This word covers all those psychological processes such as projection, pre-emptive pessimism, and wishful thinking which help to shape our judgements.

Hunch as used here is far more than mere guesswork. Pure
guesswork—for instance, in a simple yes/no choice—would have a
50 per cent chance of being right; but projection, or wishful
thinking, may entail a higher chance of actually being wrong.

Personal Contact

Politicians spend much of their lives talking to other politicians
and to those whose intellectual processes are similar to their own.
Such dialogue reinforces rather than challenges their own presup-
positions. An MP's weekdays are spent in the House with other
MPs, or perhaps with political journalists; at the weekend he or
she may visit a constituency, to talk first to the constituency
activists, another group abnormally interested in politics. An
extreme manifestation of the view that local party activists are a
necessary and sufficient guide to public opinion is provided by the
member of Labour's National Executive Committee (NEC) who
thought that his general management committee was at least as
good an indicator of public opinion as Robert Worcester's MORI
surveys were (Butler and Kavanagh 1980: 272). (The same general
management committee later deselected him.) True, there are the
constituency surgery and the canvass. But even here there is an
element of selection or of self-selection in those the politician talks
to. Those who come to an MP's surgery are likely to be better-
informed and more politically aware than those who never come.
Parties, too, tend to canvass in their own best areas, so diminishing
further the flow of challenging grass-roots questions. When politicians consciously seek to measure public opinion through personal
contact, they may talk to biased sources. Thus in 1964 one 'senior
Conservative minister cited business executives, clergymen and
doctors as the sort of people to whom he looked for assessments of
public feeling . . .' (Butler and King 1965: 51).

An unusually blatant example of biased personal contact can be
found in Churchill's tentative efforts to assess the impact of the
first of his four radio broadcasts in the 1945 election campaign.
(The famous Gestapo address). 'You ask me if I felt influenced,'
wrote his daughter, Sarah. 'If I were thinking Labour, I doubt it
would have made me vote Conservative; but it would have started
me thinking along completely new lines about Socialism' (Gilbert
1988: 35). What is remarkable is not Sarah's reply (which, taken

as a whole, was neither unbalanced nor unperceptive) but that Churchill should have turned to his own daughter for a reaction.

Perhaps more damaging, though, is not so much the content of opinion derived from partial and biased sources as the preconceptions into which this content is fitted. All of us are theorists of a sort, however practical we may pride ourselves on being. We begin with some preconceptions, usually untested and often crude, discarding or modifying evidence that does not fit.

Public Indicators

The same handicaps apply to the use of indicators such as election results. These are often ambiguous in their meaning, but not, unhappily, to all in the way they are interpreted. Politicians may give exaggerated significance to a single by-election. Thus, the huge swing to Labour at East Fulham in October 1933 was interpreted as a sign of massive public feeling against rearmament, and was invoked by the Conservative leader, Baldwin, as justification for the National government's low-key rearmament programme (Middlemas and Barnes 1969: 744–7). (This episode is discussed further below.)

Hunch

As explained already, hunch is a comprehensive term, to be distinguished from mere guesswork, and embracing a range of psychologically shaped responses. The most widespread form is projection—in this context, the politician's attribution to millions of voters of his or her own intuitions and feelings. Projection itself is close to being an umbrella term; one form is pre-emptive pessimism, a kind of inner talking-down of the chances of one's own party, and another is wishful thinking. Wishful thinkers disregard all objective signs of the unpopularity of particular policies or leaders, and adhere, sometimes passively and sometimes stubbornly, to the chosen line.

THE 1945 GENERAL ELECTION

Few contrasts are more vivid than that of the well-nigh universal expectation of the result of the 1945 general election and the actual outcome. Belief in a Conservative victory was widespread in both main parties. Hugh Dalton 'took for granted that Churchill would sweep the country if a "khaki" election were fought on party lines as soon as victory had been won' (Pimlott 1985: 363). Consequently, 'The assumption that Labour would lose any inter-party electoral contest that took place either during the war or its immediate aftermath provided a basis for all Dalton's wartime calculations' (ibid.: 365). At the end of the campaign and a fortnight before the count, Dalton thought that Labour's maximum was 290 seats, well short of an overall majority and unlikely even to make Labour the largest single party. Dalton's view was shared by Attlee (Donoughue and Jones 1973: 338).

Herbert Morrison, who prided himself on his gift for sensing the mood of the British electorate, if not as pessimistic was at least cautious. 'As the campaign progressed,' say his biographers, 'he could not help being struck by the tremendous optimism of local Labour Party workers, but he wrote that off as amateur enthusiasm' (Donoughue and Jones 1973: 338).

If Labour were not sanguine about the result nationally, few if any on the Conservative side questioned the outcome. That Labour would gain seats was widely conceded; they had done badly in 1935. No one, however, seems seriously to have disputed a Conservative victory of some kind.

Conservative complacency and Labour caution seem alike to have been misplaced, for there were enough signs to show that major changes in voting loyalties were afoot. By-elections in the spring of 1942 showed a strong anti-Conservative thrust. Independents fighting on a progressive or leftish ticket won Conservative seats at Grantham, Wallasey, Rugby, and Maldon. Next year Common Wealth, the small idealistically left-wing party led by Richard Acland, captured the National Liberal seat at Eddisbury in Cheshire, and followed this by taking Skipton from the Conservatives at the beginning of 1944. Common Wealth's biggest triumph was at Chelmsford a fortnight before the end of the war in Europe; here, with a swing of 28 per cent, Common Wealth converted a Conservative majority of over 16,000 to a Common Wealth margin of 6,400 (see Addison 1975: 248–52).

The true significance of Chelmsford lay not simply in the size of the swing but in that it was the first by-election since 1940 to be fought on an up-to-date electoral register (Addison 1975: 260).

By-elections could be downplayed; despite independent and left-wing victories, the results were patchy. In some constituencies the only opposition to the Conservatives came from the anti-war Independent Labour Party, and these candidates fared poorly. Because of the electoral truce, moreover, agreed between the parties early in the war, no contest took place between official Conservative and official Labour. Labour played the role of a passive proxy. It is, nevertheless, surprising that so few commentators discerned the shape of British politics to come. Below the surface a remarkable electoral realignment, of which the by-elections were the outward and visible sign, was in the making.

Electoral soothsayers had for long studied by-election portents. Opinion polls were a new-fangled device first developed by Dr Gallup in the United States during the mid-1930s, and then imported into Britain three years later, achieving remarkable predictive success at the West Fulham by-election of April 1938 (Wybrow 1989). However, they had as yet been untested in a general election.

In the summer of 1943 Gallup resumed its questions about voting intentions at the next general election. In June Gallup gave Labour an eight per cent lead amongst those whose minds were made up. This was a striking change since the last general election, when the Conservatives and their allies had been 15 per cent ahead. By November the figure had widened to 14 per cent, and thereafter, whether the war news was good or bad, Labour maintained a lead of above 10 per cent (Gallup 1976: 77–107).

To anyone familiar with the normal workings of the British electoral system, such figures would have seemed ominous for the Conservatives. Their publication, however, roused little or no comment. When, three weeks after polling day, the votes were counted, the political world expressed deep and widespread surprise.

In retrospect two Conservative politicians claimed to have discerned signs of a swing to the Left, but they did so on the basis of contradictory evidence. 'Although at the time of my decision I did not foresee how formidable would be the swing to Labour, I felt in my own mind doubtful of my personal success.' Harold Macmillan's doubts were prompted mainly by an awareness that five years of government office, most of it in North Africa and Italy, had forced him to neglect the constituency, and by the almost complete disappearance of the local organization, rather than by fears about the national standing of his party. What convinced Macmillan that he would lose was that his opponents treated him with 'special courtesy and consideration. Questions were few, interruptions negligible.' Such forbearance by Labour supporters sprang from their confidence in victory. Macmillan's experience in the five contests since 1923 had been that, when Labour's partisans thought it likely they would lose, 'The meetings became rowdy and violent. . . . As soon as electioneering began in earnest I knew what the result would be . . . My meetings were well attended, but dull and uneventful' (Macmillan 1969: 30–1).

Sir David Maxwell-Fyfe, Attorney-General in Churchill's care-taker government, and later ennobled as Lord Kilmuir, also appraised the public mood by reference to the behaviour of Labour supporters in the campaign in his Liverpool constituency.

Over the years, I have come to apply a simple test of how the campaign is going. If the Labour Party have their tails up, then their supporters make a row at Conservative meetings. This was specially so in 1923, 1929 and 1945. . . . The quieter the campaign the better for the Conservatives. (Kilmuir 1964: 245)

This was written of the placid contest of 1955, when the Conservatives increased their majority from seventeen to sixty. Writing specifically of 1945, he found his expectations of a good reception belied:

the wind was blowing unexpectedly cold. I was never subject to the organized howling down of Conservative candidates which occurred in many constituencies, but there was a sharpness in the questioning and heckling which surprised and disconcerted me. It was evident at once that drastic steps would have to be taken. (Kilmuir 1964: 84)

When people lack firm knowledge of what is going on, they tend to fall back on the voice of authority, however ill-founded its claims, especially if that authority offers reassurance in an uncertain environment. Astrologers flourish because the future is, by its nature, unknowable.

There was much speculation [wrote the same Lord Kilmuir, looking back upon the 1945 election campaign], as to the result. On paper the government still had a majority of some 230, so that even if we lost 100 seats, we would still have a majority of 30. It is interesting to record some well-informed opinions expressed during those three weeks. At a cocktail party given by the Russians, M Kukin, counsellor at the Soviet Embassy, asked me my view. I said that I thought we should get a majority of 100. He said, 'No, we think you will only get a majority of 60.' I then heard that the official view in the Vatican, which is usually very well-informed, was 50. (Kilmuir 1964: 85)

What is remarkable about this passage, presented without a trace of humour, is Lord Kilmuir's sense of being 'well-informed'. The main problem was not that he did not have the correct answers but that he never put the right questions. At no stage was the attribute of being well informed scrutinized or queried. Nowhere in Lord Kilmuir's account is there any awareness of the kind of information needed before such a prediction could be made. Such a forecast required a knowledge of the national division of votes between the two main parties; an understanding of the normal relationship between the votes for each party and the number of seats won in Parliament; and an estimate of the likely effects of wartime movements of population. Neither the Soviet Embassy nor the Vatican was particularly experienced in democratic elections and it is hard to see what sources either had to justify the description 'well-informed'. The kind of knowledge needed to make an observer well informed about the outcome of an election is totally different from that required to assess the reactions of a Cabinet or a Parliament.

Lord Kilmuir already held ministerial office, was to become a senior figure in later Conservative Cabinets, and, most pertinently, chaired the committee inquiring into the party's organization after the débâcle of 1945. No one can be censured for making a wrong prediction; but what Lord Kilmuir failed to do was to ask the simple question, 'What knowledge do these people have which makes them so certain?'

Elections, like war, are inherently ambiguous and for the chief actors much hinges on the outcome. They are a time of high stress for the participants, and, at least until the coming of frequent and regular opinion polls, distinguished by a lack of objective information. At such times people are likely to respond to what seems to be a clear and authoritative lead, especially when it seems reassuring. It is not so much that politicians often did not know the answers but that they rarely put the right questions. Lacking well-founded data, they fell back on obsolete 'rules of thumb'.

There is much here resembling the phenomenon which Irving Janis (1972) labelled as 'Groupthink'. Groupthink is a tendency towards uncritical concurrence-seeking which occurs particularly in cohesive groups under stress. Members of decision-making or advisory groups affected in this way seek not the right solution to their problems, but reassurance.

PARTY STRATEGY AND PARTY POLICY

How much politicians can do, in the short term, to improve their party's position is debatable. It is arguable that, in the longer term, policies pursued in government may help a party by altering the country's social structure. So Conservative support for owner-occupation, and Labour backing for council-house building, could yield a distinct if long-term pay-off. In an election campaign it is not always easy to see what a party can do if it is lagging behind its rivals, or what it should do to convert level-pegging into a clear lead. The growth of opinion-polling techniques gives a party the chance to test out the effects of both its own and the Opposition's initiatives. However limited the scope a party has, it is self-evident that it needs accurate information about the mood and concerns of the electorate.

Campaign decisions do not differ in principle from other political decisions. They share with some other decisions, such as those in international or industrial relations, the feature of being taken in conditions of ambiguity. In international relations, the motives and the capabilities of the counter-players are often unclear. No one, for instance, could be wholly sure in the 1930s whether Hitler was at heart a German nationalist seeking redress for the wrongs of Versailles, or a man bent on the domination of Europe. No one could be sure how strong an ally Soviet Russia might be. How many divisions has Stalin was an easy question to answer. How good was Soviet equipment, how high was Russian morale, how talented were the generals of the Red Army—these were altogether more difficult issues. In such conditions, decision-makers find it easy to project their own fears and their own hopes on to a potential enemy or a possible ally. The world becomes an ink-blot which portrays the anxieties and yearnings of the beholder.

Without clear-cut data about the electorate, politicians fall back on a skimpy and often outdated stock of knowledge. Their conceptualization of the electorate is crude, and is often drawn from academic or journalistic accounts of the past.

The problem, let us remind ourselves, is as much a failure to ask the right questions as to have the right information. A major hindrance to clarity of thinking about the electorate lay in the crude conceptualization of electoral change. Politicians sometimes focused on electors' propensity to change: were voters habitual partisans, or floaters? A second focus was on the ideological content of voters' beliefs: were electors moderate or extreme in their policy preferences? There was a tendency to merge two distinct dimensions.

'The floating voter' has long been part of the stock-in-trade of electoral politics. Conventionally, commentators divided the electorate into two classes: committed partisans, who rarely if ever changed allegiance, and who were divided roughly equally between the two main parties; and 'floating voters' or 'waverers', who moved from one side to the other, and by their decision were able to change the outcome of the election.

A second division lay between moderate and the more extreme voters. Such a dimension refers to the ideological beliefs of electors, not directly to their propensity to change sides. However, the two dimensions seemed to be obviously related. Moderate voters, it was said, were likely to be alienated from their traditional party if it adopted extreme policies, and would switch to the opposition. Politics was seen as being about 'the middle ground'.

Indeed, this model of the electorate has become the basis for an elegant academic treatise by Anthony Downs (1957), *An Economic Theory of Democracy*. Parties tend to converge in the centre of the spectrum of ideological preferences, because those which move too far to the extreme of either Right or Left lose support to the opposite party. Parties, therefore, have a strong incentive not to deviate too far from 'the middle ground'. True, a party which dilutes its appeal and sheds its more extreme policies may offend its more ideologically committed electors. However, such voters can hardly vote for the Opposition, whose policies are, by definition, even more objectionable. They can at worst stay at home or vote for some electorally irrelevant splinter group. Such voters have less electoral force, however, because their party loses only one vote; those switching to the Opposition add one vote to their new party and cost their old party one vote, making a difference of two.

The thesis 'British politics is about the middle ground' has long exercised a pervasive influence on politicians and commentators in Britain. In one sense it is obviously true, if only tautologically. If citizens cast their votes on policy grounds, and if opinion is heavily clustered around the midpoint of the spectrum, parties which abandon moderation will lose support. So, the Labour party under the leadership of the erstwhile left-winger Neil Kinnock has sought to regain its moderate credentials by embracing the market economy (if in qualified form), accepting considerable curbs on trade union power, renouncing unilateral nuclear disarmament, and accepting British membership of the European Community.

Note, however, the conditions, whether explicit or tacit, that underlie the validity of the 'middle-ground' thesis as conventionally expressed. It assumes a bell-shaped, unimodal distribution of opinion in which the policy preferences of electors tend to cluster about the midpoint of the ideological spectrum, with the median voter by definition dividing the population into two equal blocs. For example, we might postulate that, on the issue of restrictions on trade unions, fifteen million voters want stronger curbs, fifteen million want to relax existing legal limitations, whilst five million want to keep the status quo. The five million obviously represent the middle ground, and a party in a two-party system which called for a change in the laws governing trade unions would lose support. This presupposes that voters have accurate information about the policies propounded by the parties; and that voting, if not wholly shaped by concern for policy, must be responsive to it. Moreover, since election campaigners fight on a range of policies, we have to asume that electors cast their votes according to some kind of 'average agreement' on party policy, with the level of agreement being weighted by the importance voters attach to each issue.

The difficulty about the 'middle-ground' thesis is that there are really two 'middle grounds'—one empirical and one subjective.

The empirical middle ground relates, as Downs describes it, to the actual distribution of popular opinion on the issues of the election. However, men's and women's behaviour is not determined by reality but by their perceptions of reality. In twentieth-century British politics the 'middle ground' has, for practical purposes, been the 'middle ground' as defined by politicians. The gap between reality and perception has often been wide. After a widely publicized speech by Enoch Powell one distinguished biographer wrote:

It is a commonplace that the two big parties have to fight each other for control of the 'middle ground' but the phrase requires definition. . . . In another sense, the middle ground represents those who recoil from dogmatism of the Right or Left, and have an essentially moderate approach to politics. To that element—much larger than is often supposed, and embracing people of all ages, I.Q.s and income groups—Mr Wilson may still seem preferable to Mr Heath. . . . Mr Heath has done himself much good by dismissing Mr Powell from the Shadow Cabinet and substantially rejecting Powellism. But until he becomes Prime Minister his credentials as a man of the Centre will be subject to periodic doubt. (Grigg 1968)

The argument assumes, without empirical evidence, that British voters are distributed along a Left–Right axis, with the Centre (as defined by Grigg) holding the balance of electoral power; and goes on to assert that Mr Heath, whose personal ratings were languishing, had improved his electoral prospects by dismissing the personally popular Mr Powell, on an issue in which Mr Powell's views (or what were perceived to be Mr Powell's views) were shared by the great majority of the British people.

It has sometimes taken the salutary force of electoral defeat to waken politicians to the realization of the gap between public opinion and their view of it. In the 1950s neither party would touch the issue of immigration control, and those who raised the question were dubbed extremists. Opinion polls, however, showed huge support for a strict curb on immigration, when in 1961 the Macmillan government introduced a bill to impose such controls. Labour denounced the bill, but by the 1964 election came to accept the principle of control. The defeat of their foreign affairs spokesman, Patrick Gordon-Walker, at Smethwick in 1964, in an election in which Labour made considerable gains elsewhere, completed Labour's conversion and was reflected in the drastic measure of 1968 which excluded from the United Kingdom the Kenya Asian British passport holders.

Sometimes, however, the pay-off for pursuing unpopular policies is long delayed, and politicians fail to see the actual or potential damage that specific policies, moderate in their eyes, do to their electoral appeal.

It is easy to confuse the two dimensions of propensity to change, and ideological content. 'A party cannot win an election unless it wins the support of a high proportion of the uncommitted voters. And, as the common middle ground means the uncommitted voters, anybody who says he is not concerned with that ground is in effect saying that he does not ever want to win an election . . .' (Gilmour 1977: 140–1; also quoted in Crewe and Sarlvik 1980: 245). Floating voters are identified with moderate voters—the politically uncommitted with the ideologically middle of the road. There may indeed be a considerable overlap between the two, but this is a matter for empirical investigation, not of a priori judgement. It is not easy for example, for exponents of this thesis to accommodate the common element in Liberal and National Front support (Steed 1974: 336).

'If it is clear that "Bevanism" is in the ascendant,' confided Harold Macmillan to his diary, after the left-wing sweep of the constituency parties' section in the NEC elections in October 1951, 'a lot of Liberal and middle-class votes may come over to us' (1969: 341). It seems that Mr Macmillan must have been thinking of that section of the middle class which voted Labour in 1950, which then accounted for fewer than one-quarter of non-manual voters, and Macmillan seems almost blind to the huge Conservative lead among non-manual workers. More important, he seemed to regard the middle-class Labour vote as being distinctively moderate in its policy preferences. Nowhere does he question this assumption.

Later, indeed, Macmillan doubted his own earlier belief that Liberal voters, prompted by fears of a Bevanite Labour party, would rally to the Conservatives. In the summer of 1957 he discounted the fashionable interpretation that the substantial anti-Conservative swing of the time was caused by middle-class resentment over the cost of living and the introduction of the Rent Act, and opined that it might be attributable to propaganda about the H-bomb. 'This, combined with Suez, has drawn away from us that wavering vote with vague Liberal and nonconformist traditions which plays such an important role because it is still the no-man's land between the great entrenched parties on either side' (Macmillan 1971: 298–9).[1]

'Moderation' as the key to electoral success has inspired successive generations of Labour policy-makers. Herbert Morrison's call for consolidation in the run up to, and the aftermath of, the 1950 general election was prompted by electoral calculation. 'The crucial test was whether it [Labour] could retain and even win more floating voters from the middle-ground of politics; the housewives, the professional middle-classes, the rural vote, and the Liberals of radical inclination' (Donoughue and Jones 1973: 441). Note the explicit identification of the floating vote with the 'middle-ground'. The wide definition of floating vote is puzzling. If all of these categories constituted the floating vote, it is hard to see from where hardcore Conservative support (and the Conservatives gained almost 40 per cent of the electorate even in 1945) actually came.

Fears of a loss of middle-class support undoubtedly spurred Labour's concern to project an image of political moderation by, in particular, playing down further measures of nationalization. Middle-class electors, who had swung to Labour in considerable numbers in 1945, were believed to have deserted the party because of its socialist philosophy. Such an explanation is almost certainly too sophisticated. The continuation of rationing after the war, the shortages of food, clothing, consumer durables, and petrol, probably played a larger part in the disillusionment felt by this comparatively small section of the electorate than a reaction against Labour's supposed extremism. The marvel is not that Labour lost some middle-class (and working-class) support in 1950 but that, after the hardships of the previous five years and the repeated false dawns, it did so well.

Fear of electoral reprisals contributed to the Labour leadership's determination to crack down on left-wing rebellion.

But what kind of impression [asked Hugh Gaitskell late in 1954] will the Opposition make on the country if its Members do not stand together? ... They will not support a Party if that Party cannot rely on the loyalty of its Members in the Division Lobbies ... God knows there is trouble enough in the Party already, but in the main, because of the threat of Party discipline, we do manage to vote together in the House. (Williams 1983: 353)

This was written in the light of the party's bitter dispute about foreign and defence policy, and a few months later Aneurin Bevan once again offended against party unity. In the party discussion that followed, Gaitskell pressed strongly for expulsion: 'if we did not expel him,' he said, 'the Tories ... would use this against us in the Election.' Gaitskell admitted that the party would lose some support in the constituency party membership but thought that 'this would be balanced by the gain from marginal voters' (ibid. 391).

There is indeed considerable evidence from opinion surveys that British voters like their political parties to be united, and that moderation (however defined by the voters) is better than extremism. This is far from saying, however, that the formal apparatus of party discipline or the expulsion of leading rebels will always be congenial to the electors. What the invocation of expulsion or withdrawal of the Whip does is to draw attention to the party's disunity. At no point did Mr Gaitskell seem to ask himself how the electoral costs and gains of expelling Mr Bevan might be quantified.

The problem, put simply, is that voters do not always define moderation in the same way as political leaders do. The battle may indeed be for the 'middle ground'—but, we have to ask, for whose middle ground?

THE LIBERALS AND THE AFTERMATH OF 1945

The problems that the Liberals had in identifying the concerns of the mass electorate were an enlarged edition of those facing the two major parties.[2]

The 1945 election seemed to confirm, for the Liberals, the almost continuous decline of the previous twenty years. Only twelve Liberals were elected to the House of Commons, and only two won in genuine three-cornered fights. With neither business donations, nor trade union affiliation fees, with few constituency organizations to raise subscriptions from members, the party was desperately short of money. Its local associations had decayed and throughout urban Britain the party did not return a single MP to Parliament. The party could not have afforded to make use of modern survey techniques, even had it wanted to do so, nor, with a moribund local organization, could it use the constituency associations as listening posts to eavesdrop upon the mass electorate.

The task confronting the rump Liberal party of 1945 was immense; what was notable was the failure to assess the future course of the party in the light of accurate information about the voters. Once again, there was a failure to pose the right questions.

Should the party try to attract the members of clearly defined sectional groups or should it make an across-the-board appeal to the national electorate? Was there, indeed, any evidence to show how practicable the former approach was? Should it seek to break into the then huge, and preponderantly Labour, working class; or did the smaller, but heavily Conservative, middle class offer better pickings? How might the distinctive themes of British Liberalism—which in the late 1940s the party arranged around the issue of personal liberty—be communicated to the mass electorate of urban Britain, where the party's performance in 1945 had been so poor? How might the social composition of the new electorate be described and what were its policy preferences?

The party's leaders seemed to have no comprehension of the way the party's problems in seeking mass support might be defined, or the kind of information that might be needed. The search for increased electoral support was nevertheless a major concern of the party leadership. It was assumed that Labour were more vulnerable and that disillusioned Labour voters of 1945 could be won over. The party, however, found it hard to decide whether to court Labour's middle-class clientele or its working-class supporters, and whether the Labour government should be censured for being too extreme or for not being radical enough. No one seems to have asked what kind of evidence might help resolve these doubts (Joyce 1989: 52–4).

In the 1950 election campaign the party continued to place its hopes on tempting Labour's middle-class constituency into its ranks, without asking how large that group was, and how weak the loyalty of its members might be. Lord Samuel, elder statesman of the party, thought that many of those who had voted Labour in 1945, but had since become disenchanted, would 'want the Socialist out' without wishing to vote Conservative. 'If a Liberal candidate is there they will vote for him. If not they might abstain, or more probably vote Labour after all; but never Tory' (Joyce 1989: 65). The apparent confidence with which this judgement was made is striking. It does not seem to have occurred to Samuel that purportedly empirical statements of this kind needed to be tested against evidence.

Even more remarkable was the message of an internal memorandum circulated within the party during the 1955 campaign. The memorandum asserted that 'the greater part of the former Liberal vote' had transferred to Labour. Hence, the party must undermine Labour's claim to be a true radical party, a fit home for progressive voters (Joyce 1989: 104). No one seems to have attempted to define a 'progressive voter', to check whether such voters were former Liberals who had defected to Labour, or to find out how best such voters, if they existed in sizable numbers, might be summoned back.

As it happened, 1955 saw a halt to the party's post-war slide, and the first of the post-war Liberal surges came a few years later. After some encouraging by-elections in 1956 and 1957, the Liberals came a close second at Rochdale early in 1958, and actually won the seat at Torrington. Support then fell back, but after the 1959 election the party had a further run of by-election successes, culminating in a remarkable victory at Orpington. Hopes of a Liberal breakthrough which would overturn the two-party system revived. Here was the opportunity the party had been waiting for; what the party needed to do was to identify the new constituency which had emerged (if indeed it had an identity) and to define the appeal required to fortify the allegiance of this group.

As early as 1957 the new leader of the party, Jo Grimond, referred to the 'five or ten per cent of the new voters that come on to the register each year. They are the rising scientists and technicians, the new artisan class who are certainly not tories but are not trade union fodder of the old type' (Joyce 1989: 145). The definition is so vague, and the numbers so uncertain (does the comment refer to 5 or 10 per cent of the new voters each year, or to the new voters each year constituting 5 or 10 per cent of the electorate?) that it is hard to see how such a calculation could have been of help to a political campaigner.

After Orpington, the appeal to the new classes was renewed. It was these whom Mr Grimond described as the 'enterprising, professional, managerial and technical men and skilled workers' (Joyce 1989: 229).

In later speeches Mr Grimond became more precise, naming groups such as technicians and engineers, doctors and nurses, managers and small business people, and those building up their own businesses and their own farms (Joyce 1989: 229–30). These were the 'new men', an up-to-date version of the 'progressive voters' of the late 1950s. It was assumed that their political loyalties lay neither with Labour nor with the Conservatives; on what basis this assumption rested was never spelt out.

Similarly, a Liberal publicist emphasized the need for a party which 'understands . . . the key social group in the new technological revolution, namely the rising group of technicians, teachers, managers and scientists' (Joyce 1989: 246), whilst, even after the disappointment of the 1964 election, Mr Grimond continued to proclaim that 'the new men and women, the professional and technically trained people, the younger executives and trade unionists, do indeed want modernization' (ibid. 277).

What was lacking in such analyses of potential Liberal support was any appreciation of the territorial base of the new Liberal vote. The suburban surge of the Orpington year of 1962 had already ebbed by 1964. The general election of that year showed what had already been foreshadowed in 1959: the decisive increases in Liberal backing came, not from the new, buoyant, economically advancing parts of the country, but from the economically stagnating and depopulating rural periphery. One Liberal indeed noted that 'there was little evidence . . . of a potential majority of like-minded radicals or that a lively concern for political change permeated a large section of the electorate' (Joyce 1989: 296), but his was a lonely voice.

The changing social structure of Britain, and the vicious conflict between Right and Left in the Labour party, gave some surface plausibility to the decision to aim for a realignment of the Left. Grimond's call to the 'new men', to the 'progressive voters' was to rally support for a progressive, non-socialist, classless party, not tied to the trade unions. The Liberal party's goal, either alone or in alliance with new political forces, was to replace Labour as the party of the Left. It is again surprising that the Liberal leadership failed to absorb the most obvious lesson of electoral ecology—that Liberals did best in Conservative, and the more middle-class, seats! Liberals found it hard to make progress in Labour areas. Indeed, in 1964 Liberals contested nearly four times as many Conservative-held, as Labour-held seats, and did significantly better in the former than in the latter. The Liberals' proclaimed goal of supplanting Labour was belied by their own choice of constituencies to fight.

Nor did the Liberals draw the lessons of the published poll data—that Liberal support was drawn fairly evenly from all social classes, with a mild tendency to draw rather more from the middle classes. Nor, too, did they have any inkling of the volatility of their support. The steady base of 10 per cent, which the polls registered even in poor years, deceived the party into thinking that it had a stable electoral core. The work of Butler and Stokes (1969: 315) was to show how heavy the turnover of Liberal support was.[3]

THE ELECTORATE AND THE BUSINESS
OF GOVERNMENT

That, left to themselves, politicians are rather poor formulators of electoral strategy might seem to be a matter of little import. 'Armies only win battles because they fight other armies.' One party or other, after all, has to win.

Yet, thinking about party campaign strategy, and sources of information about voters, does highlight another, more significant problem—the gap between the élite and the mass public in making governmental, as distinct from party, decisions. Politicians may shrink from doing those things they ought to do, for fear of a hostile public response, and do those things which they ought not to, in the belief that public opinion enjoins such measures. Of course, politicians are not always, or even usually, confronted by such a severe choice; public opinion is often fluid enough to give the élites considerable leeway.

The danger, however, remains that governments fearing an electoral backlash may not always take action they deem right or necessary, a peril vividly illustrated by the events of the 1930s. A familiar defence of the failure of governments to rearm Britain in time, and of the policy of appeasement, is that public opinion would not have stood for more robust measures. In particular, commentators have seized upon the East Fulham by-election of 1933—whose result was cited by Stanley Baldwin, then leader of the Conservative party, as both a cause and a justification of the government's reluctance to rearm—as showing the unwillingness of a democratic electorate to endorse the hard but necessary choices that governments ought to make.

In October 1933 Labour won a startling victory in a by-election at East Fulham. The Conservative vote fell by ten thousand, compared with the general election of 1931, and Labour's rose by nearly nine thousand. The swing since 1931 was 29.2 per cent.

Disarmament (along with social issues such as housing) was a prominent theme of the Labour campaign. The swing was one of the largest ever recorded at a by-election since the coming of universal suffrage; a movement of votes on that scale at a general election would have swept the National (i.e. largely Conservative) government from power (see Middlemas and Barnes 1969; Ceadel 1973.)

Once the result was known, Baldwin asked for a special investigation. Arthur Baker, a journalist on *The Times* who had predicted a heavy increase in the Labour vote, undertook this task.

His report [write Baldwin's biographers, Keith Middlemas and John Barnes], made gloomy reading. Baker was convinced that the seat had been lost purely on the pacifist question; and his deductions made a profound and lasting impression on Baldwin, affecting all his calculations for months to come. A Party Leader can ignore a phenomenon of this size only through ignorance or folly.' (Middlemas and Barnes 1969: 746)

The conclusion that East Fulham was a repudiation of rearmament rested on a simple syllogism: (1) Electors vote on the issues put before them by the candidates; (2) the by-election was fought on the issue of rearmament; (3) therefore, the result was a vote for disarmament.

The first duty of a party leader or minister on reading such a report is to ask how firm is the evidence, and how sound is the reasoning, on which the conclusion has been reached. It is quite unsafe to infer that electors always cast their votes on the issues propounded by the candidates. The conventional wisdom once had it that local council election results were a verdict on local government issues, on which indeed these elections are ostensibly fought. In fact, to a considerable extent local elections are a referendum on the standing of the government at Westminster. It does not follow that, because candidates campaign on certain issues, electors vote on these.

However, there is also considerable doubt as to whether the question of armaments did dominate the by-election campaign. Disarmament was certainly espoused vigorously by the Labour candidate, but so was housing. Food prices, beginning to rise after the long slump, were another Labour theme. Neville Chamberlain, then Chancellor of the Exchequer, reflecting on the figures, confessed that he

did not lose a minute's sleep over it. The press put it all down to Housing
and lies about War. Both no doubt were factors but I heard yesterday
from a friend who had been talking to a speaker (street corner) from
Fulham what I had all along suspected, that the real attack was on the
means test. (Ceadel 1973, citing Macleod 1961)

Note Chamberlain's sources for his judgement. It is in this way
that electoral myths are made—even if, after Fulham, it was a
different myth that took hold. Party leaders in 1933 simply lacked
the information on which a valid verdict about the causes of the
huge anti-government swing could have been made. More important, they failed to pose the questions which might have been put to
those making confident but ill-founded assertions.

Nearly three years later memories of East Fulham revived when
a deputation of senior Conservative back-benchers including
Churchill, met Baldwin to voice their misgivings about Britain's
defences. Baldwin implied that, even if opinion were favourable to
more rapid rearmament in the Conservative heartland, it would
not be so in working-class areas. 'Most of you', he answered 'sit
for safe seats. You do not represent industrial constituencies, at
least not many of you . . .', (Gilbert, 1976: 776)

What evidence did Baldwin have to sustain his division into
middle-class and industrial Britain? None, indeed, from the by-
elections. Middlemas and Barnes, in their attempt to vindicate
Baldwin, argue that Fulham was but the first of a series of by-
elections, fought on disarmament, recording heavy swings against
the government. 'These constituencies covered not only the geographical distribution of the majority of the electorate but the
different patterns of voting—agricultural and industrial, town and
city' (1969: 746).[4]

Politicians may at times be excited by their own hopes but they
are equally likely to be imprisoned by their own fears.

THE NEW REALISM

The last half-century has seen a great increase in our understanding,
both of electoral behaviour and of the working of the electoral
system. This change in our knowledge reflects a shift from the
anecdotal to the statistical, from the intuitive to the systematic.
The most visible change lies in the extensive use of opinion polling,

both in monitoring the day-to-day standing of the parties and in exploring the electorate's attitudes to the issues and personalities of the time.

One of the biggest changes has been in the behaviour of the politicians themselves. The political parties now make extensive use of private polling, and, though in the interstices of election campaigning, individual hunch and personal intuition still play a part, the approach of the parties both to propaganda and to policy-making is prompted by a much more informed knowledge of the mass electorate.

The climate of opinion has been transformed since 1945; in this change the pioneering work of David Butler has played one of the foremost parts. His first book *The Electoral System in Great Britain, 1918–1951* (Butler 1953) showed that, at that time, the electoral system worked in a predictable and highly regular way. Few politicians in 1945 would have talked so confidently of a majority of fifty, or sixty, or a hundred, if they had understood the sensitivity of the system to small shifts in popular support. His monument, however, will surely be, *Political Change in Britain* (Butler and Stokes 1969). He and his co-author, Donald Stokes, used modern techniques of opinion sampling, not only to analyse contemporary British electoral behaviour with a penetration never before achieved but to reconstruct, by an unusually imaginative use of data, the electoral history of modern Britain. Together they ensured that nothing in the study of British electoral behaviour would ever be the same again.

It is easy to criticize opinion surveys. Their failures are cherished, their successes forgotten. April 9 1992, like 1970, showed that, sampling charge apart, systematic error can occur. Changes in question wording, and question order, can generate big apparent differences in attitude. Indeed, the problems arising from the phrasing of questions are numerous and diverse. The timing of a survey, too, can seriously affect responses to questions about political issues.

Such charges are well known. Those who make them seem, more often than not, unaware of the huge volume of work undertaken both by the polling organizations and by social scientists, to identify, and hopefully to mitigate or overcome, these problems.

There are three answers, at least, to charges of this kind. Faults occur, sometimes collectively, more often individually. It is unreasonable to expect any branch of work to be totally free of preventable error. There are bad biographers and bad historians. Inefficiency is hardly ground for condemning the activity in which it occurs. We do not abolish our defences because of incompetent generals.

Moreover, the pollsters and academics who run opinion surveys and similar forms of enquiry are *accountable* in a way that the intuitions and impressions of politicians can never be. Sloppily-worded questions can be identified; variations in response caused by alterations to the phrasing of questions, or by changes in question order, can be observed and measured. Poor sampling techniques or defective interviewer training can be scrutinized and corrected. Of course, no survey can ever claim absolute certainty for its findings. It is, however, likely to be closer to the truth than any other form of evidence.

Knowledge grows dialectically. It is not only through the steady accumulation of data about voting behaviour, but through the continuing debate about method amongst practitioners and academics, that greater certainty will be achieved.

We know how easily the uselessness of almost every branch of knowledge may be proved, to the complete satisfaction of those who do not possess it. How many, not altogether stupid men, think the scientific study of languages useless, think ancient literature useless, all erudition useless, logic and metaphysics useless, poetry and the fine arts idle and frivolous, political economy purely mischievous? Even history has been pronounced useless and mischievous by able men. (Mill 1861 and 1910: 254)

Notes

1. In this diary passage Macmillan shows a perceptive understanding of Bevan's political creed: 'Bevan is by nature a Radical rather than a Socialist and not at all in sympathy with the intellectual Socialists. He is an old-fashioned Radical, who 50 years ago would have been Lib/Lab, anti-Church, anti-landlord, anti-Royalty and anti-militarist. I believe that he senses all this and thinks that the bomb will be the great grappling point.' The passage as a whole, however, almost certainly exaggerates the political strength of this sort of radicalism among the mid-century electorate.

2. This section depends heavily on Joyce (1989).

3. Note, however, should be taken of a sophisticated survey of Orpington, conducted by Liberals after the by-election of 1962.

4. The treatment of East Fulham and the later by-elections by Middlemas and Barnes is defective. They seem to assume that the inferences drawn by Baker, Baldwin, and others about the causes of the Conservative rout were correct; they regard East Fulham as typical of the run of by-elections in late 1933 and early 1934; and they distinguish these by-elections from the contests of 1932, and early 1933, before the peace issue had been fully joined.

One problem is that they misuse the term *swing*. They substitute the fall in the Conservative/National government share of the vote for the normal measures of swing, without realizing that they are putting forward a different measure. Thus the swing at Skipton, which they report as 25.2% was actually 13.5%. Conversely, they actually underestimate the defeat at East Fulham.

The contrast between the autumn 1933 and spring 1934 by-elections on the one hand, and the earlier contests in the same Parliament, is overdrawn. East Fulham fell almost exactly two years after the landslide general election of 1931. There were twenty by-elections before East Fulham, but nine of these were simply not comparable with the general election, or not valid as indicators, because of the absence of either a Conservative/National government candidate, or a Labour candidate, at one or other election, or both. The five comparable by-elections of 1932 showed an average swing to Labour of 10.4%; the four in 1933 before East Fulham, of 15.2%; the eight from East Fulham in October 1933 to Portsmouth North in February 1934 show a swing of 17.4%. Anti-government feeling was there long before the raising of the peace issue, which seems to have contributed relatively little to the pro-Labour swing.

References

Addison, P. (1975), *The Road to 1945* (London: Jonathan Cape).

Butler, D. (1953), *The Electoral System in Britain, 1918–1951* (Oxford: Oxford University Press).

—— and Kavanagh, D. (1980), *The British General Election of 1979* (London: Macmillan).

—— and King, A. S. (1965), *The British General Election of 1964* (London: Macmillan).

—— and Stokes, D. (1969), *Political Change in Britain* (1st edn., London: Macmillan).

Ceadel, M. (1973), 'Interpreting East Fulham', in C. Cook and J. Ramsden (eds.), *By-Elections in British Politics* (London: Macmillan), 118–39.

Cooper, A. Duff (1953), *Old Men Forget* (London: Rupert Hart-Davis).

Crewe, I., and Sarlvik, B. (1980), 'Popular Attitudes and Electoral Strategy', in Z. Layton-Henry (ed.), *Conservative Party Politics* (London: Macmillan), 244–75.

Donoughue, B. and Jones, G. (1973), *Herbert Morrison: Professional Politician* (London: Weidenfeld and Nicolson).

Downs, A. (1957), *An Economic Theory of Democracy* (New York: Harper and Row).

Gallup, G. (1976), (ed.), *The Gallup International Public Opinion Polls: Great Britain, 1937–1975, i. 1937–1964* (New York: Random House).

Gilbert, M. (1976), *Winston S. Churchill 1922–39* (London: Heinemann).

—— (1988), *'Never Despair': Winston S. Churchill, 1945–1965* (London: Heinemann).

Gilmour, Sir I. (1977), *Inside Right: A Study of Conservatism* (London: Hutchinson).

Grigg, J. (1968), *Guardian*, 17 Oct.

Hattersley, R. (1984), *A Yorkshire Boyhood* (Oxford: Oxford University Press).

Janis, I. (1972), *Victims of Groupthink* (Boston, Mass.: Houghton-Miflin).

Joyce, N. P. (1989), *The Electoral Strategy and Tactics of the British Liberal Party, 1945–1970*, Ph.D. thesis, University of London.

Kilmuir, Lord (1964), *Political Adventure* (London: Weidenfeld and Nicolson).

Macleod, I. (1961), *Neville Chamberlain* (London: Frederick Muller).

Macmillan, H. (1969), *Tides of Fortune, 1945–1955* (London: Macmillan).

—— (1971), *Riding the Storm, 1956–1959* (London: Macmillan).

Middlemas, K. and Barnes, J. (1969), *Baldwin: A Biography* (London: Weidenfeld and Nicolson).

Mill, J. S. (1861), *Representative Government* (London: J. M. Dent).

Moran, Lord (1966), *Winston Churchill: The Struggle for Survival, 1945–1965* (London: Constable).

Pimlott, B. (1985), *Hugh Dalton* (London: Macmillan).

Steed, M. (1974), 'The Results Analysed', in D. Butler and D. Kavanagh, *The British General Election of February 1974* (London: Macmillan), 313–39.

Williams, P. (1983 (ed.), *The Diary of Hugh Gaitskell, 1945–1956* (London: Jonathan Cape).

Wybrow, R. J. (1989), *Britain Speaks Out, 1937–87* (Basingstoke: Macmillan).

5

The Natives are Restless: The Reporting of British By-Elections

DAVID MCKIE

I

In October 1933 Labour took East Fulham from the Conservatives on a swing of 29 per cent, transforming a Conservative majority of 14,521 into a Labour one of 4,840. This was the first of six by-elections defended by the National government over a period of five weeks, and the only one which Labour won, but the swings against the government were substantial in every case. These events had a profound effect on Stanley Baldwin, then much the most influential figure in the government, as he confessed to the Commons when under attack from Churchill in the debate on the Address in November 1938:

I put before the House my own views with appalling frankness. From 1933, I and my friends were all very worried about what was happening in Europe. You will remember at the time the Disarmament Conference was sitting in Geneva. You will remember at that time there was probably a stronger pacifist feeling running through the country than at any time since the war. I am speaking of 1933 and 1934. You will remember the seat at Fulham in the autumn of 1933, when a seat which the National Government held was lost by about 7,000 votes [sic] on no issue but the pacifist . . . I asked myself what chance was there—when that feeling that was given expression to in Fulham was common throughout the country— what chance was there within the next year or two of that feeling being so changed that the country would give a mandate for rearmament. Suppose I had gone to the country and said that Germany was rearming and we must rearm, does anybody think that this pacific democracy would have rallied to that cry at that moment! I cannot think of anything that would have made the loss of the election from my point of view more certain. (Ceadel 1973: 120)

But was East Fulham truly lost on 'no issue but the pacifist'? Subsequent research has challenged that view (see Ceadel 1973). The *Manchester Guardian*, while awarding the issues of peace and disarmament pride of place in the contest—'the country is roused to consciousness on international issues as it has not been since the War ended'—thought the dreadful state of housing in Fulham, where the Conservative candidate, Alderman Waldron, was a pillar of the local council, and recent rises in rents, 'which those who are intimate with the division believe to have exercised a great though silent influence', might have been crucial too. The means test, and the personal reputation of the Conservative candidate, have also been cited as contributory factors.

Much the most important press source for East Fulham was the lobby correspondent of *The Times*, Arthur Baker, who not only reported it for his newspaper but wrote a private assessment afterwards for the eyes of Conservative party organizers. The *Manchester Guardian* was rather more concerned with by-elections nearer home, at Manchester, Rusholme, and Skipton. The *Daily Telegraph* reported the routine events of the contest, like constituency speeches and leaders' messages to candidates, but the only hint in its columns of how the contest was going was its repeated insistence that, though Conservative canvassers were not lacking in Fulham, there could never be too many.

Although the Conservatives started with an advantage, in that their candidate, Alderman Waldron, was a local man, whereas the Labour man, John Wilmot, had no local connections, the seat, Baker reported, was not as safe as it looked. The Conservatives owed their imposing majority to the traumatic circumstances of 1931. Before that, this had been a Conservative marginal, and that, in his judgement, was what it was in 1933. He noted the large number of removals, the high proportion of women voters (they outnumbered men by around five thousand), and the possibly crucial effect of the Liberal party's decision not to stand. The Liberals, who had polled 1,788 votes (5.2 per cent) at the previous election, instead sent out a questionnaire to the Conservative and Labour candidates, on the basis of which the local association recommended supporters to vote for Wilmot, on the disarmament issue if on no other. On the eve of poll, Baker quoted local Conservative officials as expecting a majority of about 1,700.

In fact, the Conservative vote was roughly halved (23,438 to

12,950) and the Labour vote roughly doubled (8,917 to 17,790). *The Times* was incensed. Mr Wilmot, it said in a leader, was to be congratulated. Yet he could hardly have hoped that his opponent and the organization that supported him should have failed so hopelessly to present the strongest case ever possessed by a British government in modern times.

The biggest share of the blame belonged to those who had failed to select an adequate champion for that government. Indeed, it was doubtful whether the choice on such important occasions ought to be left in local hands. It was to be inferred that nearly all Liberal votes, much of the 'fluid' vote, and many Conservatives had been alienated. The Socialists, the *Telegraph* complained, had the better organization, the more intensive tactics, and the greatest show of enthusiasm. Their readers might perhaps have wondered why it was that such manifest imperfections had never been mentioned throughout the campaign.

II

In March 1990 Lord Deedes of the *Daily Telegraph*, who after a life in politics had returned to the trade where he began, cited East Fulham as some kind of comparison when the Conservatives were turned out from one of their safest seats on a swing of 21 per cent. In Mid-Staffs., as in Fulham, the Conservatives had been defending a 14,000 majority: in Mid-Staffs. Labour emerged with a majority of 9,449, against 4,840 in Fulham. This was one of two by-elections in the year which badly destabilized a government and a party already in delicate health. Safe though it once had been, Mid-Staffs. came on the market at a particularly difficult moment for the government. The poll tax—already in force, widely hated and widely unpaid, for a year in Scotland—was due to break over England and Wales on 1 April. The Labour lead on the polls at the start of March was 18 per cent and rising.

The Conservatives, it was cruelly calculated, were getting into territory from which no government since opinion polls began had ever recovered. On 2 March one poll put Labour ahead for the first time as the party most widely expected to form the next government. On 15 March another found two-thirds of electors wanting Margaret Thatcher to quit. Though she had beaten off a leadership challenge from Sir Anthony Meyer the previous December, there was rising speculation that another and more formidable test might be on the way. Michael Heseltine, a public scourge of the poll tax, was ominously on the prowl. Mrs Thatcher dismissed such talk as 'poppycock', but some of her colleagues were not so sure. The loss of the seat on 22 March, though predicted, increased back-bench alarm. Some commentators forecast that, if the May local elections went badly, more and more back-bench MPs might decide that the only way to save their political lives was by terminating hers.

Thanks to skilful public relations, concentrating media attention on good results in the London boroughs of Wandsworth and Westminster, that threat was averted. But on 18 October the Conservatives lost Eastbourne, in a contest occasioned by the assassination of Mrs Thatcher's friend, Ian Gow, to the Liberal Democrats. Five weeks later she had gone. The immediate causes of her downfall—the divisions over Europe, the demotion of Geoffrey Howe, her outburst in the Commons after the Rome summit, Howe's resignation and resignation speech, Heseltine's decision to run—had nothing to do with Eastbourne. But the by-elections had sapped her. They had made the invulnerable vulnerable.

In time to come, historians may well pore over Mid-Staffs. and Eastbourne as they do over Fulham, asking how much they contributed to the end of an epic reign in British politics. But will they be better served by the press reports of the day than those who have sought to excavate East Fulham?

III

In 1964 the editorial management of the Westminster Press group of provincial newspapers invited David Butler down from Oxford, where they published the *Oxford Mail*, to talk to assembled editors. He used the occasion to lecture them on the failings of their political reporting. You report the politicians, he said, but you rarely tell us anything much about what voters are saying. Should you not now and then, especially during elections, attempt to assess that too? Why not send reporters out to talk to them and try to gauge the political mood? Even if it cannot be done in large numbers, it would add a new dimension to your reporting.

The consequences were disastrous. As a London office reporter, I was summoned and told to proceed to Devizes, where a by-election was in progress within the circulation area of one of the group's evening newspapers, the *Swindon Evening Advertiser*. With the help of two local reporters, I would carry out a poll. In vain was it protested that this was not what Dr Butler had advocated—that he had been talking of tasting opinion, not of anything so grand or so scientific as an opinion poll. Enough of that, it was said. Go down to Devizes and do as you're told, and we'll have a look at the outcome.

The outcome was a set of figures showing a Conservative lead much bigger than the one they were defending, in a contest which almost everyone thought they were going to lose. The figures were clearly incredible. But the *Swindon Evening Advertiser* had cleared the front page and was waiting for copy. The only course in the circumstances was to find some way of adjusting the figures. Accordingly we devised an Error Factor, based on the record of how people said they had voted at the previous election (few people were aware at that time how deeply unreliable such figures usually were). By weighting the figures accordingly, we produced a result which put the Conservatives two points ahead. That should have been the end of this adventure, especially when a real poll in the *Daily Mail* the following day put Labour ahead. But the voters of Devizes inadvertently kept it alive. The Conservatives won on the day with a lead of 4 per cent. In the coming election, it was immediately ordered, these polls must be carried out in every town where the group had an evening newspaper.

The results were not very good. Some were roughly accurate. The announcement from Bath made us look spot on—until the Returning Officer published a correction. Others were very inaccurate—as in Oxford, where a letter from Nuffield College asked awkward questions about the methodology. The people of Darlington learnt to their astonishment that the town was on the verge of a Liberal landslide. They were not to know that the reporter in charge of the exercise had multiplied where he should have divided.

In another sense, though, the Butler method was vindicated. Slogging round the doorsteps with clipboards gives you a firmer sense of how people vote than any amount of academic instruction. I can still recall, for instance, the lane in Tidworth, Wiltshire, where an old agricultural labourer told me why he always voted

Conservative: the Conservatives, he said, were people who had money, so they knew how to handle it. (And if things got bad for the country, he added, they could always dip into their pockets to help.) Or the woman at Wootton Bassett, the first of many, who, when asked how she intended to vote, said her husband had not yet told her. And, above all, the joyful thirst among white-collar workers on Teeside, in ICI country, for a Labour government, after Harold Wilson's speeches on science and technology and the end of the grousemoor era. It was almost as if, fifteen years before the Conservatives promised people the right to own their own homes, Harold Wilson had promised them the right to own their own lives.

IV

The following year the Butler thesis was once again put to the test in Northumberland Road, E17. The Leyton by-election was called after Patrick Gordon Walker, Wilson's choice as Foreign Secretary, failed to hold Smethwick in a general election contest so ugly and so full of racial tensions that Wilson dubbed the Conservative victor 'a parliamentary leper'. So the search began for some amenable elderly MP who would give up his seat to let Gordon Walker back into Parliament, and in time the choice fell on Reginald Sorensen, who, apart from a four-year gap (1931–5) had represented the area since 1929. He was 73. It was said that, when the notion was put to him, he replied: 'Heavens above! God forbid.' But he duly complied.

The *Guardian* dispatched to cover the contest its reporter Tony Geraghty, who in his early reports saw little reason to doubt that Gordon Walker's return to the Commons was a formality. Suggestions that the issue of race had followed the candidate from Smethwick to London were swiftly dismissed. 'A snap opinion poll conducted among police, probation and education and public health authorities indicated that the coloured population was normally healthy and educated and less than normally criminal,' Geraghty reported on 5 January. Two days later, things were changing. Racialism, 'which until yesterday had seemed a spindly phobia in Leyton, limited to the imagination of a few hoarse fanatics', had now become an issue between the parties. Conservative canvassers were said to be stirring it up. Gradually, and against the trend of much other reporting, as well as an NOP poll which showed a solid Labour victory, Geraghty began to suspect that things were going badly for Labour. On 12 January he reported the results of a house-to-house canvass in Northumberland Road. Of his sample of fifteen, four expressed opposition to coloured immigration; three were past Labour voters opposed to Gordon Walker because of his reputation for racial tolerance.

Later Geraghty returned to Northumberland Road to check the main parties' canvass returns against his own. Labour's figures were Labour 62 per cent, Conservatives 14, Liberals 5, doubtful 19. His own were Labour 40, Conservatives 28, and Liberal 13.5. 'The disparity of the various estimates', he wrote, 'may be attributed to the politeness of the English voter which is lethal to the accuracy of most political soundings. The voters, particularly the lady voters, cannot say "no".' By now he had also picked up the other, neglected, theme of this by-election: resentment that Reg. Sorensen was being bundled into obscurity (i.e. the House of Lords), with a stranger supplied in his place, for no better reason than the Labour party's convenience. Though he failed to predict the Conservative victory (so for that matter did the Conservative candidate), his time on the doorsteps had shown him truths which most other reporters had missed.

V

In 1966 there occurred a contest which produced perhaps the most abject example of pre-Butlerianism in modern election reporting. Despite the enthusiasm on Teesside, Labour had been elected in 1964 with only a thin majority, and was considering calling another election to build a solid majority. The Hull North by-election in January 1966, where the party defended a seat which in 1964 had produced a 1,181 (2.5 per cent) Labour majority, was seen as a test of what could be done. It seemed, as reporting began, that Wilson was in for a bad disappointment. Labour's campaign, the press agreed, was disastrous. 'The most self-effacing candidate I have ever met,' said the man from the *Financial Times* of Kevin McNamara. The reporter of *The Times* castigated the Labour campaign and the failure of the candidate to emerge from obscurity

in such forthright terms that protests arrived from party
headquarters.

The *Guardian*, meanwhile, appeared obsessed with the Radical
Alliance candidate, Richard Gott, who had resigned from the paper
to fight predominantly on the issue of Labour's support for US
action in Vietnam.

From today, [its reporter wrote on 10 January], the framework on which
the three main candidates . . . have to build their campaigns will gradually
be submerged in a forest of guile. Already the fronds of confusion are
slithering among the girders. . . . Mr Gott and his freebooting campaign
over the Vietnam war have so far won more publicity, intellectual and
'pop' alike, than all the other candidates put together.

He outshone all other candidates, the paper later reported, in a
United Nations Association forum on foreign affairs. 'Mr Gott a
highly important factor in Hull North', a *Guardian* headline
announced on 19 January.

Yet when, Geraghty-like, you started knocking on doors, the
story was rather different. On 25 January Dennis Johnson reported
for the *Guardian* on a canvass of two Hull streets, one leafy and
privileged, one 'a sort of Coronation Street'. In terms of prediction,
the results were not very helpful, since they showed little slippage
in anyone's vote. Even so, that did not sustain the consensual myth
that Labour was on the slide. And it also confirmed what should
have been suspected: that very few people raised foreign affairs;
that, when they did, it was Rhodesia rather than Vietnam; and that
neither street showed any great interest in Richard Gott.

By now both *The Times*—'everything points to a Conservative
victory'—and the *Telegraph* had abandoned all hope for the
Labour party. In the event, Labour took the seat with a swing in
its favour of 4.5 per cent; Richard Gott took 253 votes. And
Wilson got the signal he needed to stage a second election, which
he won with a solid majority.

VI

The reporting of by-elections has moved on since then. The pattern
of most reporters' days has not altered much. The day always
begins with a round of party press conferences, usually staged close

enough to each other to enable the media to get to each one every day—though the parties often like to spin things out a little to encroach on their rivals' time. The platform will usually consist of some star of the party leadership (in those parties, that is, which have enough stars to go round), the candidate, and the candidate's minder. The last is a relatively new development, made a general rule because of past indiscretions by candidates unskilled at resisting the wiles of the press. The minder, normally an MP of some seniority, will try to intercept questions beyond a candidate's reach, or will intervene when a candidate's answer falls short of the mark, or offends against party policy, with a swift explanation that what George really means is this . . .

The visiting star will normally do most to set the agenda for the national press—the candidate will have more success with local issues for the local media—and will usually be there more to catch the eye of a national audience on lunchtime television than to talk about the particular problems of Stragglesville. But the media will also use these occasions to test the candidate, sometimes pretty cruelly. These are daunting occasions for people fresh to this world, and some do not survive them. The *Daily Telegraph* used to employ a leprechaun-like Irish reporter called A. J. (Paddy) Travers, who specialized in questions with an innocent opening and a lethal twist to their tail. In cricketing terms, he took his wickets with spin, not pace. One Labour candidate in the late 1960s would visibly tremble when Travers came into the attack. At Crosby in 1981 the Conservative candidate John Butcher had such daily travails with two reporters (both from Conservative newspapers) that a decision was taken to abandon the daily press conference: it was quickly rescinded on orders from Central Office. At Mid-Staffs. the Labour candidate, Sylvia Heal, came under early attack for her stylized, unspontaneous answers. Paddy Ashdown tagged her 'Barbie Doll'. On 14 March, under the headline, 'Would you vote for Barbie Doll?', the columnist George Gale wrote in the *Daily Mail*: 'In close on 40 years of covering by-elections I do not recall any candidate expected to overturn a huge majority as feeble as Mrs Heal.' The Conservative minister Michael Howard took up the theme at that morning's Conservative press conference. Had Mrs Heal, he demanded, taken a Trappist vow? But Jon Hibbs of the *Daily Telegraph*, whose reporting from this election was a model of fair-mindedness, wrote the next day: 'Unfortunately for the Conservatives, Mrs Heal is beginning to blossom under pressure. With a week to go, she is displaying increasing self-confidence.'

At Bradford North in November 1990 it was the Conservative candidate, Joy Atkin, who became the target for press attack.

Whoever's effigy was going to be burned at the Idle Conservative Club's bonfire night in Bradford North yesterday, Miss Joy Atkin was determined it was not going to be hers [Hibbs reported on 6 November]. With just three days before polling the Tory candidate suddenly came out of her corner fighting . . . Stung by what had been written about her, she hit back in kind. 'Your frightened rabbit is fighting back' she snapped at the *Daily Telegraph* after dominating the morning press conference with a selection of forthright views.

Having sunk to third place on polling day, she was not retained as candidate for the general election.

Through the rest of the day the parties stage events which they hope will catch media (which above all means television) attention. Visiting stars go on walkabout through the constituency and are pictured, heads slightly cocked, the models of attentiveness, listening to local complaints. If they are Jeffrey Archer, without whom no self-respecting by-election campaign in 1991 was complete, they will stride through the town accepting the people's plaudits and dishing out manly advice. He always gets plenty of space in the newspapers. There may be factory-gate meetings at lunchtimes, visits to old people's homes, or opportunities to go canvassing with the candidate and note down, in the case of the government party's candidates, the insults they have to take for the nature of government policies and quite often their party's leadership. Most reporters will file to their offices in late afternoon, since their pieces will normally go on inside pages which have earlier deadlines.

In the evenings there will often be meetings, though these are not what they were. Except on special occasions—the great Alliance triumphs of 1981–2, for instance—you rarely get packed halls, more huddles of the faithful. Only a few politicians are still guaranteed crowd-pullers. Michael Heseltine got hundreds in Mid-Staffs. where Cecil Parkinson played to an audience of about thirty-five. And, even then, the turn-out may be misleading. In the Crosby by-election Tony Benn, having arrived to find a full school hall and a packed overflow meeting, returned to London to report that things were going much better than press reports had suggested. But reporters saw the event less as a constituency meeting than as a rally of the Merseyside Left. Labour's candidate polled 9.5 per cent of the vote and lost his deposit.

There is also, in the evenings, a certain amount of living it up. After the Mid-Staffs. election, Colin Brown produced in the *Independent* an astonishingly copious guide to the local restaurants and pubs. Some of the grandees of the lobby, he reported, had fled the constituency altogether for an Egon Ronay-listed hotel in Stafford: 'Staff here are prepared for expense account living, but one waiter did a double take when one senior member of the visiting press corps, having ordered 'surf 'n' turf'—steak and lobster slices—complained about the lack of lobster, then insisted on three chocolate eclairs with cream for dessert.'

The greatest change in by-election coverage is the attention now paid to the polls—not least because it is now accepted that, by triggering the tactical vote, the polls may virtually settle the shape of a by-election. Whereas, in Leyton and Hull North, newspapers did not bother to pick up each other's polls, now, in any constituency where the result is in doubt—and even in some, like Mid-Staffs., where it is not—stories will be written, and the day's information possibly superseded, by what newspapers treat as the latest 'prediction'.

Twenty years ago there were many people in newspapers who distrusted all such proceedings. Young arrivals who had grown up on Butler and Robert McKenzie and knew about swing were frowned on as if for preaching heathen practices. Such techniques, it was complained, were taking the poetry out of politics and turning election-reporting from an art to science. A few retain that scepticism. But you cannot take that line any longer without trouble from your news desk. The reporting of polls, even so, remains undeveloped. Despite a constant stream of letters from Robert M. Worcester of MORI, the information is often treated uncritically. Polls with tiny samples conducted by people with no track record (the successors, perhaps of the Westminster Press poll in Devizes) are reported alongside real ones. On 8 March 1990 the *Daily Telegraph* reported two new polls from Mid-Staffs.: one, a telephone poll with a sample of 928 conducted by students at Wolverhampton Poly, put Labour on 37 per cent and the Conservatives on 27, while the other, which appeared in the *Birmingham*

Post but whose origin was unstated, gave Labour 49 and the Conservatives 41. The fact that one set of figures excluded 'don't knows' while the other did not was left unexplained. 'There is controversy in the constituency over the accuracy of these polls,' the *Telegraph* added helpfully.

This resort to polling evidence is both a blight and a blessing: a blight in that it further highlights the horse-race aspect of by-elections—the question 'who's going to win'—while neglecting the equally necessary question: 'and why?' The blessing is that, with a few outstanding exceptions, reporters are much more likely now to report a climate of local opinion which corresponds with the facts than to rely, as they so often did in the days before psephology, on the pricking of their thumbs.

VII

Hardly anyone doubted that Labour would win Mid-Staffs. Labour began the campaign as 5 to 1 favourites, and polls throughout the campaign underlined the bookmakers' wisdom. Trawl as they might, the Conservatives and their eager allies in the national press could do nothing to shake Labour's dominance. The *Daily Mail* made great play of the poll-tax riots and Militant's involvement. Here, they said, was a dangerous issue for Labour. 'A desolate Neil Kinnock stood amid the ruins of his poll tax dreams last night,' the paper asserted hopefully on 10 March, after some Labour back-benchers had come out in favour of non-payment. On 13 March the Home Office minister, John Patten, warned the people of Lichfield and Rugeley, the two biggest towns in the constituency, to 'batten down the hatches . . . some unpleasant and malevolent people are coming here to cause as much trouble as they can.' This unfortunately coincided with a burst of speculation about whether or not Michael Heseltine would be visiting the constituency.

The *Mail* tried another tack. 'Hysteria about Mrs Thatcher's future is uniting Tories behind her in the by-election,' it declared. 'Conservative canvassers claim that many have been jolted to stick with her because of what they see as ill-founded speculation that she might resign.' But most reporters knew better. The contest was cut and dried.

The second question—why was this happening—was less successfully answered. In the early days much of the daily reporting seemed to portray a single-issue election: an election fought on the poll tax. 'Tory faithful deserting Thatcher in the Poll Tax election,' the *Observer* declared in a headline over a piece which told a rather more subtle story. 'It is a two-horse race and a one issue campaign,' wrote a *Sunday Telegraph* correspondent after a fleeting visit. But it was not. A one-horse race in a two- or three-issue campaign would have been nearer the truth. A MORI poll for *Times* newspapers, published on 19 March, found 88 per cent of respondents naming the poll tax among the issues which most concerned them. But 31 per cent were worried about interest rates and 31 per cent about the health service, and 78 per cent of respondents disapproved of the government generally. Opposition to the poll tax was by no means the only motive for the great Conservative retreat, as a second *Sunday Telegraph* writer noted: 'I found one or two Tory deserters with £50,000 mortgages whose interest payments were almost £200 a month more than in 1988,' he reported. 'By comparison with that, the community charge is negligible.'

A leader in the *Mail* in February, reflecting on a fresh wave of increases in mortgage-interest rates, fitted the context well: 'It is the Thatcher stalwarts, whom statisticians call the skilled and semi-skilled Cs, who are hardest hit by the mortgage payment increases. Among them it is those aged between 25 and 34 who suffer most of all.' The BBC's *On the Record* programme established that the constituency had twice as many young mortgaged families with children as the national average. You had only to see the smart new estates of Lichfield to see how well that judgement fitted Mid-Staffs. They glowed with the pride of ownership. The people who lovingly maintained them had once been Thatcher's people; but now what had formerly been a source of joy and self-fulfilment, a liberation, had become a burden, generating apprehension and fear.

The poll tax, resented though it was, could not alone have created the alienation so plainly written across the face of Mid-Staffs. It came as the conclusive blow on top of a lot of others: mortgages, the state of the National Health Service, the return of inflation, big price hikes from newly privatized industries. Sylvia Heal put it well to the political editor of the *Spectator*, Noel Malcolm: 'They come up to me and they speak about the poll tax and then they start talking about the general nature of Government policy.' Malcolm was unimpressed. He was generally unimpressed by a candidate who looked 'like a cross between a clothes-conscious headmistress and Glenys Kinnock on valium'. Had he listened, he might have learnt.

Malcolm's account of Mid Staffs., published on 17 March, belonged to the loftiest pre-Butlerian traditions of by-election reporting. The huge evidence of Tory disaster took second place to his instincts. 'If the election were held now, of course,' he wrote 'all the evidence suggests that Labour would win.' But Charles Prior—'red, beefy features, an engagingly goofy boggle-eyed grin, a forthright style of public speaking and a willingness to admit mistakes'—was by no means out of the race.

Given Labour's huge lead on the polls it is hard to foresee anything other than a Labour victory here. Nevertheless I believe it will be a much closer thing than the pollsters are allowing at present. A rise in support for Mr Jones [the Liberal Democrat candidate], a slackening of interest in Mrs Heal's inertial, line-toeing campaign, and above all the superior organization of the local Tory workers in getting the vote out: all this suggests to me a very narrow margin. Mr Prior is still in with a chance.

In his column the following week the failure of this forecast went unmentioned. Mr Malcolm, it seemed, shared the candidate's forthright style, but unhappily not his frankness over mistakes.

VIII

Eastbourne, unlike Mid-Staffs., was unforeseen—except, perhaps by the *Daily Mail*'s astrologer, who, as the paper proudly claimed after the result, had predicted two years earlier that the Liberal Democrats would be in an ideal position to win a by-election on 18 October 1990. In any other circumstances it might have looked like a good Liberal Democrat prospect. They had a strong base in local government, with thirteen of the thirty seats on the local council, and had outpolled the Conservatives by 40.5 per cent to 35.1 per cent in the local elections in May. But the fate of Ian Gow seemed to cancel out all that. By-elections where an MP had died in such tragic circumstances were not expected to produce huge swings or sensational results. Some newspapers thought there should not be a contest at all, though in the event the only intending candidate to retire from the scene was Screaming Lord Sutch.

The contest was very lightly reported. That was partly because nothing much was expected of it, and partly because of the conference season. It was only on the Friday before polling day that most political reporters got away from Bournemouth, where the Conservative conference had been dominated by speculation on the party leadership and the news that Britain was joining the Exchange Rate Mechanism. The heavy papers confined themselves to three or four reports. The *Mail* produced an unbylined story on 15 October, saying the Conservative candidate, Richard Hickmet, was 'in little danger', and a second unbylined report, recording Mrs Thatcher's tribute to Ian Gow, the following day. On 17 October its assessment was a little gloomier. But the Gow factor, it expected, would dispose of any possible revolt over the poll tax.

Still, as the final week developed, a consensus emerged: the Conservative majority was going to be badly cut. One reason was Hickmet: Richard Saladin Hickmet, as the papers liked to call him, whose Turkish connections had not pleased the town's Greek Cypriot community and whose touch was less than sure (at one point he saluted the work of a local hospital which in fact had already closed). Mrs Thatcher did not help. One reporter, canvassing with Hickmet, picked up a typical exchange. ' "No, you can't count on my support," said the lady at number 52. "Why? Because I feel decrepit and unwanted. Mrs Thatcher's the worst disaster the country has ever had." ' The condition of prosperous Eastbourne was causing dismay: the boarded-up shops, the eight abandoned hotels on the promenade. Of five factories which the Liberal Democrat candidate, David Bellotti, had visited in the 1987 election, only one remained.

But what most caught the media's eye was the Conservatives' apparent mishandling of the 'Gow factor'. A Conservative broadsheet declared: 'Every one of us must remember that whatever the other parties may say, this election will be seen around the country in the light of Ian Gow's murder. Any result other than a massive vote for Richard Hickmet will be a moral victory for terrorism. The people of Eastbourne must avoid sending such a message at all costs.' The tasteless overplaying of this issue, Alan Travis reported for the *Guardian* on 17 October, was now threatening the Conservatives' majority. But with the only poll of the campaign looking inconclusive, no one quite expected the Tories to lose.

A lot of the most powerful descriptions of Eastbourne did not appear till the contest was over. The *Mail* produced no fewer than three separate pieces to explain what had happened. 'A crass Tory campaign,' Paul Johnson complained. With a record pension increase, John Fisher reported, the Conservatives had assumed the town would be safe. But the poll tax, the effects of the recession on hotels and shops, the state of community care, the failure to clear the seafront after the gales—all had contributed. Like the readers of *The Times* and the *Telegraph* after Fulham, the *Mail*'s clientele were surely entitled to ask: why weren't we told this before?

An NOP exit poll filled out the picture. Health, education, interest rates, and the general state of the economy had hurt the Conservatives, along with the poll tax and the clumsy attempt to invoke Ian Gow. But Ivor Crewe, in *The Times*, thought the swing to the Liberal Democrats might have been greater but for the way that Ian Gow died.

IX

So how did the newspaper fare on the test which David Butler had set back in 1964 in these two elections? Not, overall, as well as they should have done. Some of their ancient failings now seem to have been cured: the Gott fallacy, for instance, where, because an independent is lively and personable, it is assumed he is spellbinding voters as he is the visiting press. The psephological evidence is far better heeded, though with due understanding of the fallible record of by-election polling. (The words 'Remember Brecon' are engraved on many a heart.) But the papers still listen too much to the politicians and not enough to the voters. Their agenda is too candidate-led. The pattern of most reporters' days is set by the parties. Even canvassing with the candidate, which gets you on to the doorstep, is an over-rated pastime: it is the candidate, not the reporter, who usually asks the questions and determines what is discussed.

Here were two elections which caught a political movement and a political idea at its lowest ebb: on the eve, perhaps, of disintegration. Margaret Thatcher's MPs would not have turned on her had the country not done so first. And here, most of all in Mid-Staffs., with its shining new estates and its air of Middle England, were test beds where the moment of historic rejection could be usefully explored. The people who wrote the daily reports, tied as they were to daily routines and deadlines and editors' expectations, had less of a chance to do what was needed than the heavyweight pundits and columnists, with their far more generous rations of time and space. Yet those who dissect these things in twenty years' time will find hardly a piece which so fully captures the moment that they are able to say: yes, this is why the people turned on her; this is what it must have been like.

Meanwhile, at the loftiest levels of journalism, the old pre-Butlerian traditions survive. At the Monmouth by-election of May 1991 the press mostly got it right, plotting the growing entrapment of the Tory campaign in voters' fears for the National Health Service, properly weighing the polls, and predicting Conservative defeat. Yet here is Alan Watkins, in his *Observer* column, on the Sunday after polling day: 'At Monmouth I got the majority right but the party wrong' (he had tipped the Liberal Democrats). 'Ah well. There we are. At least I was able to collect a bottle of champagne from Mr Peter Jenkins, who made a bet with me that the Conservatives would retain the seat.'

What a splendidly full confession! Though rather less splendid, ultimately, than reading the signs aright.

Reference

Ceadal, M. (1973), 'Interpreting East Fulham', in C. Cook and J. Ramsden (eds.), *By-Elections in British Politics* (London: Macmillan), 118–39.

6

Expressive versus Instrumental Voting

RICHARD ROSE and IAN MCALLISTER

The role of the people is to produce a government
Joseph A. Schumpeter (1952: 269)

Our approach is in the main dependent on the point of view of the actor.
Angus Campbell *et al.* (1960: 27)

Every vote has a double significance: it expresses the state of mind of an individual elector and it is an act in an instrumental process for determining control of government. The two functions are related but very different (Rose and Mossawir 1967; Pammett 1988).

For students of voting, the state of mind of an individual is of first importance; the ruling dictum is expressed in the epigram above from the path-breaking University of Michigan study *The American Voter*; the emphasis should be upon individual motives and behaviour. For students of government, however, the critical question is which party gains control of office. The primary consideration is the transformation of votes into seats in Parliament and thus into seats in Cabinet. Schumpeter's perspective is appropriate to the parliamentary tradition, focusing on elections as instruments in élite struggles for power.

The instrumentalist view of elections as a means of choosing government is particularly congenial to the British parliamentary tradition. If electoral competition is seen in terms of one of only two parties winning control of government and each party representing a distinctive social class (e.g. Beer 1965; Butler and Stokes 1969), then it can be both expressive and instrumental. An individual's vote may be interpreted as expressing an identification with family and class loyalties, and concurrently endorsing the governing party remaining in office or being evicted. However, in a multi-party system, in which governments are formed by coalitions of parties; then the instrumentalist model of voters producing government is irrelevant, since voters cannot be sure which parties will form the coalition government resulting from post-election haggling.

While democracy is a universalistic norm, the actual forms of electoral systems and party competition are diverse. In the first section of this chapter the differences between the macro-level instrumental theory of voting producing government, and the micro-level expressive theory of voting as an expression of individual outlooks, are set out. The instrumentalist theory is then tested by evidence from the 1987 British general election, which was atypical in meeting the conditions for determining which theory motivates most voters. Since the instrumentalist theory is rejected, the third section tests what voters are trying to express—family loyalties, class ties, or political values. The conclusion considers the implications of voters giving representation priority over the production of government.

MACRO-MICRO DIFFERENCES IN THE FUNCTIONS OF VOTING

The instrumental view of voting is a macro perspective; the main function of an election is the production of government. Given this, it is assumed that the motive of individual voters is to keep the governing party in office, or to turn it out and put the Outs in. By contrast, the expressive theory of voting is micro-level; the function of an election is to give individuals an opportunity to express their preferences. The choice of government is subsidiary or ignored.

Instrumental Voting

Writing when democracy could not be taken for granted, Joseph Schumpeter (1952: 269) rejected the idea that the object of democracy was to allow people to choose representatives to carry out their collective preferences. Schumpeter defined the object of democracy as the production of government: 'free competition for a free vote' gives voters the opportunity to choose a government from competing teams of political leaders; once in office, leaders could then decide what policies to follow.

Competition for votes was expected to be oligopolistic: 'In economic life competition is never completely lacking, but hardly ever is it perfect.' Freedom to compete for office is 'free in the same sense in which everyone is free to start another textile mill' (Schumpeter 1952: 271, 272 n. 6). Just as many producers do not provide exactly what each individual consumer may wish, so it is impossible for an election to represent individuals; the 'will of the people is a mosaic' (ibid.). In a producer-oriented oligopolistic market for votes, the choice of many voters will be reduced to a second-best choice between lesser evils.

Like many of his generation, Schumpeter took as his model of democratic politics what he called 'the classical English practice' (1952: 274). Disraeli and Gladstone facing each other in the British House of Commons was the paradigm example of duopolistic competition for votes between leaders. Shortly before his death, Schumpeter wrote to Arthur Smithies: 'I never really could understand anyone with the least chance to play some role at a measurable distance from Downing Street doing anything else' (1951: 11).

In language that marketing experts repeat when advising politicians today, Schumpeter saw competition for votes as about winning office, and not about advancing policies and political principles. Parties were said to have principles and make policies 'incidentally, in the same sense as production is incidental to the making of profits' (Schumpeter 1952: 282). The 'business' of a party is to win control of government, and not to advance capitalism or socialism or to reduce inflation or unemployment. Such actions are only instrumental means to the end of winning and holding office.

Competition is an active process, for the electorate has not only the right to produce a government but also 'the function of evicting it' (Schumpeter 1952: 272). Duopolistic competition remains competition between Ins and Outs, and even a nominally one-party system offers a degree of choice, endorsing or refusing to endorse the government of the day, or discriminating between candidates of the governing party (Hermet 1978). Just as a businessman is driven to adapt his products if there is a threat of losing customers to a competitor, so governors are seen as responding to the potential loss of votes and office (cf. Hatschek's 'law of anticipated reactions') (Friedrich, 1941: 589 ff.). Sartori describes Schumpeter's model as a 'competitive-feedback theory' (1987: 153).

Although Schumpeter's instrumentalist views gained him a reputation in his day as a cynic (see Wright 1951: 130), his realism has since appealed to scholars raised in a behavioural or public-choice tradition. Robert McKenzie concludes his study of leadership in *British Political Parties* by rejecting Michels's idea that parties ought to represent the mass of their supporters, instead endorsing as 'more realistic' Schumpeter's view 'that the essence of the democratic process is that it should provide a free competition for political leadership' (McKenzie 1963: 646). In *Political Man* S. M. Lipset bases his definition of the democratic order upon Schumpeter, describing it as a political system in which the mass of the population can exercise the right of 'choosing among contenders for political office'. (1960: 45).

The micro-level foundations for the instrumental theory of voting were spelt out by Anthony Downs (1957; cf. Almond, 1990: 117 ff.) in *An Economic Theory of Democracy*. He followed Schumpeter in defining democracy as voters choosing between parties competing for control of government. Downs explicitly rejected the idea that parties seek office to express the views of voters, quoting approvingly the passage from Schumpeter cited above in which policies are described as incidental to the profits of office (Downs 1957: 29, 284).

The theory of retrospective voting is a contemporary evocation of Schumpeter. V. O. Key saw the electorate as making a retrospective judgement on the performance of governors: 'Voters may reject what they have known; or they may approve what they have known', (1966: 61). Given minimal awareness of what has happened under the incumbent party, voters need not be concerned with the prospective 'direction in which society should move'; they can assign responsibility for producing government by a simple reward–punishment calculus based on past performance (Fiorina 1981: 6). Fiorina (1981: 197 ff.) also notes that voters may also hold prospective expectations of what competing parties may do after entry into office.

While Schumpeter's instrumental model of democracy is widely known, the conditions in which it applies are so restrictive that they are not met in most contemporary democratic systems. In most countries the model is not wrong; it is simply not relevant. Three conditions must be met:

1. The authority of government is centralized in a set of offices determined by a single ballot. This condition is met in parliamentary democracies in which the executive is formed as a consequence of the election of Parliament. But, in a separation-of-powers system such as in the United States or France, individuals have two votes, one for a representative assembly and the other for a President. Lane (1962) interprets such an election as offering a chance to express conflicting views that prevent the production of a responsible single-party government; individuals can vote for an authoritative President and a Congress acting as a check upon this authority. In a system offering voters a multiplicity of votes for a multiplicity of offices, no one vote determines the government: 'collective responsibility has leaked out of the system' (Fiorina 1981: 210).

2. Two parties are clearly recognizable as the governing party and the Opposition. The use of a first-past-the-post electoral system encourages the reduction of choice to a single In and a single Out party. As long as there are only two parties in Parliament, the electorate can easily discern how to vote for or against keeping the In party in office. By contrast, in a proportional representation system, up to half a dozen parties usually win seats and are 'relevant' for producing a government, and the largest party normally must govern as part of a coalition (Sartori 1976: 121 ff., 300 ff.).

Since most parliamentary systems are multi-party systems, a voter has a choice between opposition parties and between governing parties. Coalitions can be temporary marriages of convenience, with office changing hands between elections as a result of coalition reshuffling. In most elections involving a coalition government the verdict of the voters is ambiguous or even contradictory, for some partners in the coalition gain votes and seats while others lose votes and seats (cf. Browne and Dreijmanis 1982; Rose and Mackie 1983).

3. The choice of parties in a voter's constituency is the same as the choice of government in Parliament. In a two-party parliamentary system this condition is met; it is also met in a presidential election in which two candidates are the principal opponents nation-wide. But in a multi-party system the two principal parties

competing may differ from one constituency to another. Belgium is an extreme example, since linguistic divisions result in the choice in Flanders being different from that in French-speaking Wallonia. In Canada the two principal parties differ from province to province. In the days of the American Solid South the choice in one-fifth of the Union was different from that between Republicans and Democrats (Key 1949). In the United Kingdom there are different systems of party competition in England, Scotland, Wales, and Northern Ireland (McAllister and Rose 1984).

When more than two parties are relevant to the choice of a coalition government, voters are offered a choice between several In and several Out parties. Whereas two-party competition lends itself to increasingly intense public-relations campaigns to mobilize the support of a mass electorate that effectively produces the government, coalition government encourages bargaining for office in a 'cloakroom style' or *kuhhandel* politics (cf. Bogdanor 1983; Lijphart 1984).

Expressive Voting

Expressive voting is consistent with any form of free elections. Even in the absence of parties, individuals may still vote express-ively, using the ethnicity, gender, locality, or other attributes of candidates as a cue to casting a ballot in favour of the candidate deemed most likely to express the elector's outlook.

What exactly are individuals trying to express when casting their ballot? Three different answers are given: social cleavages, socio-psychological identification, and proximity to a party's position on issues.

Social-cleavage theories describe parties as appealing for votes along lines of class, religion, language, race, or other social differences (see, for example, Lipset and Rokkan 1967). In casting a vote, an individual expresses commitment to a class, a church or anti-clerical stance, or a linguistic or ethnic group. The production of a government is not particularly relevant; a minority group can maintain an intense commitment to a permanent Out party, as Catholics do in Northern Ireland. The introduction of proportional representation around the time of the First World War in continen-tal Europe institutionalized a multiplicity of parties expressing class, religious, and other cleavages, preventing an election being reduced to a simple choice between Ins and Outs (Lipset and Rokkan 1967: 32 ff.; cf. Wald 1983).

Social psychological theories of identification focus upon the small-group basis of party choice. Within a small group, typically the family, an individual learns to identify with the party that is dominant. Party identification is shaped in pre-adult political socialization; youths become aware of their parents' party identification long before they are old enough to vote, and this identification is carried forward into adulthood. When casting a ballot, an adult need not be making a choice between the policies of parties competing for control of government, but expressing loyalty to family upbringing. This is particularly important if an individual is upwardly mobile in class terms, or develops views about issues or government performance at variance with a long established party identification (see Campbell *et al.* 1960, Butler and Stokes 1969).

A third alternative is that individuals vote for the party that best expresses their political values or views on issues. This is often presented as a spatial-distance model of voting, in which parties are arrayed along a left-right dimension, with each voter inclined to favour the party that is located closest to his or her position on this continuum (see Downs 1957; Dalton *et al.* 1984). The clusters of values may exist in more than one dimension (see Inglehart 1977). The important point is that the actions of voters express value or issue preferences. Instead of parties appealing for votes on non-directive themes such as 'competence' or 'it's time for a change', they are reckoned to compete by expressing values or stands on issues.

Voting is seen not as an instrumental means of choosing a government but as a means of giving expression to an individual's subjective identification and tastes. From this perspective there can be no such thing as a 'wasted' vote. Just as people have a right to express a preference for strawberry or banana rather than the two most popular kinds of ice cream, so they can express a taste for a party that has no chance of forming a government.

Instrumental and Expressive Voting Compared

In logic, the two approaches to voting can point to the same conclusion. Given a right-wing government in office, a middle-class elector with right-wing parents and right-wing views is likely to want to support the In party, and a voter with a contrasting class, parental, and ideological orientation to vote for the Out party. Thus, either theory would appear to explain voting behaviour.

In the overwhelming majority of democratic political systems, voters must act expressively, for there is a multiplicity of parties competing, and there is no simple swing in votes between an In and an Out party (Rose 1991a). If Schumpeter had looked at France or Weimar Germany rather than Disraeli's and Gladstone's Britain, he would have seen that party competition need not be restricted to two oligopolistic parties; instead, it can represent a bazaar in which a multiplicity of 'retail-size' parties cater to a wide variety of tastes, albeit at the cost of confusing responsibility for government.

For two generations after the eclipse of the Liberal party in the 1930s Britain did meet conditions for both instrumental and expressive voting. Control of government was consistently in the hands of one party with a majority in the House of Commons. The Liberal party usually did not fight half the constituencies, thus ensuring that the choice of voters at constituency level was the same as the choice of government in Parliament. Furthermore, Conservative and Labour candidates finished first and second in nine-tenths or more of all constituencies (Craig 1989: Table 14.13, p. 15).

INSTRUMENTAL VOTING: THE EXCEPTION NOT THE RULE

Britain today affords a clear and unusual opportunity to test the relative importance of instrumental as against expressive voting. Since 1974 there has been multi-party competition, due to the rise of the Liberal party, the creation of the Social Democratic party and of the Liberal–SDP Alliance, and the shift to the extremes of both the Conservative and Labour parties. By the 1987 election a situation had arisen in which instrumental and expressive calculations led to opposing predictions of voting by a large portion of the electorate, and this remains true after the 1992 election.

Instrumental Choice Differentiated from Expressive Choice

Just as only one party can finish first in a constituency, so only one party can be in second place. Finishing second is important, for the

TABLE 6.1. *Patterns of party competition in England, 1983–1987*

Party order	1983	1987
Con. 1st; Alliance 2nd	249	226
Con. 1st; Lab. 2nd	113	132
Lab. 1st; Con 2nd	131	139
Lab. 1st; Alliance 2nd	17	16
Alliance 1st; Con. or Lab. 2nd	13	10
TOTAL	523	523

Source: Centre for the Study of Public Policy, Election File.

party that is second in a constituency is the alternative to the incumbent there. A voter who wants to turn the incumbent MP out will find the second-place party the best instrument for doing so. In a first-past-the-post electoral system, success in challenging the governing party at the constituency level is a necessary condition of a parliamentary opposition becoming the government.

The 1983 election result repudiated condition 3 in the two-party model of instrumental voting: the ordering of choices at the constituency level was not that of the parties in Parliament. Labour's vote fell to its lowest since 1918, just 2 per cent more than the Alliance, and its number of parliamentary seats was the lowest since 1935. Although the electoral system awarded Labour almost ten times as many MPs as the Alliance, the Alliance parties finished second to Conservative MPs in more than twice as many constituencies as did Labour. In 249 of the government seats, the Labour candidate was in third place in 1983.[1] Labour candidates were more likely to finish third than second in a constituency. Only the Conservative party met the conventional assumption of instrumental politics, finishing first or second in 96 per cent of the constituencies in England (Table 6.1).

In the 1987 election the wasted-vote argument—a party is not an instrumentally credible government if it cannot win a majority of seats in the House of Commons—could be used to dismiss the Labour Opposition in two-thirds of the constituencies held by Conservative MPs. If in 1987 Labour had won every seat in England where it had finished second in 1983, it would still have lacked sufficient MPs to constitute a majority government. In March 1987 only 10 per cent of the electorate thought that Labour was likely to win the forthcoming election, and 46 per cent did not even think Labour could finish first or second in their constituency (*Gallup Political Index* No. 319, March. 1987: 6–7).

At the start of the 1987 general election there were two two-party systems in England, one in which the choice between Ins and Outs involved Conservative and Alliance candidates who had finished first and second at the previous election, and the other in which the choice was between Conservative and Labour candidates as incumbent and instrumental challenger. Just as voting for an Alliance candidate was not instrumental in some constituencies, so voting for Labour, the official Opposition in Parliament, was a wasted vote in hundreds more. The 1987 general election confirmed the existence of two different two-party systems, for competing patterns of party competition persisted (Table 6.1), and this was reconfirmed in 1992, when Liberal Democrats finished second in 154 seats, and Labour in 192.

How Much Instrumental Voting in 1987?

The 1987 British general election offers an unusual test of the extent to which voters will cast their ballots instrumentally, as the macro-theory predicts, or continue to vote expressively, as the micro-theory predicts, for in the majority of constituencies a substantial portion of voters were predisposed to support a party that could not contribute instrumentally to determining whether the Conservative government held or lost its majority in the House of Commons. The instrumental theory predicts that the great majority of voters would vote instrumentally, or 'tactically', to use the common phrase. The expressive theory predicts that tactical voters would be a minority of those subject to conflicting cues.

There are a number of different ways to test hypotheses about the extent of instrumental voting. Since each method involves estimates or inferences, none by itself is authoritative. Yet, in so far as all support the same conclusion, then we can confidently assess the importance or unimportance of instrumental voting.

Self-reported instrumental voting.   During the 1987 election campaign the Gallup Poll asked its weekly sample how they would vote if the party they favoured was doing badly in their constituency and the party that they disliked most was going to win. Three choices were offered: an expressive choice (stick to own party); an instrumental choice (vote for second-place party); and a cognitive dissonance response (would not vote). The response was clear-cut: 70 per cent said they would stick to their own party, as against 22 per cent showing a predisposition to vote instrumentally; the remainder were uncertain or abstainers. There was only a 5 per cent difference in commitment to expressive voting among Conservative, Labour, and Alliance supporters.

When the 1987 British Election Survey asked voters to state the main reason for their choice of party, only 7 per cent said that they were tactical voters preferring a second-best party because their first choice had no chance of winning in their constituency. The great majority endorsed an expressive answer.

Changing votes. Since we know the order in which parties finished in each constituency in 1983 and their share of the vote, we can test instrumental voting by examining how voting behaviour differed in 1987 with the character of constituency competition. The instrumental theory predicts that, where a party was the second-place challenger in 1983, it would gain a substantial number of votes in 1987, and where it was third, it would lose votes as those supporting it on expressive grounds switched to a more effective alternative.

The proportion of instrumental switching between second- and third-place parties in 1987 should have been high, since the 1983 election was held in circumstances in which it was not clear to voters which party was likely to end up in third place. Confusion was caused by a major split in Labour ranks, a new third party receiving great national media attention, and new constituency boundaries following redistribution. By contrast, in 1987 the parties and the media gave considerable attention to the tactical position of the parties in each constituency, and those who had not realized that they were 'wasting' a ballot by voting expressively in 1983 could switch to a second-best alternative.

At every election some voters will always change parties; hence, to test the extent of tactical voting in 1987, we must control for the effect of party defections independent of constituency effects. In seats in which Labour finished second, 18 per cent of its former supporters defected in 1987; in seats where the party was third to the Conservatives, the percentage was 11 points higher. For the

TABLE 6.2.   *Change in mean constituency vote by type of party competition, 1983–1987 (% change in vote)*

Party order in constituency (no.)	Con.	Lab.	Alliance
Con.–Alliance–Lab. (226)	0.0	+1.2	−1.1
Con.–Lab.–Alliance (132)	+1.7	+3.1	−4.5
Instrumental vote	n.a.	1.9	3.4

Source: Centre for the Study of Public Policy, Election File.

Alliance parties, the defection rate was 8 per cent higher in seats where it was third than in seats where it was the second-place challenger (Rose and McAllister 1990: Table 6.6).

When we examine constituency results, there is evidence of instrumental voting in the predicted direction, but the scale of instrumental voting is very limited (Table 6.2). In 1987 the Labour vote rose in constituencies where it had been third as well as where it had been second. An indicator of the extent of instrumental voting is that where Labour was second its vote rose by 1.9 per cent more than where it had been third. The vote for Alliance candidates fell in seats where the party had been second as well as in seats where it had finished out of the running in 1983. The Alliance vote fell 3.4 per cent less where it was a second-place challenger than where it started as an also-ran behind a Labour challenger.

The continuing importance of expressive voting is shown by Labour's vote going up where it had been third in 1983 as well as where it had become established as the second-place challenger to the Thatcher government. Similarly, where Alliance candidates were challengers in second place to a Conservative MP, the Alliance vote went down. The recovery of Labour support occurred across all types of constituencies, and the slump in Alliance support occurred even where it could claim an instrumental advantage as the challenger to a Conservative MP.

The direction of change in seats where Alliance had been third in 1983 provides a reminder that instrumental voting need not involve an anti-government coalition to turn the In party out. Voters can also shift from a third-place candidate to support an incumbent in order to keep the second-place challenger from winning. Where the Alliance had finished third in 1983, an average of 4.5 per cent of voters left the Alliance ranks. Of the net defectors two out of three voted Labour to put the Conservative incumbent out, and one in three voted Conservative to keep the Labour challenger from winning (Table 6.2). The net gain of Labour from the decline in also-ran Alliance support was 1.4 per cent. There was a similar net gain by Labour from Alliance in constituencies where the Alliance had finished second in 1983.

Whatever the indicator, instrumental voting appears to be limited. Only one-tenth to one sixth of those who vote for a third-place party may change their votes because their party has no chance to influence the composition of the House of Commons or the government. When the electorate as a whole is considered, the extent of instrumental voting is bound to be small, for by definition the proportion of the electorate voting for a third-place party will be less than that voting for parties finishing first and second. If we measure the size of the instrumental vote, it is a fraction of a fraction. The estimated 1.9 per cent disadvantage that Labour suffered by being in third place rather than second in a constituency in 1987 is less than one-eighth of the 16 per cent share of the vote it polled there. The 3.4 per cent share of the vote that 1987 Alliance also-ran candidates are estimated to have lost is one-fifth of the vote where Alliance had been third in 1983 (cf. Table 6.2). Only a few per cent of the total vote was cast on instrumental rather than tactical grounds in 1987, and the same was true in 1992.[2]

Cognitive Barriers to Instrumental Voting

Like Walter Bagehot, Schumpeter had a low opinion of the political knowledge of the ordinary voter. Formulating democracy as competition between two teams of leaders limits the amount of information that a voter requires, for politicians can absorb the cost of thinking what the government ought to do.

As long as competition is confined to two and only two parties, instrumental theory makes a minimum of cognitive demands on the ordinary voter. It is only necessary to tell the In party from the Out party in order to choose between them. Voting can become simpler still if an elector is content simply to decide whether the In party should remain in office or be voted out.

The amount of information that a voter requires is substantially increased when there is a disjunction between competition in the House of Commons and competition at the constituency level. In a first-past-the-post electoral system voters must then know how the three parties finished in their constituency, and cues from the national media about which party is the challenger may conflict with the facts of the situation in the constituency.

In the absence of knowledge of which party is the challenger and which is a third-place also-ran, instrumental voting is not possible; expressive voting is the only alternative. We can even formulate a *cognitive-ignorance* hypothesis: if a voter does not know the position of parties in the constituency, a vote is more likely to be cast for a third-place party.

Paradoxically, Schumpeter's theory of minimal information overestimates the cognitive awareness of the majority of the electorate. More than two-thirds of the electorate cannot vote instrumentally because they do not know the position of all three parties competing in their constituency. Before the 1987 election only 31 per cent knew this; 46 per cent did not know the position of any party, and the rest only knew the first-place party (Table 6.3).

TABLE 6.3. *Influence of cognitive ignorance on voting for losers* (%)

| Order | Correctly knows constituency position of parties | | | |
	All	One	None	Difference
First	56	57	32	−24
Second	29	20	38	9
Third	15	24	31	16
As % of all respondents	31	23	46	15

Source: 1987 Gallup Poll campaign surveys.

Those who did not know the pattern of competition in their constituency were more than twice as likely to vote for a third-place party as those who correctly understood that; 31 per cent voted for a third-place party, compared to 15 per cent doing so knowing that it was out of the running. The conclusion is clear: ignorance of constituency competition further depresses the predisposition to instrumental voting.

EXPRESSIVE VOTING: A LIFETIME OF LEARNING

The low level of instrumental voting indicates that electors use their vote to express something—but it has not identified what that is. Many explanations of expressive voting appear reasonable at first sight. Psychology can be invoked to explain why voting should express family loyalties. In England it has long been thought normal for voting to express class loyalties; in Northern Ireland, expressing religious identification is the norm. Proponents of universal suffrage assumed that a mass electorate would develop political values that would be expressed through the ballot box. Geographers use maps to demonstrate the correlation between voting and spatial groupings. Others argue that current events in Parliament and the media are immediately most important. While each of the foregoing appears a plausible reason, some must be more influential than others.

Lifetime Learning Model

The outlook of ordinary people is not formed by momentary events viewed on television or by the actions of government during a single Parliament. In his seminal discussion of party images, Graham Wallas emphasized that, because party politics is of peripheral significance to ordinary people, loyalties are slow to form: 'The indifferent and half attentive mind which most men turn towards politics is like a very slow photograph plate. He who wishes to be clearly photographed must stand before it in the same attitude for a long time' (1908: 95).

Current political outlooks express the accumulation of a lifetime of learning. Awareness begins in the home. Incidental remarks made by parents can teach a youth to identify a party as the one for 'people like ourselves', and to think of another party as somehow unacceptable. Learning continues after a young person leaves school, and settles into a job and a life-style expressing socio-economic interests. Experience of public policies and social problems leads individuals to formulate political values about how the country ought to be governed. The events of a single Parliament or an election campaign are the final step in a lifetime of political learning. On election day, a voter is at the exit point of a 'funnel of causality', concentrating a lifetime of learning in a single act (Campbell *et al.* 1960: 24).

The academic division of labour encourages the author of an article to concentrate upon a single influence: thus, different authors examining the same electoral data can offer very different interpretations of what determines voting. If an author decides to concentrate upon the influence of pre-adult socialization, then any evidence of family influence will be held to justify this theory. Another author may find in the same data a real but limited correlation between class and party or a large but potentially spurious correlation between evaluations of party leaders and party preferences. What is needed is a theory that integrates the major influences upon the expression of voters, so that the simple cross-tabulation of two classes by two parties can be replaced by more appropriate multivariate statistics that discriminate between influences that are large and small, and those that are real or spurious.

The lifetime learning model of voting does just this; it draws together all the major influences that can affect an individual during a political lifetime (Fig. 6.1). Each influence first becomes evident at a different point in an individual's life history: parental influences are earliest, and the current performance of the parties is most recent. Although each step can be analysed separately, the important point is that their influence is linked and cumulative. Family upbringing influences a person's adult class and political values, and political values in turn influence what people talk about to neighbours, and how they evaluate an election campaign.

Within the framework of lifetime learning, three sets of influences are expressive. Family loyalties are first in point of time. Youthful political socialization is indirect; yet in the home a child can learn that the family identifies with a particular party without knowing anything else about it. (Butler and Stokes 1969). Even if a child does not think about social class, the parents' class affects the environment in which a youth develops, and his or her educational opportunities. What is learnt as an adult can be evaluated in the light of pre-adult experiences.

An adult's position in the social structure reflects individual efforts and choices as well as family background. Theories of class voting stress the importance of socio-economic structure; occupational class, however measured, is normally considered dominant. However, occupation is not the only socio-economic influence

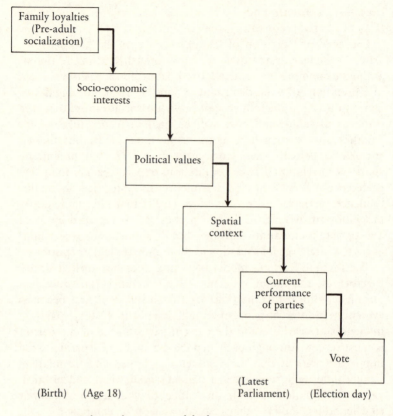

FIG. 6.1.   *Lifetime learning model of voting*

upon voting. Trade union membership can stimulate a sense of
solidarity with Labour, and home-ownership can make a person
more Conservative. For the occupationally mobile, adult class can
be an influence independent of the home.

It is easier for people to have values than to have an understanding of particular public policies. People can have opinions about
the relation of business and labour, government spending on social
programmes, abortion, or race relations without being experts on
such subjects. Even if a person does not take much interest in
politics, in the course of a lifetime of learning people can formulate
relatively durable values independent of their family background
or their social-economic status. On election day, individuals can

then express these values by voting in favour of the party that appears closer to their own primary political values.

In so far as spatial context influences electors, then their vote is not an expression of individual identification but a reflection of environment. If where a person lives affects how a person votes, then a change of address can change a vote. Theories of instrumental voting are based upon a variant of this assumption: a person who wanted to protest against the Thatcher government would have voted Alliance in some constituencies and Labour in others.

Another way in which an individual can vote instrumentally is to react to the current performance of the governing party and the Opposition. Economic theories of voting assume that current economic conditions are important without regard to predispositions shaped by a lifetime of political learning. On election day a person need only compare the current performance of government and Opposition parties to choose a government as Schumpeter prescribed. Media advisers assume that how a party projects itself is more important than what it does. The voting of individuals is assumed to be a transitory preference rather than an expression of a lifetime of learning.

Testing the Model

The lifetime learning model is open not closed; it recognizes that a multiplicity of influences can affect voting. Each step in a lifetime of political learning adds predispositions to voting. The steps in the model occur in sequence in a lifetime; we know that parental influences come before adult occupation, and that long-term values are formed before election campaigns, and thus influence responses to short-term stimuli. An appropriate way to test the influence that each step has upon the expression of party preference is to use stepwise multiple regression, because it calculates how much (or how little) of the variance in vote between the Conservative, Alliance, and Labour parties is explained at each stage, after taking into account the influence of preceding stages in a lifetime of learning (for full details of the statistical analysis that follows, see Rose and McAllister 1990).

Voting is first of all an expression of political values, which accounted for almost 28 per cent in the variation of the vote at the 1987 British general election (Table 6.4). That values explain more

TABLE 6.4 *Influences in a lifetime of political learning, variance explained, 1987* (%)

Influence	Con.–Alliance–Lab. vote
Expressive	
Family loyalties	19.7
Socio-economic interests	9.3
Political values	27.9
SUB-TOTAL	56.9
Other	
Social and political context	1.7
Current performance of parties, leaders	10.5
Party identification	3.4
SUB-TOTAL	15.6
TOTAL OVERALL	72.5

Source: Rose and McAllister (1990: Table 8.2), stepwise hierarchical regression analysis of 1987 British Election Survey data.

variance than any other step in a lifetime of learning is particularly striking, since their impact is calculated only *after* the impact of family loyalties and socio-economic interests has been taken into account.

The values that are important are familiar enough in British politics; they express judgements about trade unions, the privatization or nationalization of industries, the welfare state, the power of business, and other socio-economic concerns. These values are not an instant assessment of the situation of the moment; for the median voter, they are the cumulative reflection of almost twenty-five years of experience in the world of work. Given political values, an individual does not need to take much interest in the current issues of the day, or even in the personalities projected through the media. Titbits about current events can be interpreted in the light of what a person already believes.

Political values are not just another label for socio-economic interests, for values tend to be formed across class lines. The growth in the size of the middle class has not meant an increase in what were once considered middle-class values, that is, conventional Tory principles. Such media as Channel 4 and the *Independ-*

ent symbolize the appeal of non-Tory values among a significant and materially prosperous portion of the middle class, just as the success of the *Sun* is a reminder that working-class people are not necessarily inclined to the Left. The autonomy of political values from class ties is particularly striking, given that the values that count most electorally are familiar Left versus Right economic concerns rather than non-economic concerns such as attitudes towards race, traditional morality or internationalism.

A second major expressive influence is the parental home: family loyalties account for almost one-fifth of the total variance in the vote. Father's party preference is the single most important influence in the family, and is independent of class. Even before becoming old enough to vote, an individual forms loyalties in the home which indirectly as well as directly influence voting. Net of other influences, a voter with Conservative parents is 32 per cent more likely to express Conservative support as an adult than a person whose parents are not Conservatives.

Although the family influences a youth's opportunities for obtaining an education or a first job, it is not a ticket for life. The Butler and Stokes (1969: 45) theory that adult voting expresses pre-adult socialization is inadequate. It fails to explain more than four-fifths of the variance in the vote; 58 per cent do not vote as parental influence would direct. One reason is that a third of the electorate does not know how both its parents vote.

Contrary to many generalizations about class politics (see Pulzer 1967), voting is not an expression of social structure. Even though its impact is here reckoned *before* political values, it accounts for less than one-tenth of the variance of the vote. The most important socio-economic influence is home-ownership, not occupational class. Family income and union membership—both subject to variations within as well as between classes—are the other influences. For the most part, adult socio-economic interests tend to reinforce what has already been learnt from parents about parties, and incidentally about class.

If voting were an expression of socio-economic class influences, then it would account for a third to two-fifths of the total variance of the vote, since the stepwise regression methods used here would attribute all the influence of political values to objective positions in the social structure, as is assumed in theories of social structure determining the ideological outlooks of individuals (but cf.

Scarbrough 1984). We can infer very little about the values that individuals express at the ballot box simply on the evidence of occupational class or trade union membership.

Altogether, the three primary motives of expression—family loyalties, socio-economic interests, and political values—account for nearly 57 per cent of the variance in voting Conservative, Alliance, or Labour at the 1987 election—and they have been important at every election since 1964. When the residual influence of party identification is included, the total influence rises above 60 per cent.

The instrumental idea that voters are trying to express a judgement on the performance of the government of the day is misleading, because élitist. It is the introverted perspective of the world of SW1, the world of politicians, journalists, and their followers. This perspective may be justified in studying aspects of policy-making, where participation is invariably selective and narrow. But it is hardly appropriate to studying the behaviour of more than forty million electors.

To interpret the current performance of the parties as significant is a misleading half-truth. It is noteworthy and noted by a portion of the electorate, if only as a headline on the evening news. But of far greater importance are the criteria by which current events are evaluated. The judgements that voters express are not, like those of news editors in the media, formed in the light of events of the past twenty-four hours. They are formed in the light of a lifetime of learning.

Hence, the current performance of parties—that is, the actions taken since the last election in dealing with issues and the personality and image of each party—together account for only 10.5 per cent of the variance in the vote. A person predisposed by a lifetime of learning to vote Conservative will interpret actions of a Conservative government more favourably than a person predisposed to vote Labour; this is true of political personalities too. Social context is even less an independent influence; it reinforces rather than causing party loyalties. The multivariate analysis shows that the position of Labour as second or third in a constituency accounted for only 0.4 per cent in the variance of the vote, making a person 3 per cent less likely to vote Labour net of other influences

Given a choice between voting for the party that best expresses its outlook and a second-best instrumental alternative, the great majority of the British electorate votes expressively. From this perspective, the idea of a 'wasted' vote is meaningless. A vote is not wasted if it expresses what the elector wants to say on the one occasion when individuals can register their political views.

REPRESENTATION BEFORE GOVERNMENT

Effective government is the stated purpose of elections in the instrumental theory of voting, and every British general election since 1945 bar one has manufactured a majority for one party in the House of Commons. But this outcome at the macro-level is not the intent of the electors; it is a consequence of the electoral system. It is empirically false as well as logically fallacious to infer individual intent from aggregate consequences.[3]

Individuals want to express their own values, whether they will influence control of government or not. Some Scots and Welsh voters express values that they know will be in a minority at Westminster, when they vote in support of a nationalist party promoting independence. In Northern Ireland the absence of British parties denies the whole of the electorate any instrumental vote; Ulster voters express fundamental values of religion and national identity.

The primary motives in voting are expressive, but the values expressed are in opposition to each other. Those who vote Conservative express a positive evaluation of business and a negative evaluation of unions, and the opposite is true of those who vote Labour. Opinion polls during the election campaign make this evident, and each party seeks to express popular values that are distinctively identified with it.

However, the outcome of a parliamentary election is 'repressive', in so far as none of the powers of government is given to those parties supported by the votes of up to 55 per cent of the electorate or more. This is the price that must be paid for concentrating responsibility for government in the hands of a single party, enabling voters to know who is to be held responsible for the condition of the country at the next election.

Every system of government must strike a balance between the expressive and the repressive elements. The eighteenth-century authors of the US Constitution believed in decentralizing power;

they thus introduced concurrent elections for Congress and the Presidency. The district of a Member of Congress is only 1/435th of the nation; its elected representative can express very different views from the President, the sole official elected nation-wide (see Fenno 1978). For generations the outcome was nominally party government, that is, Congress and the White House were usually in the hands of the same party.

For the past generation election outcomes in the United States have rejected the simpler Schumpeter idea that instrumental choice equals party government. Instead, there is divided government, with Congress in the hands of the Democratic party and the White House in the hands of Republicans (see Jones 1991). To argue that divided government is what most voters want is fallacious. Individuals cannot know what the nation-wide outcome of Congressional elections will be when voting in their district. The argument is also empirically false. Since 1968 an average of 72 per cent has voted a straight ticket in Presidential and Congressional elections; divided government is a consequence of ticket-splitting by only one-quarter of voters (Wattenberg 1987: 66; cf. Jacobson 1990).

A different critique of party responsibility as the basis of instrumental government is offered by David Mayhew's analysis of the enactment of major Congressional activities in periods of divided as against single-party government. He finds that it makes very little difference to what Congress does. Even when control of both branches is nominally in the hands of the same party, 'enacting coalitions are hard to assemble even if party control is unified, and awkwardly stitched together compromises can occur anyway' (Mayhew 1991; see also Powell 1991).

In Eastern Europe in 1991, after two generations of totalitarian suppression of dissent in a Communist one-party system, primacy is clearly given to expressing diverse opinions. Free elections are held on the basis of proportional representation. Since more than a dozen different parties have normally contested the first free election in many decades, the result is that no one party can by itself enjoy the centralized authority of a single governing party. Voters are not seeking to produce a government but to express rejection of the past, and a desire to end decades of one-party Communist rule (White 1990; Herzmann 1991; Rose 1991b).

Free elections allow Britons to express whatever they want to express—but they do not guarantee all expressions of opinion an equal weight in government. For virtually the whole of the post-war era, the aggregate consequence has been single-party government. But, because this is a by-product of voting, it is not a commitment of principle. The great majority of Britons, however, use their vote to express diverse views without regard to the instrumental effect of their actions. The Liberals, on grounds of interest as well as principle, have long campaigned for a proportional representation system that would match representation in the Commons with party preferences expressed in national vote totals, and there is a growing group in the Labour party arguing in favour of giving more expression to the views of voters, even at the expense of risking an end to single-party government (cf. Plant 1991).

The first-past-the-post electoral system, as Schumpeter and others have emphasized, is effective in creating single-party government. But this is not a necessary condition of democracy. If it were, the great majority of countries holding free elections would have to be labelled undemocratic. Even British voters do not accept that elections are a choice between the first party past the post with a parliamentary majority, and the second-place party, a basic condition of Schumpeter's view that the purpose of elections is to produce a government. The strongest support for the Schumpeterian model comes, not from the mass of the electorate, but from politicians in the two largest parties at Westminster, the groups that reap the most benefit from holding all the power of government at least part of the time.

Notes

1. The following discussion excludes Scotland and Wales, where the existence of Nationalist parties fighting every constituency offers further grounds for discriminating between instrumental and non-instrumental voting, and Northern Ireland, left uncontested by all parties seeking to form the government of the United Kingdom. Effectively, the battle to oust the Conservative government was concentrated in England, for in both 1983 and 1987 the results in England gave the Conservative party absolute majority in Parliament.
2. The point is confirmed by using multiple-regression analysis to compare

the actual versus the predicted vote for parties finishing second and third (on methods, see McAllister and Rose 1984: especially appendix A). A multiple-regression analysis using socio-economic indicators to predict constituency voting finds that, where Labour was third in 1983, its 1987 share of the vote was 2.5 % less than would be expected from the socio-economic composition of the constituency, and where the Alliance was third, its 1987 vote was 2.7 % less than expected. Only a portion of this shortfall in the base vote can be attributed to instrumental voting; it also reflects the influence of other ecological variables, such as the predominant social milieu of the constituency.

3. Even if parties alter their positions to represent better the views of more voters, this is *not* evidence that electors are trying to achieve this effect when voting. The above evidence indicates that, except in a few university constituencies, those voting Alliance were not doing so in order to reform the Labour party but because they identified the Alliance with their own values. A strategy of reforming Labour may win it more votes—but that decision remains one that must be taken by party élites (see Rose and Mackie, 1988; Tsebelis, 1990).

References

Almond, G. A (1990), *A Discipline Divided: Schools and Sects in Political Science* (Newbury Park, Calif.: Sage).

Beer, S. H. (1965), *Modern British Politics* (London: Faber and Faber).

Bogdanor, V. (1983) (ed.), *Coalition Governments in Western Europe* (London: Heinemann).

Browne, E. C., and Dreijmanis, J. (1982) (eds.), *Government Coalitions in Western Democracies* (New York: Longman).

Butler, D. E., and Stokes, D. E. (1969), *Political Change in Britain* (London: Macmillan).

Campbell, A., Converse, P. E., Miller, W. E., and Stokes, D. E. (1960), *The American Voter* (New York: John Wiley).

Craig, F. W. S. (1989), *British Electoral Facts, 1832–1987* (Aldershot: Parliamentary Research Services/Gower).

Dalton, R. J., Flanagan, S. C., and Beck, P. A. (1984) (eds.), *Electoral Change in Advanced Industrial Democracies: Realignment or Dealignment?* (Princeton, NJ: Princeton University Press).

Downs, A. (1957), *An Economic Theory of Democracy* (New York: Harper and Row).

Fenno, R. (1978), *Home Style: House Members in their Districts* (Boston: Little, Brown).

Fiorina, M. P. (1981), *Retrospective Voting in American National Elections* (New Haven, Conn.: Yale University Press).

Friedrich, C. J. (1941), *Constitutional Government and Democracy* (Boston: Little Brown).

Hermet, G. (1978), 'State-Controlled Elections: A Framework', in G. Hermet, R. Rose, and A. Rouquié (eds.), *Elections without Choice* (London: Macmillan), 1–18.

Herzmann, J. (1991), 'Die Ersten Freien Parlamentswahlen in der DDR, in Ungarn und in der CSFR' (Prague: Public Opinion Research Institute, Federal Statistical Office, typescript).

Inglehart, R. (1977), *The Silent Revolution* (Princeton, NJ: Princeton University Press).

Jacobson, G. C., (1990), *The Electoral Origins of Divided Government* (Boulder, Colo.: Westview Press).

Jones, C. O. (1991), 'The Diffusion of Responsibility: An Alternative Perspective for National Policy Politics in the US', *Governance*, 4/2: 150–67.

Key, V. O., Jun. (1949), *Southern Politics in State and Nation* (New York: Alfred A. Knopf).

—— (1966), *The Responsible Electorate* (Cambridge, Mass.: Harvard University Press).

Lane, R. E. (1962), *Political Ideology* (New York: Free Press).

Lijphart, A. (1984), *Democracies* (New Haven, Conn.: Yale University Press).

Lipset, S. M. (1960), *Political Man* (New York: Doubleday).

—— and Rokkan, S. (1967) (eds.), *Party Systems and Voter Alignments* (New York: Free Press).

McAllister, I. and Rose, R. (1984), *The Nationwide Competition for Votes* (London: Frances Pinter).

McKenzie, R. T. (1963), *British Political Parties* (rev. edn., London: Heinemann).

Mayhew, D. R. (1991), *Divided We Govern: Party Control, Lawmaking, and Investigations, 1946–1990* (New Haven, Conn.: Yale University Press).

Pammett, J. (1988), 'Framework for the Comparative Analysis of Elections across Time and Space', *Electoral Studies*, 7/2: 125–42.

Plant, R. (1991), *Democracy, Representation and Elections* (London: Labour Party, Interim Report of Working Party on Electoral Systems).

Powell, G. B. (1991) (ed.), 'Symposium on Divided Government', *Governance*, 4 3.

Pulzer, P. G. P. (1967), *Political Representation and Elections in Britain* (London: George Allen and Unwin).

Rose, R. (1991*a*), 'The Ups and Downs of the Electorate, or Look Before You Swing', *PS*, 24/1; 29–34.

—— (1991*b*), *Escaping from Absolute Dissatisfaction: A Trial-and-Error Model of Change in Eastern Europe* (Glasgow: U. of Strathclyde Studies in Public Policy No. 192).

—— and McAllister, I. (1990), *The Loyalties of Voters* (London: Sage).

—— and Mackie, T. T. (1983), 'Incumbency in Government: Asset or Liability?', in H. Daalder and P. Mair (eds.), *Western European Party Systems* (London: Sage). 115–137

—— —— (1988), 'Do Parties Persist or Fail? The Big Trade Off Facing Parties', in K. Lawson and P. Merkl (eds.), *When Parties Fail* (Princeton, NJ: Princeton University Press), 533–58.

—— Mossawir, H. (1967), 'Voting and Elections: A Functional Analysis', *Political Studies*, 15/2; 173–201.

Sartori, G. (1976), *Parties and Party Systems: A Framework for Analysis* (New York: Cambridge University Press).

—— (1987), *The Theory of Democracy Revisited* (Chatham, NJ: Chatham House).

Scarbrough, E. (1984), *Political Ideology and Voting* (Oxford: Clarendon Press).

Schumpeter, J. A. (1952), *Capitalism, Socialism and Democracy* (4th edn., London: Allen & Unwin).

Smithies, A. (1951), 'Memorial: Joseph Alois Schumpeter, 1883–1950', in S. E. Harris (ed.), *Schumpeter, Social Scientist* (Cambridge, Mass.: Harvard University Press), 11–23.

Tsebelis, G. (1990), *Nested Games: Rational Choice in Comparative Politics* (Berkeley, Calif.: Univeristy of California Press).

Wald, K. R. (1983), *Crosses on the Ballot* (Princeton, NJ: Princeton University Press).

Wallas, G. (1908), *Human Nature in Politics* (London: Constable).

Wattenberg, M. P. (1987), 'The Hollow Realignment', *Public Opinion Quarterly*, 51/1.

White, S. L. (1990) (ed.), 'Elections in Eastern Europe', a special issue of *Electoral Studies*, 9/4; 275–366.

Wright, D. M. (1951), 'Schumpeter's Political Philosophy', in S. E. Harris (ed.), *Schumpeter, Social Scientist* (Cambridge, Mass.: Harvard University Press) 130–5.

7

Valence Politics

DONALD STOKES

Communication between leaders and led is a central, problematic element of political democracy. The importance of this element at the dawn of the democratic idea is shown by the inclusion of rhetoric among the liberal arts preparing the citizen for the civic role. But democracy took root in little places, like Athens or Thebes, where direct discussion was possible. Its extension through representative institutions to the colossal states of the modern world makes still more problematic the communication of alternative leaders with those they would represent. The rise of political parties has always been seen as partly a means of easing this problem, and the study of parties and electoral systems has been partly a study of communication between the leaders who compete for public support and the public that, by giving support, clothes these leaders in legitimate authority.

I return here to an analysis of the nature of the discourse of leaders and led that David Butler and I incorporated in *Political Change in Britain*. Although the framework of 'valence' issues is conceptually simple and reflects pervasive aspects of modern politics, it has yet to enter at all fully into the repertoire of academic or journalistic interpretations of political change. I will describe this framework by contrasting it with the widely used models of 'spatial' competition among parties or leaders, review the mixed acclaim that this alternative 'valence' framework has enjoyed among academic specialists, and explore some further insights into contemporary politics that this framework provides.

SPATIAL COMPETITION AS A FOIL

Although the framework of valence issues had a prominent place in the collaborative analysis David Butler and I undertook in

Political Change in Britain, especially its later editions on the two shores of the Atlantic, I began thinking about this problem before setting out for Oxford in the early 1960s. What led me to it was the spreading enthusiasm for the spatial conception of party competition formulated by Downs (1957), on the earlier work of Hotelling (1929) and others, especially Smithies (1941). Although I admired this effort to formalize a vision of political competition that goes back to the French Revolution, I offered a critique of the spatial modelling of party competition (Stokes 1963) that called attention to four implicit axioms of such models for which there is scant empirical support.[1]

The first of these, the assumption of *unidimensionality*, was in many ways the least troublesome, and this assumption was subsequently relaxed by a flood of work extending this line of reasoning to multiple dimensions. The second axiom, the assumption of *fixed structure*, ignored the fact that the issue content of politics, even if matched to a spatial representation at a given time, changed markedly in ways not easily accommodated by the spatial apparatus, unlike the competitive spatial markets of economics. A fourth axiom, the assumption of *common reference*, overlooked the fact that the 'space' of political competition can be differently perceived by leaders and led—and, indeed, by different individuals and groups within the ranks of leaders and voters, again unlike the spaces for which Downs's economist forebears had modelled the location of firms and the choices of consumers.

But it was a third uncertain axiom, the assumption of *ordered dimensions*, that led me to note the existence of 'valence' issues with a structure radically different from the 'position' issues that lent themselves to the spatial framework. The frailty of this axiom was the most fundamental critical point I raised about the spatial models. If these models had been easily and routinely linked to measured data, I would have spoken of their assumption of *cardinal* dimensions, since they presumed that voters and leaders make judgements about such things as the relative ideological distance of voters from two or more parties. But the difficulty of linking models to data had restricted the discussion largely to a theoretical or conceptual level, and I did not want my critique to turn on the difference between cardinal and ordinal data. It went rather to the difference between the ordered dimensions required by spatial models and the simpler structures, lacking the property of ordered dimensions, by which voters often evaluated the parties and leaders who sought their support. 'The machinery of the spatial model will not work if the voters are simply reacting to the association of the parties with some goal or state or symbol that is positively or negatively valued' (Stokes 1963: 373).

To get at this root difference, I distinguished *position* issues, on which parties or leaders are differentiated by their advocacy of alternative positions on an ordered dimension, from *valence* issues, on which parties or leaders are differentiated not by what they advocate but by the degree to which they are linked in the public's mind with conditions or goals or symbols of which almost everyone approves or disapproves. This distinction requires some explaining, since my terminology, borrowed from chemistry by way of Lewinian psychology, was obscure and my conceptual reasoning easily missed.

Let me begin with the idea of a *position* issue. It could be argued that in the liberal democracies all of the great issues underlying lasting alignments between the parties are of this kind. The alignment that emerged from the American Civil War, for example, was formed from a polarizing position issue of extraordinary power—the Negro, slave or free? Before, during, and after the war, the Republicans drew support from those who were hostile to slavery and its legacy; their opponents from those who were less so. Similarly, in the sectional realignment of the 1890s the Republicans drew support from those who favoured high rather than low tariffs on manufactured goods; in a broader sense, from those who wanted to use the power of government to favour the interests of the modernizing, industrial north-east and mid-west rather than the traditional, agrarian south and west. And in the realignment of the 1930s the Democrats drew support from those who wanted the government to protect the interests of the poor and working class rather than the more affluent in American society. In Britain, popular response to position issues such as Home Rule for Ireland and church versus chapel shaped the alignment between the Liberals and Conservatives until this cleavage was displaced by the alignment in which a rising Labour party avowedly championed the interests of the working class.

Some of the position issues involved in these alignments presented a number of alternative positions that could be ordered along a dimension of policy choice. This was true, for example, of the issue of high or low tariffs on manufactures in the United States of the late nineteenth and early twentieth centuries. But in the argument I set out, an issue qualified as a position issue if popular support for the parties or leaders was based on their advocacy of one or another of at least *two* positions that also divided the electorate (the western territories, slave or free? Britain and Europe, in or out?).

The observation that led to the quite different valence framework is that some of the issues swaying the electorate do not present even two alternative positions that divide the parties and leaders on the one hand and divide the electorate on the other. A prime example of such a single-position issue is economic prosperity. We do not have one party advocating good times and another bad. There is no constituency for economic distress; in the liberal democracies, all of the parties and the whole of the electorate endorse good times. The issue acquires its power from the fact that the parties may be very unequally linked in the public's mind with the universally approved condition of good times and the universally disapproved condition of bad times, and the difference between electoral success and disaster may turn on the parties' ability to strengthen or weaken these bonds or *valences* in the public's mind.

Examples abound. Another that has a deep historical resonance in the United States is the issue of corruption. When there is a call to 'throw the rascals out', its impact does not depend on where the parties position themselves along a dimension extending from honesty to dishonesty but rather on how closely the rival parties are linked with the universally approved symbol of honesty and the universally disapproved symbol of corruption. There are many other illustrations. If the parties have credible grounds, they may, for example, tout the strength or steadfastness of their leader and the weakness or irresolution of a rival leader, knowing that there is as little constituency for weakness and irresolution as there is for corruption or economic distress.

The consensus of leaders and led on the values involved in valence issues is an empirical matter and is in no sense logically necessary. There *could* be a constituency for economic hard times or, for that matter, for corruption or irresolution in high office. As David Butler and I observed:

There are in British society isolated individuals who see genuine moral values for others, or even for themselves, in a degree of severity to economic life. This view was expressed to us by an ageing widow in Poole, who said, 'It's awfully good for one to have to get along on less, isn't it?' Indeed, at an élite level one can find some very conservative observers as well as some doctrinaire Socialists who view with ambivalence the rising affluence of recent years. But such views are the perquisite of a tiny minority. The goal of economic betterment enjoys overwhelming mass support and any values that may lie in economic adversity are not visible to most people. (Butler and Stokes 1974: 370–1)

The possibility of change in the degree of value consensus is illustrated by the ebb and flow of popular feeling toward nationalist, patriotic symbols. These were probably universal positives for the US public in the early 1960s, the Kennedy years, and may have regained this hold on popular feeling by the time of the Gulf War in the early 1990s. But they were sharply controversial in the late 1960s and early 1970s, during the years of intense conflict over the Vietnam War.

Moreover, a valence issue can be displaced by a position issue if political debate centres on a disagreement as to the *means* to reach an agreed-upon end or if the public sees a trade-off between *two* high-consensus goals or ends. The issue of the economy again provides examples:

It is of course true that the relationship between rival economic goals does offer possible dimensions of political conflict. The classic example of this in most western economies lies in the 'trade-off' between economic expansion and price stability; all too often governments can buy economic expansion only by allowing inflation, or stable prices only by limiting expansion. For a nation as dependent on international trade as Britain, there are further trade-offs between domestic expansion on the one hand, and the balance of international payments on the other. The dilemma of choosing an appropriate position on such a continuum has faced Conservative and Labour Governments alike. Moreover, if an understanding of the relationships between these goals were to reach more deeply into the public's consciousness, the dialogue between parties and electorate on economic issues might involve genuine position dimensions, with the parties manoeuvring for the support of electors who had very different preferences between, let us say, economic expansion and stable prices. (Butler and Stokes 1974: 371)

Indeed, the trade-off between expansion and price stability has the potential of becoming a class issue, since unemployment tends to work a greater hardship on the working class, inflation on the middle class. But the electorate in Britain and elsewhere sees the provision of fatter pay packets and steady prices not as ends to be traded off but as separate, high-consensus goals. The Phillips curve expressing this trade-off is as visible to the governments confronted by this policy choice as it is generally invisible to their electorates.

These examples suggest that the quest of political leaders for popular support is at times better described by a valence framework than it is by the theory of spatial voting. Political leaders often see their strategic problem as one of choosing from a large number of potential issues those that will maximize their identification with positive values and their opponents with negative ones, rather than of positioning themselves in a space of ordered dimensions. And the electorate often chooses between alternative leaders primarily by selecting the party or candidate identified with the greater number of symbols that are positively rather than negatively valued, including the symbol of success.

Indeed, valence campaigning is not some rarely seen limiting case of position campaigning, one where parties and voters that are usually distributed along ordered dimensions happen to be concentrated at a single, consensus point. The parties typically can choose from a wide variety of generally approved values or symbols ones that will help them make their valence appeals, and their choice among alternative values or symbols is one of the most pervasive characteristics of modern campaigning. We may, therefore, speak of a *valence politics*, in which the parties mount their appeals by choosing from a larger set of potential valence issues those on which their identification with positive symbols and their opponents' with negative symbols will be most to their advantage. This communication between leaders and led is quite unlike a *position politics*, in which the parties see their strategic problem as one of finding the electorate's centre of gravity within a space defined by a series of policy dimensions.

Valence issues typically involve pairs of positive and negative symbols—good times and bad, honesty and corruption, strength and weakness; the greater ease of accommodating 'negative campaigning' within the valence framework, a point I develop below, underlines how much of modern campaigning is left out of the spatial theory of voting. A valence issue will deliver maximum support for one of the parties or leaders if its symbolic content is of high importance to the electorate and there is complete identification of the party or leader with the positive symbol and of the rival party or leader with the negative symbol. We can, therefore, deepen our insight into valence politics by enquiring further into the symbolic content of valence issues and the processes that form the valences that associate these symbols with the parties or leaders who are contesting for public support.

THE SYMBOLIC CONTENT OF VALENCE POLITICS

A good deal of the symbolic or semantic content of valence politics is, to begin with, supplied by conditions or goals or states of the world that are positively or negatively valued by the electorate. As I have suggested, the classic illustration is good economic times and bad. But the parties or leaders are at times linked to peace and war, internal order and crime, and many other conditions that are positively or negatively valued. Although their bonding to economic conditions goes back to the early nineteenth century, the conditions that provide the symbolic content of valence politics have progressively expanded with the scope of government in the twentieth century.

A second element of the symbolic content of valence politics is supplied by positive and negative qualities of the parties or leaders. A democratic electorate inevitably responds to those seeking its support in terms of their perceived strength and weakness, honesty and corruption, warmth and aloofness, and many other qualities. And the parties and leaders see the strategic problem of campaigning a good deal as one of claiming positive qualities for themselves and fixing negative qualities on their rivals, as I have noted.

A pervasive third element of the semantic content of valence politics, one that overlaps the categories of conditions and qualities, is supplied by the symbols of success and failure. This is very much the way the issue of economic good times and hard times plays out. This issue strongly moves the party balance when the electorate rewards a governing party for its success in bringing prosperity or holds a governing party responsible for its failure to avoid hard times. There is the keenest interest between elections in the pollsters' indexes of how well the public thinks a party, or President or Prime Minister, is handling the economy. These indexes gauge not the economic positions taken by the government, or advocated by the Opposition, but the strength of the bond formed in the public's mind between those running the country and the symbols of economic failure and success.

David Butler and I invoked the idea that in valence politics nothing succeeds like success, or fails like failure, to offer what probably should be described as an extended conjecture about the role of another economic goal in unexpectedly denying Labour the victory in the 1970 election that would have capped their party's remarkable six-month recovery (Butler and Stokes 1974: 399–402). Since Harold Wilson had repeatedly promised that he and his Labour colleagues would get the balance-of-payments figures right, Labour paid a heavy price when the last trade figures went wrong just before the election. Despite Mr Wilson's facile explanation that the figures were distorted by the unexpected arrival of jumbo jets from the United States, he and his colleagues had failed to reach their self-advertised goal. With a major prop on which Labour were leaning kicked away, a small margin of swing voters may have felt that this failure rubbed enough of the gloss off the government's handling of the economy to cost Labour the election.

The role of success and failure as symbols in valence politics by no means stops with the economy, or at the water's edge. In foreign affairs there is a good deal of evidence that it is the association of the parties—particularly, again, of the governing party—with the scent of success or the smell of failure that moves the electorate. This was first brought home to me when my Michigan colleagues and I were puzzling over the role played by the Korean War in the first of Eisenhower's victories over Adlai Stevenson, in 1952. Since the new President would be confronted by critical choices on the war, we might suppose that the parties would seek public support by advocating policies along a dimension that ordered the altern- ative positions of pulling out of Korea, settling on the current line between the forces, or mounting a wider offensive against the Chinese by bombing their Manchurian bases. Douglas MacArthur tried to structure the debate in these dimensional terms by advocat- ing the third of these alternatives before and after his dismissal by President Truman. In the event, however, Eisenhower rode to victory on a tide of popular feeling that the Democrat's handling of 'Truman's War' had failed. In this he profited handsomely from public confidence in his military experience; the valence issue of Korea involved a prospective, as well as a retrospective, calculus of results. But Eisenhower played the issue in pure valence terms, never committing himself to one of the policy alternatives. Only after this strategy carried him to the White House did he opt for a negotiated settlement and bring the fighting to an end on the Panmunjom line, a result the electorate quickly decided had the sweet smell of success.

The public may respond to an international issue largely on the valence terms of failure and success even when political debate seems to be focused on a dimension of policy choice. This was to a remarkable degree true of the Vietnam War, which hung over US politics in the late 1960s and early 1970s. As Vietnam became a paramount issue, public debate seemed to be overwhelmingly structured by a 'hawk-dove' dimension. This dimension seemed particularly to structure the debate within the Democratic party as Senator Eugene McCarthy challenged President Johnson's handling of the war in the presidential primaries of 1968, and Senator McCarthy eloquently pressed the 'dove' position when he delivered Johnson a mortal blow in the Democratic presidential primary in New Hampshire. But the Democratic voters in New Hampshire responded to Vietnam as a valence rather than a position issue, believing that the Johnson administration's handling of the war had failed. The post-primary polls found those registering this protest to be astonishingly unclear as to where President Johnson's challenger stood; almost as many thought Senator McCarthy was a hawk as a dove (Converse and Schuman 1970).

The parallels with British reaction to the Falklands War, although not close, are suggestive. The Falklands episode was brief enough to cut off the emergence of a clearly defined dimension of policy choice, which might have extended from acquiescing in the claims of the Argentinians on one extreme to using full military means to restore the status quo ante, the course the Thatcher government took, on the other. It was none the less impressive how disinclined the British public was to respond to the issue in position, rather than valence, terms. At the outset, there was little public sense that it was wrong to have explored the possibility of an agreement with Argentina to end British sovereignty, although this policy, fitfully pursued by the Foreign Office, was thought to have failed when Argentina seized the islands, and Lord Carrington paid with his office. Yet the course the government then took by no means rested on a deep public conviction about the appropriateness of military action. Despite the initial rally to the government, Mrs Thatcher's policy might have engendered a Vietnam-type reaction if the military campaign had been long and not gone well, with heavy British losses. Instead it achieved its goal early, with few British casualties, and strongly bonded the Thatcher government with success.

HOW ARE VALENCES FORMED?

The parties and leaders have sought to associate themselves with positive symbols and their rivals with negative symbols from the dawn of modern electioneering; the nineteenth century's image-makers helped elect Lincoln president by portraying a prosperous railroad lawyer as a rail-splitter who was born in a log cabin. But the evolution of the mass media has brought this aspect of campaigning to a high burnish. At the outset of the race for the Presidency in 1988, for example, the public's view of George Bush and Michael Dukakis was sufficiently plastic for the savage television spots on Willie Horton and Boston harbour to link Governor Dukakis with crime and environmental failure, while a carefully scripted and well-delivered acceptance speech diminished the sense of Mr Bush as an ineffective leader. Some months earlier the Labour party had exploited television's potential to associate their leader, Mr Kinnock, with a series of positive symbols.

But it would be a mistake to think that the parties and leaders are bonded to positive and negative symbols only by campaign artifices. The electorate is more likely to be moved by valences it *learns* from its experiences with the parties and leaders, and the results they achieve, over time. This was understood in the economic realm as long ago as the election of 1840, when Martin Van Buren paid with his office for the distress following the panic of 1837. It has been understood by all modern British governments that have wanted to go to the country with their economic house in order.

This learning extends to non-economic results of government actions and to qualities of the parties and leaders as well, as the electorate tries to make sense of government.

Even fairly generalized perceptions of a leader as 'able' or 'trustworthy' help the voter to say something about future actions of government on the basis of the leader's past handling of issues. These inferences may be less sure than they would be in a presidential system; the French peasant who trusted De Gaulle may have had a surer guide to the future so long as the President loomed large in it. (Butler and Stokes 1974: 294–5).

If the Falklands War did not give the British public its first glimpse of Mrs Thatcher as a strong leader, it reinforced this aspect of her image, although there is no reason to think she went to war to produce this result. By contrast, George Bush's military decisions as President may indeed have been influenced by his desire to be seen as strong. In his years as Ronald Reagan's Vice-President, he was tormented by the public's feeling that he was weak, and the view of him as a 'wimp' was not eliminated by his harshly negative campaign against Governor Dukakis. His intense frustration over this bonding with the negative symbol of weakness almost certainly played a role in his decision to invade Panama and seize Noriega, as it may have played a role in his choice of military action against Saddam Hussein.

It would caricature the President's decisions to say that he chose military means only to repair his image as a weak leader. But close observers have said that a desire to turn the page on this aspect of his reputation was among the reasons he was more bellicose than all of his senior civil and military advisers. However strongly he may have wanted to 'kick the Vietnam syndrome', he and his political advisers also wanted to 'kick the wimp factor'. Although the invasion of Panama did so only to a limited degree, the Desert War greatly attenuated the valence that linked Bush with the negative symbol of weakness and shored up the valence that linked the President with the positive symbol of strength. The clearest modern parallel is the dramatic effect of the Cuban missile crisis in lessening the image of weakness, of not being master in his house, that John Kennedy carried over from the Bay of Pigs. In that case, too, the desire dramatically to alter the valence politics of the day was part of the backdrop of major decisions of state.

Since the learning that forms the valences between the parties or leaders and positive or negative symbols lies in the past, it is natural to think of judgements based on these bonds as *retrospective*. And since the electorate's experience with a governing party or leader seeking a renewal in power is likely to be more important than experience with its rivals, it is natural to think of these judgements as centred mainly on a government or administration. In the economic realm:

The type of connection that has dominated both academic and more popular views of the electorate's response to the economy is one under which voters reward the Government for the conditions they welcome and punish the Government for the conditions they dislike. In the simplest of all such models the electorate pays attention only to the party in power and only to conditions during its current tenure of office. (Butler and Stokes 1974: 372)

But we did not suppose that judgements based on valence issues were purely retrospective or purely focused on those in government. Although past learning underlies these valences, the electorate is making judgements of the future as well as the past. And these judgements can involve parties or leaders now in opposition as well as those now in power. Both things were true of the issue of Korea in the presidential election of 1952. From its experience with General Eisenhower during the Second World War, the electorate had ample reason to believe that he would know how to deal with the Korean War, even if it had no idea what he would do. Hence, its judgement in that year was prospective as well as retrospective and embraced the candidate Republican as well as the candidate Democratic leadership. Similarly, four years later, the electorate still remembered the misery of Hoover's depression and the return of good times under the Democrats, even if it learnt from Eisenhower's first term that the accession of a Republican president did not automatically turn back the clock to the Great Depression. As a result, perceptions of which party was more likely to bring prosperity still cut in the Democratic direction in the 1956 election. Judgements based on the economy were prospective as well as retrospective and directed towards both parties, rather than the Republicans only.

READINGS BY THE CRITICS

In view of how often the dialogue of leaders and led conforms to the framework of valence politics, it is noteworthy how little attention has been given this framework by academic specialists and by more popular interpreters of politics. Its obscure terminology has not helped. Neither has the fact that the argument was begun almost as an aside in my original critique of spatial models and was continued as one of the many themes in *Political Change in Britain*. Having no more than glimpsed this conceptual hare, the critical hounds have not surprisingly gone off in varied directions. A number have picked up the scent only as they were chasing what they thought were other game, despite the substantial overlap of their quarry with my own. But these ideas have also been resisted as discordant with the search for a rational pattern in electoral politics, one that accords either with the theory of spatial voting or with other interpretive traditions. It will, therefore, give further insight into the valence framework to review what the critics have said.

The citations are many, due no doubt in part to the obscure nomenclature. In some cases my critique of spatial models has spurred important further work. Perhaps the most impressive is the research of Rabinowitz and MacDonald (1989), who are also sceptical of the universal applicability of a traditional spatial theory of elections, which remains 'the dominant paradigm for understanding mass-élite linkage in politics'. They note that, although the spatial model 'has been extended to overcome several elements of the Stokes critique, it has largely failed to take account of his "ordered dimensions" criticism, which questioned the assumption that voters perceive a set of ordered alternatives on the relevant issues (dimensions) of the campaign. (Rabinowitz and MacDonald 1989: 93–4). I will not summarize their 'directional' theory of voting, 'based on the ideas of symbolic politics', which deserves to be read in the original. They demonstrate the uses of a symbolic, directional approach even when there is not full consensus on the direction policy should move, in a sense extending the valence approach to cases where the direction or goal of policy is at issue.

A reading by Giovanni Sartori mirrors the subtleties of thinking conceptually about this area:

Stokes brings out the interesting distinction between position and valence issues. In essence, a valence issue is a nonpartisan issue, an issue on which there is no disagreement, and yet *is* an issue in that one party accuses another of being untrue to its verbal stands. Pressing the point further we arrive at the question: Why is one party 'believed' while another is not? A first reply is that electors are not fooled by what the parties say. But there is more to it. So-called valence issues point, it seems to me, to the juncture at which issue perceptions become largely monitored by party images and identifications. Ultimately, the question hinges on whether identifying with a party establishes—first and above all—'the authorities', indeed the cognitive authorities, on whom mass publics rely for believing, or not believing, in what they are told. (1976: 330–1)

A retired member of the Michigan group needs little persuading that party identification is at times a screen that helps identifiers to form the valences that bond the parties with positive and negative symbols. But this reading leaves out of account the importance of other experiences, such as the demonstrated success or failure of a government in getting the economy right, in forming these valences—and persuading the electorate that the valence appeals of one party are, for the moment, believable, while those of another party are not.

Two readings that bear the marks of the fragmentary and scattered development of the original argument are offered by members of the team that assembled at the University of Essex to continue the election studies David Butler and I launched from an Oxford base. Having caught sight of the valence framework, David Robertson resists the idea that this framework undercuts the spatial representation of policy stands by attributing to me the 'mistake' of equating a dimension with an issue:

If one does this it is very common to end up with a rather peculiar dimension on which only one position can be adopted. Stokes' example is corruption in government, which he says was a major issue in the American election of 1948 [my example was actually 1952]. Of course there is only one acceptable position, to be against corruption, but . . . Stokes' argument that there is only one conceivable position does not hold. For it is, to voters as much as to political scientists, obvious that no one can actively support corruption, but it is altogether another matter how one proposes to deal with it, and how one accounts for its existence. In 1948 [*sic*] positions could have varied all the way from a proposal for Constitutional change predicted on a theory that corruption was endemic to a log-rolling federal legislature, to the idea that the President had been misled and there was no cause for worry over something that was 'objectively trivial'. (1976: 61)

This odd indictment reflects Robertson's more general enthusiasm for spatial reasoning ('statistics is, by its very nature, best thought of as dealing with the relationships between points in space' and 'geometry [is] the only adequate intuitive understanding of statistical relations' (1976: 56)). But he could more easily have read our discussion of valence issues as *affirming* the presence of dimensions that may be associated with valence issues. Indeed, I clearly was readier than Robertson to imagine at times a constituency for corruption. And David Butler and I clearly saw the potential for policy dimensions displacing valence issues as well as the possibility for trade-offs between separate values making valence issues into position issues (the trade-off between economic expansion and price stability illustrates both possibilites). Yet it is by no means a 'mistake' to ask not whether a policy dimension *might* have organized the dialogue of leaders and led about corruption (or about Korea) in the 1952 election but whether it *did*. The empirical evidence is clear that it did not, either about corruption or about Korea. Both these exceedingly potent issues were conspicuous examples of valence politics in that year.

Robertson's complaint is echoed by James Alt, another worker in the Essex vineyard, who also felt that I had somehow missed the point that 'consensus on ends does not imply consensus on means' (1979: 14). To this Alt adds the equally odd complaint that David Butler and I somehow made the 'theoretical claim . . . that [our] model is superior to any other: not only is it a valid model, but it is the only valid model of the electoral consequences of the economy' (1979: 9). Once again, it would have been more faithful to read what we actually wrote as saying exactly the opposite, and Alt, in another passage, concedes as much: 'Finally, Stokes argues that "whether a given problem poses a position- or valence-issue is a matter to be settled empirically and not on *a priori* logical grounds"' (1979: 9)—as David Butler and I believed and wrote on the issue of the economy too.

I should add that Alt, having joined in this oddly conceived attack on the logic of the valence framework, goes on to a perfectly reasonable disagreement with one of our particular applications of the framework, our conjecture that Labour in 1970 ultimately undid itself by asking to be judged by the goal of righting the balance of payments. To Alt this conjecture is unpersuasive, especially in view of how far the balance of payments is from the everyday experience of voters. This issue was fairly joined. How it is resolved depends on what is made of our evidence—first, that Labour's recovery during the six months prior to the election coincided more nearly with the turnabout in the balance of payments than it did with any of the economic indicators closer to everyday experience and, secondly, that, after Mr Wilson's balance-of-payments triumph was punctured by the eleventh-hour trade figures (without any deterioration in the other economic indicators), Labour lost an election that every pre-election poll suggested it was poised to win. But Alt's rendering of the Scots' verdict of 'not proven' on this strong-plausibility argument is a perfectly fair one.

An important query about the valence framework is made by Morris Fiorina (1981), in a long aside that appears in *Retrospective Voting in American National Elections*. As Fiorina was launched on this work, he became aware of the overlap between the ideas in my 1963 discussion of valence issues, which David Butler and I extended in *Political Change in Britain*, and his own ideas about the way the electorate judges parties or leaders by results. Seeing this, he spliced on to his first chapter on 'Theories of Retrospective Voting' a conceptual 'addendum' on 'Valence Issues and Retrospective Voting' (1981: 17–19). This quotes our characterization of the simplest model of the political impact of the economy, one in which the electorate pays attention only to the party in power and only to conditions during its current tenure of office, and notes that this quotation is a 'restatement' of what he termed 'the traditional, reward-punishment theory of retrospective voting' (ibid.: 18). Fiorina therefore asks 'whether the distinction between traditional retrospective and prospective voting is simply the behavioral manifestation of the distinction between position and valence issues.' (ibid). He perfectly reasonably answers no, it is not, on grounds that retrospective voting may encompass position issues as well as valence issues. It is not quite right to conclude from this, as Fiorina does, 'that the class of valence issues is considerably smaller than the class of issues on which citizens may vote retrospectively' (ibid.), since it might equally be noted that valence issues may encompass prospective as well as retrospective voting.

This addendum leaves the reader with a sense that Fiorina is responding to the valence framework as a host might respond to an unexpected dinner guest, one who must be dealt with before the party can go on. Although his conclusion, that retrospective voting is not simply 'the behavioral manifestation' of valence issues, is unexceptionable, it leaves unexplored the question of whether this guest might make a contribution to the party, particularly his attempt, in the tradition of V. O. Key, to find a bounded rationality in the electorate's judging of those who seek its support by the results they achieve. I will return to this question below.

The valence framework is bound to discomfit public-choice theorists, who incline to the economists' conception of rationality and find the spatial theory of voting an admirable means of aggregating individual voter preferences into collective policy choices. But commentators who are sceptical of parts of the spatial theory and are groping for a softer, more realistic rationality have also been uneasy about this framework. One is Samuel Popkin(1991), in *The Reasoning Voter*. In the course of characterizing the 'practical reasoning about government and politics in which people actually engage' as 'low-information rationality', he offers an extended note that manages both to regret the valence framework's departure from Downsian assumptions and its tendency 'to confuse and mislead most researchers into worries about whether the presence of common symbols, or valence issues, in elections is ... evidence of irrational and nonideological voting [and] a sign of lack of concern with policy and government performance' (1991: 248). My reading of the commentaries leaves me sceptical that the valence framework has had this effect. Certainly it left Fiorina unworried. A more accurate judgement would be that David Butler and I used this framework simply as a tool of positive analysis and left the normative question of rationality unaddressed. But this is an interesting question, and I will return to it in a moment.

INSIGHTS FROM THE VALENCE FRAMEWORK

Although these readings by the critics help clarify the valence framework, the key to its wider use will be the belief that it gives important new insights into electoral politics. I therefore close by sketching a variety of ways this view of the dialogue of leaders and led can strengthen our understanding of contemporary democracy. This will give a sense of how interesting a board can be spread, even if no more than a few morsels are set out here.

The amplitude of electoral swings. Valence politics has almost certainly contributed to the fluidity of party support and the greater amplitude of electoral swings. The position issues associated with the old-time alignments, including those of class, put a ceiling on how high a victorious party could fly, since the victors could not escape alienating those who held to the 'opposite' positions on the issues they stressed. A party could not win the support of those who wanted to extend slavery to the Western territories without losing the support of those who wanted these territories to remain free. But position issues equally put a floor under a defeated party's fall, since the losers would hold on to the voters anchored to the party by its support of positions they believed in.

Neither such a ceiling nor such a floor is imposed by valence issues. Part of the appeal of valence-campaigning to the electoral strategists is that an artfully chosen valence issue need not cost *any* votes. A brilliantly successful valence campaign, such as Jimmy Carter's drive for the Democratic presidential nomination in 1976, can soar very high indeed. But when the tide turns and the support brought by issues of this kind melts away, as it did for Mr Carter long before he was taken hostage by the valence issue of his weakness before the revolutionary guards, the free fall can be breathtaking, far greater than in an era of position politics. It is likely that the wider role of valence issues in modern campaigns has helped produce the cycle of high expectations/low realization that has beset so many presidents and prime ministers.

The weakening of partisan loyalites.   The trend towards valence politics is plainly correlated with the weakening of the old-time party loyalties, which were rooted in strong position issues. It is less clear whether the decline of party loyalties is cause or consequence of the rise of valence politics. The class alignments that had such a hold on party allegiance in an earlier day have been weakened by the transformation of society and the economy in a post-industrial age rather than by any change in the style of political campaigning. In this respect valence politics may simply be filling a void left by the decline of an important kind of position issue. Yet it is often said that the empty and kaleidoscopic symbolic appeals of the parties or leaders, and the relentless effort to bond rival parties or leaders to negative symbols, have diminished the appeal of the parties for this generation of voters.

The media and the dialogue.   Even the span of one generation has brought a profound change in the means of the communication between leaders and led. Earlier in the century campaigns still had important face-to-face elements, with large numbers of people attending outdoor rallies or indoor meetings where there was a genuine exchange between speakers and audience, although the print media played a vital role in this sort of communication from the time the suffrage was extended to a literate general electorate. The changes of recent decades involve a dramatic fall-off of the face-to-face element and an equally dramatic shift from the print to the electronic media, especially television. It is hard to believe that these changes are not linked to the rise of valence politics. It was very difficult in an old-time campaign meeting to make a speech devoid of position issues, and issues with this structure were the grist of the leading articles and angled news coverage of the partisan press. But it is very easy to produce a thirty-second television spot that is free of position issues and seeks merely to bond parties or candidates with positive or negative symbols.

The trend to negative campaigning.   Negative appeals were no strangers to position politics. The symbols of class campaigning have always been mainly negative, both in Britain and in the United States. But the structure and symbolic content of valence issues are admirably suited to negative appeals, and valence campaigning in a television age, particularly in the United States, has brought a torrent of mutual negative assaults on the parties and their leaders. This trend is pronounced enough to be offered as one of the reasons for the weakening hold of the parties and the declining participation of the electorate.

The role of single-issue groups.   The gravitation of the parties and their candidates towards valence politics has widened the role of single-issue groups, particularly in the United States. Position issues that demand attention and a place in political discourse do not simply disappear in an age of valence politics. On the western shore of the Atlantic—and the shores of the Pacific—issues such as abortion or property tax relief have increasingly been captured by interest groups focused on a single, or a very few, position issues. This trend is carried to an extreme in the US states with elements of direct democracy that wire the single-issue groups into policy-making via the initiative and referendum, devices that further relieve the party leaders from having to deal with position issues that divide the country.

Valence campaigns and position mandates. Although valence issues may appeal to the campaign strategists, position issues will face a government in power. For this reason, parties or candidates who may succeed in valence campaigns will have strong motives for discovering, after the victory is won, that it was a position mandate they sought and received. An interesting example of this is supplied by Ronald Reagan's victory over Jimmy Carter in the 1980 presidential election. It would be wrong to suggest that Mr Reagan mounted a campaign free of position issues in that year. But his gifts as a valence campaigner were well in evidence when he summed up in his television debate with President Carter.

Jimmy Carter came first. Believing, as any spatial theorist might, that Mr Reagan was vulnerable in ideological terms, Mr Carter told his listeners that they faced a choice between two positions on a Left–Right or liberal–conservative dimension. He declared himself the mainstream candidate of the mainstream party and called his opponent an extreme candidate of the extreme right-wing party. If they belonged to the American mainstream, he told his audience, they should vote for *him*. When it was Mr Reagan's turn to sum up, he told his audience the choice they faced was nothing like that. They should instead ask themselves whether they were better off four years ago than they were today, whether the country was more respected in the world and better led at home. If their response was 'yes' to these carefully contrived valence questions, they should vote for Jimmy Carter. But if their response to any of these questions was 'no', they should vote for Ronald Reagan. His summing-up capped a wonderfully skilful valence campaign.

Yet the most striking part of this saga was what happened next. Once Mr Reagan's victory was assured, the two parties abruptly traded places in their interpretation of the choice before the country. As the President-elect and his lieutenants geared up to put their programme through Congress, they claimed the electorate had given them a radically right-wing ideological mandate to reduce taxes, shrink the size and domestic responsibilities of the government, build up the military, and take a tougher stand towards the Soviets. The Democrats, on the other hand, were now the ones to say that the electorate had rendered a very different judgement: that they were less well off than they had been four years before and that Jimmy Carter's leadership had failed—a judgement, in other words, in valence terms. Winning parties will always have motives for discovering after an election the position dimensions lurking behind valence issues, for seeking retroactively to find a position mandate in an electoral victory that may have been sought and won in valence terms.

Bounded rationality and democratic responsiveness. The valence framework has normative implications that reach well beyond negative voting and other presumed pathologies of modern campaigning. This framework so often describes the communication between leaders and voters because it gives the public a more manageable problem of choice. If an election were fought in a Downsian framework, we would need no more than two parties and a single evaluative dimension to put severe pressure on the capacity of voters to get and use the information they need to reach a fully rational choice—on the basis of the relative distance of each of the competing parties from the voters' own ideal position on the evaluative dimension. There is some irony in this, since Downs viewed the spatial theory of voting so much as a means of reducing the information required by the voter. By contrast, the simpler tasks of valence politics, including judging a governing party on the basis of its bonding with the symbols of failure and success, require of the electorate only a kind of bounded rationality, in Simon's phrase.

This difference in the normative implications of position and valence politics echoes the most famous distinction in the normative theory of representation, Burke's distinction between the role of *instructed delegate* and *trustee*. Parties or leaders who seek electoral support by positioning themselves in a dimensional space essentially play the role of instructed delegates, committing themselves to the positions they advocate and inviting their constituents to punish them for gaps between this advocacy and their behaviour in office. By contrast, parties or leaders who identify themselves with generally approved values, and their opponents with generally disapproved ones, are playing a role closer to that of trustee of the electorate's interests. They are by no means divorced from the electorate's review. But they ask to be judged not by the policy content of their decisions, involving matters that were in Burke's view best resolved by those possessing the detailed information in government, but by the demonstrable success of this trusteeship of their electors' interests. Burke argued the greater rationality of the trustee's role, since it allowed the decisions of government to be based on reasoned debate and the full information available to those in authority. For Burke, too, the key to this difference lay in the limits to the voters' capacity to get and use information.

An awareness of these limits has guided the efforts of a number of commentators to find a realistic solution to the modern problem of democratic responsiveness and control. It was a cornerstone of V. O. Key's (1966) analysis in *The Responsible Electorate*. It is equally a cornerstone of Fiorina's (1981) *Retrospective Voting in American National Elections*, and of Popkin's (1991) *The Reasoning Voter*. The valence framework does not stand apart from these efforts, as the reception of the unexpected guest at dinner by Fiorina's addendum might suggest. By probing the dialogue of leaders and led under a valence and a position politics this framework can help us to understand the ways the parties and leaders respond to a democratic electorate and the ways the electorate itself can be said to control those to whom it gives legitimate authority. This insight into the problem of democratic responsiveness and control requires us to understand the *structure* of valence issues and not only the learning by which valences are formed, the aspect of the problem that is stressed by students of retrospective voting.

Although an appreciation of valence politics supplies an important corrective to the still-dominant spatial theory of voting, the valence framework has a broader importance than this. It calls attention to several persuasive yet under-recognized aspects of contemporary politics. A clear view of the structure and symbolic content and development of valence issues gives insight into a number of trends in recent politics, including the greater amplitude of electoral swings, the weakening of party loyalties, the rising importance of television, the spread of negative campaigning, and the role of single-issue groups. Beyond this, the valence framework can lead to a more realistic understanding of the possibility of democratic responsiveness and control.

Notes

Although none bears responsibility for any of the errors of my ways, I gratefully acknowledge the encouragement and detailed comments I have received from Douglas Arnold, Fred Greenstein, Stanley Kelley, and Anthony King, and the skilled assistance of Frank Hoke. I should also note how much I enjoyed thinking through these ideas with David Butler some years ago, although it is clear that he had no hand in any fresh errors here.

1. These ideas were more visible for a US scholarly audience when my initial article was included in Campbell *et al.* (1966). This line of thinking also drew on my earlier work in modelling the components of the choice of individual voters and whole electorates (see, e.g., Stokes 1966). It was impossible to cast my net at all broadly without finding issues structured very differently from traditional position issues.

References

Alt, J. E. (1979), *The Politics of Economic Decline: Economic Management and Political Behaviour in Britain since 1964* (Cambridge: Cambridge University Press).

Butler, D., and Stokes, D. (1974), *Political Change in Britain* (2nd edn., London: Macmillan).

Campbell, A., Converse, P. E., Miller, W. E., and Stokes, D. E., (1966), *Elections and the Political Order* (New York: John Wiley).

Converse, P. E., and Schuman, H. (1970), ' "Silent Majorities" and the Vietnam War', *Scientific American*, 222 (June); 17–25.

Downs, A. (1957), *An Economic Theory of Democracy* (New York: Harper and Row).

Fiorina, M. P. (1981), *Retrospective Voting in American National Elections* (New Haven, Conn.: Yale University Press).

Hotelling, H. (1929), 'Stability in Competition', *Economic Journal*, 39: 41–57.

Key, V. O. (1966), *The Responsible Electorate* (Cambridge, Mass.: Belknapp Press).

Popkin, S. L. (1991), *The Reasoning Voter: Communication and Persuasion in Presidential Campaigns* (Chicago: University of Chicago Press).

Rabinowitz, G., and MacDonald, S. E. (1989), 'A Directional Theory of Issue Voting', *American Political Science Review*, 83: 93–121.

Robertson, D. (1976), *A Theory of Party Competition* (London and New York: John Wiley and Sons).

Sartori, G (1976), *Parties and Party Systems: A Framework for Analysis* (New York: Cambridge University Press).

Smithies, A. (1941), 'Optimum Location in Spatial Competition', *Journal of Political Economy*, 49: 423–9.

Stokes, D. (1963), 'Spatial Models of Party Competition', *American Political Science Review*, 57: 368–77.

—— (1966), 'Some Dynamic Elements of Contests for the Presidency', *American Political Science Review*, 60: 19–28.

8

Electoral Pacts in Britain since 1886

VERNON BOGDANOR

I

One of David Butler's greatest gifts is his ability to open up new areas of study for scholarly investigation. He is, of course, the founding father of British psephology, and the study of electoral behaviour in Britain owes an enormous amount to his pioneering work with Donald Stokes, *Political Change in Britain*, first published in 1969. Yet, precisely because he is so closely identified with psephology, his contribution in other areas has been inadequately recognized. It is, however, David Butler who has opened up the study of *Coalitions in British Politics* (1978), of *Referendums* (1979), and of the history of the British electoral system.

In his doctoral thesis, first published in 1953 as *The Electoral System in Britain, 1918–1951*, David Butler was the first to draw attention to the search for an agreement between the Labour and Liberal parties during the second Labour government of 1929–31. 'It is impossible', he concluded, 'fully to disentangle the complications of the relationship between Liberals and Labour' (p. 62). One central theme, however, was the search by the Liberals for either an electoral pact with Labour or, alternatively, electoral reform. In *The Times* on 21 January 1930 Lloyd George is quoted as saying that one of the conditions for co-operation with Labour 'should be an understanding that . . . members of the Liberal party should not be assailed by Government nominees, or . . . as an alternative, there should be a *bona fide* promise that a measure of electoral reform would be carried by the Government at an early date' (quoted in Butler 1953: 62–3). Lloyd George's instinct—that either an electoral pact or electoral reform was needed to save the Liberal party—was correct, as was his belief that they were, in the short run at least, *alternatives* to each other. Yet, while there has been extensive examination by political scientists of electoral reform,

and even of the history of the electoral-reform debate, there has
been hardly any study of the working of electoral pacts in Britain.
This chapter is intended as a first contribution to such a study.

II

An electoral pact is an agreement between two (or more) distinct
and separate parties to co-operate electorally. Such pacts frequently
occur in the multi-party systems of the Continent, but they have
been much less frequent in Britain, especially since 1931. The
purpose of this chapter is to explain why national electoral pacts
have become so rare, and to argue that they perform an important
function in giving elasticity to the party system, and in making it
adaptable to social change.[2]

On the Continent, pacts are frequent since most democracies are
both multi-party and bipolar, with the main cleavage lying between
parties of the Left and parties of the Right. This means that, to
maximize its influence, a party does well to co-operate with like-
minded parties from the same bloc, so as to defeat the greater
enemy which lies on the opposite bloc. This co-operation is often
assisted by particular features or mechanisms of the electoral
system.

It is, in fact, precisely because the majority of democracies—
with Switzerland being the most notable exception—possess bipolar party systems, in which a left party or bloc of parties confronts
a right party or bloc of parties, and yet are also multi-party, that
most electoral systems make provision for co-operation between
two or more like-minded parties. The type of provision made will
differ with the electoral system.

The German electoral system allows the voter to distribute his
or her first and second votes between two different parties, thus
indicating the political colour of the coalition which the voter
favours. This has proved a crucial factor in creating an electoral
basis, first for the Social Democrat–Free Democrat coalition in the
years 1969–82, and then for the Christian Democrat–Free Democrat coalition which has ruled West Germany, and now Germany,
since 1982. Without the willingness of electors to cast their first
votes for the Christian Democrats and their second votes for the
Free Democrats, this coalition might well not have been possible,

since the Free Democrats might not have been able to surmount the 5 per cent threshold. Moreover, the pact enables Free Democrat voters, knowing that their party was unlikely to win a constituency seat, to cast their first vote for the party to which it was allied, the Christian Democrats. In the 1983 election, for example, no less than 58 per cent of those who had voted Free Democrat on the second vote supported the Christian Democrats on the first vote, as compared with only 29 per cent voting Free Democrat on the first vote (Bogdanor 1984: 66).

The single-transferable-vote system allows the voter to signal a coalition through the way in which preferences are distributed; this was a crucial factor in the construction of the National Coalition of Fine Gael and Labour which governed the Irish Republic between 1973 and 1977. Fine Gael voters, hitherto a conservative force in Irish politics, showed through their pattern of transfers that they were prepared for their party to co-operate with Labour; while supporters of Labour, whose party had abandoned the politics of isolation for co-operation with a 'bourgeois' party, proved willing to use their later preferences to secure the election of Fine Gael candidates.

Other proportional systems may allow *apparentement*, a provision by which separate parties can declare themselves linked for the purposes of vote-counting and seat allocation. The votes of these separate parties are then counted together, as though they had been cast for a single list (Williams 1964: ch. 2). A further possibility is *panachage*, as employed in the electoral systems of Switzerland and Luxemburg, by means of which the voter can distribute his or her votes in a multi-member constituency system, across more than one party list.

The majoritarian electoral systems—the alternative vote and the second ballot—also provide for co-operation. The alternative vote is, in this respect, analogous to the single transferable vote, while the second ballot emphasizes the importance of co-operation by allowing for bargaining amongst parties between the first and second ballots. In Fifth Republic France, the second-ballot electoral system has proved of considerable importance in encouraging agreements between the parties of the Left—Socialists and Communists—and, to a somewhat lesser extent, the parties of the Right—Gaullists and Giscardians—particularly for presidential elections.

All of these mechanisms serve to reward co-operative parties and penalize the intransigent. Other things being equal, a party which is prepared to ally itself with others is likely to secure more seats for a given percentage of the vote than an extremist party which avoids co-operation with others, and with whom others do not wish to co-operate. It is for this reason that, in the multi-party systems of the Continent, pivot parties such as the German Free Democrats enjoy such tremendous influence. Proportional representation can ensure that each vote carries the same weight; but it cannot ensure that each vote will carry the same weight in the process of government formation. Votes cast for parties which are prepared to co-operate together will carry more weight than votes cast for intransigent parties.

Under the plurality system, however, co-operation is much more difficult, for it can only be achieved by reciprocal withdrawal of candidates on the part of the parties which seek to co-operate. The candidates of party A must withdraw from constituencies p, q, r, etc. in exchange for the candidates of party B withdrawing from constituencies u, v, w, etc. This gives rise to two main problems.

The first problem is that, in a political system such as the one in Britain, where local constituency parties are autonomous, a headquarters agreement between the leaders of the two parties, A and B, although it might influence the stance of constituency parties, cannot determine them. In pre-democratic times, before parties existed as mass organizations, the stance of a party could be largely determined by its leaders. This would make it relatively easy to construct an alliance. The shifts and manœuvres of the Peelites between 1846 and 1859, when they finally cast their lot with the Liberals, would not be possible today, since the leaders would, at every stage, have to convince their members in the country of the correctness of the stance they were taking. The more parties have developed as mass organizations, the more their freedom of manœuvre to form electoral alliances has been limited.

The essential pre-condition of a pact—the reciprocal withdrawal of candidates—cannot, therefore, under modern conditions, be decided upon by the leaders of a party alone. The decision as to whether or not to run a candidate lies with local constituency parties, and national headquarters cannot force a constituency party to withdraw its candidate. Indeed, a constituency party will often regard the running of a candidate as part of its very *raison d'être*, and will be loth to ask its candidate to stand down, even in the wider interests of the party. The candidate, also, will often be unwilling to make the supreme sacrifice. The following *cri de côeur* of a Liberal candidate, who had been asked to stand down in the interests of a candidate from the Social Democratic party, made at the SDP's Council for Social Democracy, at Great Yarmouth, in 1982, is perhaps not untypical:

Seven years ago, when I became prospective parliamentary candidate for this constituency, we sold a home we all dearly loved to move to live in the constituency, our youngest left her school and all three children eventually went to school locally. My wife changed her job to teach in the local comprehensive school and we accepted the upheaval because we both believed that for me the only way to nurse the constituency was to live in it and become part of it. (Josephs 1983: 155).

Moreover, even if a constituency party can be persuaded not to put up a candidate, and the candidate can be persuaded to stand down, the purpose of the exercise might still be frustrated by an independent candidate of the same political tendency, a John the Baptist figure, channelling away votes which would otherwise be given to the other party in the pact. That, in fact, was what happened in a number of constituencies in Britain in 1918, when, despite the existence of the coupon determining the allocation of Conservative and Lloyd George Liberal candidatures, eighty-three uncouponed Conservatives stood, of whom fifty were successful. One of these successful uncouponed Conservatives defeated the former Liberal Prime Minister, H. H. Asquith, in East Fife. Asquith had been granted the coupon, but opposition to him was so strong that local Conservatives insisted upon putting up a candidate. Similarly, in 1931, local Conservatives were much more willing to stand down for Simonite Liberal Nationals, than for Samuelite Liberals, who continued to support Free Trade. (Simon himself had not been opposed by a Conservative in either the 1924 or the 1929 general elections.) For this reason there were contests between Conservatives and Liberal Nationals in only four constituencies, but seventy-nine contests between other Liberals and Conservatives (Thorpe 1991: 177). In 1951 there was no national electoral pact, but Conservative constituency associations were encouraged to make deals with Liberals, where these would assist the anti-Labour cause. Seven Liberal candidates, and five of the six MPs elected, faced no Conservative opposition; and, when the Conservatives issued their first list of prospective candidates, these included the Liberals in all the uncontested seats (Butler 1952: 94). But Conservatives were more willing to stand down for Liberals who had opposed the Labour government than for those who had supported it. Indeed, of those who had opposed Labour, only Jo Grimond faced Conservative opposition. A pact, if it is to be successful, therefore, must go with the local grain of constituency opinion; it cannot be imposed by party headquarters.

Secondly, even when a pact has been agreed and approved by party headquarters, and accepted by the constituencies, it does not follow that it will have a determining influence upon party supporters and electors. A party is not like a disciplined army which can order its supporters to transfer their votes in accordance with decisions made by a party organization. There must be some overriding reason—defeating Home Rule in 1886, preserving financial stability in 1931—which persuades voters to follow the advice of their parties. A pact, if it is to be successful, must go with the grain, not only of local constituency opinion, but also of local electoral opinion.

III

It is perhaps surprising, given the difficulties attending the formation of an electoral pact under a plurality electoral system, that they have played so important a part in British politics since 1886. There have, in fact, been five national electoral pacts during this period.

1. The pact between Conservatives and Liberal Unionists in 1886, a pact which lasted through seven general elections until the two parties merged in 1912.

2. The pact between the Liberal party and the Labour Representation Committee (LRC), forerunner of the Labour party, in 1903, often known as the Gladstone–MacDonald pact. This pact was operative only during the general election of 1906, but it continued in the shape of an informal understanding during the two general elections of 1910.

3. The pact between the Conservatives and the Coalition Liber-

als, during the 'coupon' election of 1918. This pact would, it was hoped by the party leaders, encourage fusion between the two parties, but fusion was rejected, probably to the relief of the Conservative party in the country, by the Coalition Liberals in March 1920.

4. The pact between the parties comprising the National government—the Conservatives, Liberal Nationals, Liberals, and National Labour—during the general election of 1931. The National government also fought a second general election in 1935, by which time the Liberals had left the government, and the Liberal Nationals and National Labour, with whom the Conservatives maintained an electoral pact, had become almost indistinguishable from the Conservatives.

5. The pact between the Liberals and the Social Democratic party, creating the Alliance, in 1981–2. This pact held for the general elections of 1983 and 1987.

These pacts have been of considerable importance in British politics. Each of them, except the last, secured a period of electoral hegemony for the dominant party in the pact. The 1886 pact ensured the dominance of the Unionist alliance for a period of twenty years, and the defeat of Home Rule. The Gladstone–MacDonald pact of 1903 gave the Liberal party a period of electoral dominance until the outbreak of the First World War. The 'coupon' election of 1918 prefigured the period of Conservative dominance between the wars, by confirming the split in the Liberal party; while the arrangements made in 1931 ensured that Labour would be faced, in the vast majority of constituencies, with a single National government candidate, so that it would be unable to benefit, as it had in 1929, from a split vote amongst the parties opposing it. Only the pact forming the Liberal–SDP Alliance failed to achieve its object, which was to 'break the mould' of the political system, although it came nearer to doing so than any party or grouping since the Liberal party under Lloyd George in the years 1929–31.

It is noticeable that the Liberal party has been involved in each of these pacts. That ought not to be particularly surprising. Since the end of the First World War the Liberals have been the centre party in British politics; and, in a three-party system, it is the party in the centre which is most likely to be sought as a coalition partner, or a partner in an electoral pact. In 1886, also, it was the Whig element of the Liberal party, the most centrist group in the political constellation, which formed the dominant element in the Liberal Unionist party. Not only is a centrist grouping in a plurality electoral system ideally placed to pursue an electoral pact; but, because the plurality system discriminates so severely against it, such a pact may well be the only way in which it can survive as an electoral force.

Labour has only participated in one pact at national level—the Gladstone–MacDonald pact of 1903. Its attitude towards pacts, or indeed any form of co-operation with other political parties, has been deeply conditioned by the trauma of 1931. David Butler has often said that the most powerful figure in modern British politics is the ghost of Ramsay MacDonald; and the events of 1931 have led Labour to take the view that any leader who seeks to co-operate with other parties in peacetime is guilty of a form of betrayal.

There were signs, admittedly, after Labour's third electoral defeat in 1987, that attitudes within the party were changing. The party showed an increasing willingness to consider a change in the electoral system, and the Scottish Labour party proposed, to the Scottish Convention, that a future Scottish Parliament be elected either by the alternative vote or by the additional-member system of proportional representation. Either of these systems would almost certainly require co-operation with other parties for Labour to be able to govern Scotland with a majority. After another election defeat in 1992, however, the party might well prove more willing to consider reform of the electoral system, and, possibly, some form of electoral pact with the Liberal Democrats. Such a pact, however, would be more likely to take the form of a series of local arrangements, as seems to have occurred between the Conservatives and Liberals in 1951, rather than a fully-fledged national pact. After the 1987 general election, Michael Steed, a Liberal psephologist, advocated just such a limited pact, covering '30 or so carefully selected seats on either side' which 'could be presented as a form of insurance, thus not inhibiting or damaging a Labour thrust for outright victory' (Steed 1987: 11). Such a limited pact would have little effect with a Conservative vote of over 40 per cent; but, if the Conservative vote 'came down to about 40 per cent, it would decide whether or not we had a Conservative government in the mid-1990s' (ibid.). Predictably, however, the call for a limited pact fell on deaf ears amongst the Labour leadership during the 1987–92 parliament.

Were Labour's attitude to change, this would do no more than put the party in line with other European Social Democratic parties. In 1933, one year after they had begun their long period of electoral hegemony, the Swedish Social Democrats, in a minority in the lower house of the Rikdsdag, reached an agreement with the Agrarian, now Centre party, to combat unemployment in exchange for the introduction of price supports on agricultural products— the so-called 'Red–Green Coalition'. In Germany, as we have seen, the Social Democratic Party were able to come to power in 1969 with the aid of the Free Democrats; while the hegemony of the French Socialists was made possible by co-operation with the Communists, co-operation which was, of course, facilitated by the second-ballot electoral system.

If Labour's attitude towards electoral pacts must remain in some doubt, there can be no doubt that the predominant tendency of electoral pacts in Britain since 1886—with the Gladstone–MacDonald pact of 1903 being the main exception—has been to benefit the Conservatives, enabling them to gain power with the aid of satellite parties, splinters from their opponents such as the Liberal Unionists, Liberal Nationals, and National Labour. Indeed, it can be argued that, between 1886 and 1951, the only general elections won by the Conservatives as an independent party were those of 1922 and 1924. As late as 1975 Harold Macmillan was able to declare:

the last purely Conservative Government was formed by Mr Disraeli in 1874—it is the fact that we have attracted moderate people of Liberal tradition and thought into our ranks which makes it possible to maintain a Conservative government today. A successful party of the Right must continue to recruit its strength from the centre, and even from the Left Centre. Once it begins to shrink into itself like a snail it will be doomed . . . (1975: 18–19)

The electoral pacts of 1886, 1918, and 1931 each prefigured long periods of Conservative hegemony, a hegemony granted to them by political leaders—Joseph Chamberlain, Lloyd George, and Ramsay MacDonald—who were anything but Conservative in the traditional sense, who never saw themselves as Conservatives, and who were never comfortable working with the Conservative party.

Yet they helped ensure that the Conservatives remained the natural party of government in Britain.

IV

The Gladstone–MacDonald pact of 1903 was drawn up primarily because the Liberal party, having lost the two previous general elections, did not believe that it could win the next without an ally in the form of the support of the Labour movement. Labour, especially in Lancashire, the stronghold of the 'Tory working man', could secure votes for the 'Progressive alliance' which the Liberals would not be able themselves to win. The LRC for its part realized that it could not survive in a world of three-cornered fights, without an agreement. It badly needed an ally if it was ever to establish a foothold in the inhospitable environment created by the plurality electoral system. The pact was greatly assisted by the fact that the 1884–5 settlement, establishing the single-member constituency as the norm, had nevertheless retained forty-six double-member boroughs. In these constituencies it was possible for an LRC candidate and a Liberal to fight in tandem, just as Whigs and Radicals had been able to fight together in double-member constituencies before 1885. Indeed, of the twenty-nine seats won by the LRC in 1906, no less than eleven were in the double-member constituencies.

In the 1906 general election the pact fulfilled its function for both parties. Of the fifty LRC candidates, all but eighteen enjoyed a straight fight with a Conservative opponent; and all but three of the LRC MPs in England and Wales (the pact did not operate in Scotland) were elected without Liberal opposition. Thus, the pact both enabled Labour to gain a secure foothold in the Commons, and allowed the Liberals to contain Labour within areas where it was already naturally strong. Although there was no explicit renewal of the pact for the two general elections of 1910, there was a tacit understanding, on the part of the two-party leaderships at least, that they would do their best to avoid splitting the 'Progressive' vote. In January 1910 Labour fought just twenty-seven seats against Liberal opposition; and in December 1910 a mere eleven (Blewett 1972: 241, 262). In this latter election the only Labour candidates elected were those without Liberal opponents. The understanding was assisted by the fact that Labour was finding itself unable to win seats against Liberal opposition; indeed, in every three-cornered by-election in a Liberal-held seat between December 1910 and 1914, Labour came bottom of the poll. For so long as the two parties co-operated, however, the hegemony of the Left was assured, and it is difficult to see how the Conservatives could have broken it. One cannot, of course, know whether the understanding between the two parties could possibly have survived the expansion of the franchise and the massive changes induced by the First World War; but the fact that it did not survive enabled the Conservatives to dominate the inter-war period.

The other four electoral pacts have been the result of party splits; and they have served to confirm those splits. When the first meeting of the Liberal Unionist party was held in the House of Commons in May 1886, the Marquess of Hartington, who was in the chair, was able to harden the resolve of MPs to oppose Gladstone's Home Rule Bill, 'by reading a message from the Conservative Chief Whip giving an absolute undertaking on behalf of that party not to contest at the next election the seat of any Liberal member who voted against the Bill' (Chilston 1961: 77).

The pact of 1886 determined the shape of British politics for the next twenty years. By giving the Liberal Unionists a free run against Gladstonian candidates, the Conservatives allowed the Liberal Unionist party to survive, confirmed the Liberal split, and made Liberal reunion extremely difficult. The Liberal Unionists were crucial to the success of the Unionist alliance, because there were voters opposed to Home Rule who would, nevertheless, not be prepared to vote for a Conservative candidate. Nearly ten years after the pact, in 1895, Joe Chamberlain could write to his son, Austen, 'No one who has not worked among the electors can be aware how strong are old prejudices in connection with party names and colours and badges. A man may be a good Unionist at heart, and yet nothing can persuade him to vote "blue" or give support to a "Tory" candidate' (Blewett 1972: 15).

The Conservatives thus gained considerably from the pact of 1886. They helped to engineer a split in the Liberal opposition with the aid of a party which could never aspire to more than satellite status, and whose seats were largely in areas which Conservatives could not hope to win. The Liberal Unionists were confined to their 1886 position, and would not be allowed to expand from their bridgehead into Conservative territory. Thus, the number of seats which they won in 1886–77 represented their ceiling. They never succeeded in winning so many seats again. The Liberal Unionists were to prove a most valuable adjunct, but never a competitor, to the Conservatives; and in 1912 the two parties formally merged.

In 1918 the 'coupon' election actually helped to *create* a new political identity, for the differences between Asquithian and Lloyd Georgian Liberals were not crystallized until the machinery of the coupon arrangements forced them to stand in opposition to each other. Indeed, part of the purpose of the electoral agreement was to assist in the creation of a new political identity in the post-war world, an identity which would be neither Conservative nor Liberal, but a fusion of the two. The old issues which divided the parties—Home Rule, Tariff Reform, Church disestablishment— would, hopefully, be submerged under this new dispensation. Bonar Law, the Conservative leader, went so far as to confess to A. J. Balfour in 1918 that he was 'perfectly certain, indeed I do not think anyone can doubt this, that our party on the old lines will never have any future again in this country' (Bonar Law 1918). Austen Chamberlain, who succeeded Bonar Law as Conservative leader in 1921, hoped that the Conservatives and Coalition Liberals would merge, as the Conservatives and Liberal Unionists of his father's generation had done. Yet, in March 1920 the Coalition Liberals had already rejected 'fusion', and it is doubtful if Conservatives in the country could ever have been persuaded to accept it, even if their leaders had pressed it upon them with more tact than Austen could summon. In the event, the Coalition collapsed, through a revolt by local Conservative constituency associations who were already choosing candidates to oppose Coalition Liberals, and through the hostility of back-bench Conservative MPs and junior ministers. When the Conservative leaders sought to overcome these objections by summoning a meeting of Conservative MPs at the Carlton Club in 1922, they were soundly defeated, and the Coalition came to an end.

In October 1931 the National government, composed of the Conservative, Liberal National, Liberal, and Labour parties, formed just two months previously, fought the general election as a government, in striking contradiction to the pledge made at its formation, that 'The election which may follow the end of the Government will not be fought by the Government but by the parties' (Samuel 1931). By contrast with 1918, however, no formal 'coupon' was issued endorsing particular candidates with the imprimatur of the government. Instead, there were negotiations between party headquarters, which sought to influence their respective constituency parties. These methods of informal persuasion left just eighty-eight constituencies out of 615 in which there were contests between candidates supporting the National government (Thorpe 1991: 177). As Andrew Thorpe, the historian of the 1931 general election has remarked, 'Given the poor relations which often prevailed, the wonder is perhaps not the number of constituencies in which National candidates ultimately stood against each other as the number of straight fights achieved' (ibid.: 166). That there were not more clashes is probably due to the overriding fear of a Labour victory and the financial instability to which it was thought a Labour victory would give rise.

The National government's decision to go to the country as a government confirmed and finalized the splits in the Labour and Liberal parties. It made reunion between MacDonald and his former colleages impossible, while it showed that the Liberals were split three ways—between the newly formed Liberal National party, willing to support the National government unconditionally even if this meant abandoning Free Trade; the Samuelite Liberals, offering conditional support to the National government, provided that it made no serious departures from Free Trade; and the Lloyd George family group, which came out in root-and-branch opposition to the National government, and advocated support for Labour. From this threefold split, the Liberal party never recovered.

In 1981 the formation of the Social Democratic party confirmed the split in the Labour party. Indeed, David Steel, the Liberal party leader, has confessed that he persuaded potential defectors *not* to join the Liberal party, but to form a new party, precisely in order to maximize the number of Labour defectors, and widen the Labour split. Labour MPs would, it was thought, be willing to defect to a party calling itself 'Social Democratic', even if it was to be virtually indistinguishable from the Liberal party, but not to a party called 'Liberal'. Steel admitted this strategy in an article written for the Liberal journal, *New Outlook*, entitled 'The Alliance: Hope and Obligation', published in September 1981.

I do not deny that my role, as I saw it, in encouraging a social democratic break-out from the Labour Party and the formation of a new party was, and is, a high-risk strategy. But I also believe that it is the approach which provides us with the only chance to break the existing two-party system and present the electorate with a credible alternative government, in one move, at the next General Election.

I know that some will argue that my job a year ago should have been solely to encourage Labour dissidents to join the Liberal Party as the only agency capable of change. Had I pursued that line I do not believe that the Labour Party—and British politics—would have been shaken to anything like the same degree by the earthquake caused by those willing to quit the Labour Party.

The possibility of a new Social Democratic grouping maximised the numbers of those prepared to cross that divide. The presence of an SDP, whose leaders and membership recognise an ally and friend in the Liberal Party, maximises the potential appeal of the forces of realignment'. (quoted in Bogdanor 1983: 278–9)

The Alliance, formed of the Liberal and Social Democratic parties, followed the precedent set by Lloyd George and Bonar Law, in 1918, in allocating seats by means of a signed agreement, negotiated by the two parties. These are, in fact, the *only* two occasions on which the allocation of constituencies has been decided in this way (Hart 1990: 34–5). Guidelines were drawn up by party headquarters as principles to help determine a fair allocation of seats, and an independent arbitrator was called in at the end of the process to sort out contentious cases (Josephs 1983: Appendix B). The whole process proved long drawn out and difficult, but, eventually, success was achieved. In the 1983 general election there were only three constituencies in which candidates from the Liberal and Social Democratic parties stood against each other.

V

In Britain, electoral pacts have proved to be essentially temporary arrangements. They have led either to merger or to separation. The Liberal Unionists merged with the Conservatives in 1912, the National Labour party wound itself up shortly before the 1945 general election, while the Liberal National party signed, with the Conservatives, the Woolton–Teviot agreement in May 1947, urging the merger of Conservative and Liberal National constituency associations. In 1948 the Liberal Nationals, by now indistinguishable from the Conservatives, renamed themselves the National Liberal party, and in 1966 became an integral part of the Conservative party. The Social Democratic party agreed, by majority vote, to merge with the Liberals in 1987, although the minority, led by Dr David Owen, the party leader, formed a 'continuing' SDP, which, however, wound itself up in 1990. Thus, one wing of the SDP merged, while the other separated only to find itself extinguished by the iniquities of the electoral system.

The Gladstone–MacDonald pact of 1903 did not lead to a merger between the Liberal and Labour parties, nor did Labour ever intend that it should. After 1918 it proved impossible to recreate the pre-war arrangements. Labour proposed to run candidates over the whole country, refusing any longer to be confined by a pact with the Liberals. Arthur Henderson hoped that co-operation with the Liberals could still be secured and declared in December 1917 that 'he would depend on the alternative vote and on a friendly understanding between Liberalism and Labour to give each other their second choice' (Wilson 1970: 317). With the defeat of the alternative vote in 1918, however, there was no machinery to help secure co-operation between the Liberal and Labour parties, and Labour's refusal to co-operate with the Liberals ensured that the Conservatives were in power, either alone or with allies, for all but three years of the inter-war period.

The 1918 'coupon' election was seen by the party leaders, if not by the rank and file, as a step toward merger, but this, as we have seen, failed to come about. In 1931 the components of the National government eventually merged with the Conservatives, except for the Samuelite Liberals, who, unlike their former colleagues, the Simonites, refused to countenance any departure from Free Trade, and resigned from the National government in September 1932 in protest at the Ottawa agreements which established a protective tariff.

Electoral pacts, then, have either proved a means to party realignment, or have not lasted. Where, as in 1886 and 1931, an electoral pact has made possible the survival of a splinter party, that party has proved short-lived. It has been little more than a satellite or client party, performing the function of a resting-place for MPs who would eventually cross the floor, but were unwilling to do so immediately. These satellite parties—the Liberal Unionists,

National Labour, and the Liberal Nationals—made it easier for both MPs and voters to swing towards the Conservatives without feeling that they were sacrificing their political identity. But the impression which these parties gave of having an independent identity of their own was deceptive. Parties such as the Liberal Unionists, the Liberal Nationals, and the National Labour party could never be regarded as serious competitors for power in the way that the Conservative, Liberal, and Labour parties have been. None of these satellite parties was ever able to put up a full slate of candidates. They would never have been able to increase their representation in the Commons, and the effect in each case of the electoral pact was to ensure their survival at the cost of confining them to a narrow bridgehead. British politics, under the plurality electoral system, is inherently dualistic in nature. No third choice is possible. In 1886 one either supported Home Rule, or opposed it, in which case one had no alternative but to sustain a Conservative government. Similarly, in 1931, one either supported the National government or opposed it. In each case, what seemed like a third choice, of supporting a Conservative-dominated government, but preserving a separate political identity, proved illusory.

The only way in which electoral pacts could have proved permanent would have been if the electoral system had been altered. This would have enabled co-operating parties to survive as independent entities. In retrospect, it is perhaps surprising that electoral pacts did not give rise to stronger pressure for reform of the electoral system.

There is some evidence that support for proportional representation amongst Liberal MPs in 1884 corresponded with incipient Liberal Unionism. Fifteen of the twenty-three Liberal members of the Proportional Representation Society who remained in the Commons in 1886 voted against the Home Rule Bill, while another fifteen members of the Society were to emerge, after 1886, as Liberal Unionists (Jones 1972: 103). Yet, neither Hartington nor the other Liberal Unionist leaders ever showed much interest in proportional representation.

After 1903 the Gladstone–MacDonald pact would have been assured of permanence if the electoral system had been changed to either proportional representation or the alternative vote. Yet the Liberals, while not wholly unsympathetic to the alternative vote— the first draft of the abortive franchise bill of 1912 provided for its adoption—were nevertheless unwilling, without pressing necessity, to allow Labour to extend its organization into Liberal territory; and, until 1914, the danger from Labour did not seem so great as to make electoral reform an urgent matter. Labour, on the other hand, under MacDonald's leadership, believed that it could eventually become the dominant party in the state. When that stage had been reached, the plurality system would work to Labour's advantage and enable it to obtain power without having to share it with other parties. So Labour, almost uniquely amongst European socialist parties, continued to support the plurality system.

After 1918 the Coalition Liberals could have retained their independent existence by means of proportional represenation, but Lloyd George hoped and believed that the coalition would lead to fusion. In April 1917 Lloyd George had told C. P. Scott, editor of the *Manchester Guardian*, that proportional representation was a 'device for defeating democracy . . . and for bringing faddists of all kinds into Parliament, and establishing groups and disintegrating parties' (quoted in Wilson 1970: 274); and he had been instrumental in ensuring that the unanimous recommendation of the Speaker's Conference in 1917, calling for proportional representation in borough constituencies, was defeated. By November 1925, however, Lloyd Geroge was telling Scott that 'Some one ought to have come to me . . . in 1918 and gone into the whole matter. I was not converted then. I could have carried it then when I was prime minister. I am afraid it is too late now' (quoted in ibid.: 484).

In 1931 the formation of the National government actually frustrated the chances of electoral reform. Earlier in the year an electoral reform bill, providing for the introduction of the alternative vote, had been introduced by the minority Labour government and passed by the Commons. It was, however, rejected by the Lords; and, under the Parliament Act procedure as it then stood, two further sessions were required before it could be passed into law over the Lords' veto. Samuel, the Liberal leader, sought to persuade the leaders of the National government to persist with the alternative vote, but was brushed aside; while the Liberal Nationals, identifying their future with the Conservatives, felt no interest in proposing a measure which was anathema to their coalition partners.

VI

The pact between the Liberals and the SDP, which was in large part intended to secure proportional representation, is the only post-war example of a national pact in British politics. The failure of the Liberal–SDP Alliance to 'break the mould' of British politics, and the ending of the political careers of the vast majority of the Labour MPs who defected in 1981, will probably ensure that it is a long time before a similar party split takes place. In the fifty-three years before the Second World War, by contrast, there were four national electoral pacts, as well as a number of proposed pacts which failed to materialize—such as a pact between Liberals and Unionist Free Traders in 1903–4, a pact between Liberals and Labour in the 1920s, and a 'Popular Front' between opponents of the Baldwin–Chamberlain governments in the 1930s. Why is it that pacts have become so rare a phenomenon in British politics?

One part of the answer has already been hinted at. The growth of party organization has made it impossible for party leaders to negotiate a pact without the support of the grass roots of the party. Yet, to party activists, any suggestion of an agreement with another party which involves the withdrawal of candidates will seem like a confession of defeat, an acceptance that their party cannot win an election on its own. This attitude has been widespread, in post-war Britain, even in the Liberal party, although members of the party cannot seriously have ever entertained any prospect of being able to win a general election on their own. When Jo Grimond, in the early 1960s, sought realignment, he found that 'The prospect of coalition . . . scared Liberals out of their wits', and, paradoxically, those who cried most loudly for electoral reform were 'also the most adamant against any Coalition with other Parties', although, 'if electoral reform led to the results for which Liberals hoped and which statistics foretold, that is fifty to seventy MPs to which our vote entitled us, then if government was to be carried on, coalitions of some sort would often be essential' (1979: 211–12). Between the two general elections of February and October 1974, Jeremy Thorpe adamantly refused to countenance any discussion of coalition; while, in 1977, David Steel had to exert all his influence to persuade the Liberals to accept even the very limited parliamentary arrangements contemplated in the Lib.–Lab. pact.

There is a further aspect of modern party organization which explains why electoral pacts have become rare. Under modern conditions, political parties feel, if they are to be national parties, that they have to contest every constituency. Until the Reform Act of 1832, by contrast, 'the *preponderant tradition* in English electoral practice was probably *the tradition of uncontested elections*' (Edwards 1964: 185; emphasis in original) and even between 1885 and 1922 an average of 138 seats at each general election remained uncontested (Craig 1974: 584–5; see also Butler and Butler 1986: 224). To fight every constituency was not then, as it is today, a virility symbol for a political party. The Conservatives, therefore, were perfectly willing to withdraw candidates in 1886 or 1918 if it were to their political advantage; while the Liberals did not feel fearful that, if they stood down in a few constituencies for LRC candidates in the general election of 1906, they would be accused of lacking confidence in their electoral prowess. On the contrary, the psychological effect of the pact, secret though it was, would, they believed, boost their prospects of electoral success. 'The main benefit', declared Jesse Herbert, private secretary to the Liberal Chief Whip, in 1903, of a pact 'would be the effect on the public mind of seeing the opponents of the Government united. It would give hope and enthusiasm to the Liberals making them vote and work. It would make the Tories fearful and depressed and rob them of energy and force' (Poirier 1958: 189).

Today, however, a corollary to the claim that a political party is a national party is the further claim that there is no type of seat which it is unable to win, even if the psephological facts suggest otherwise. The only exception to this—and the exception to almost all generalizations about UK politics—is Northern Ireland, where Conservatives, Labour, and Liberals have been content, with rare exceptions, not to compete. Until 1972, the Ulster Unionist party took the Conservative whip at Westminster. Northern Ireland, however, is the exception which proves the rule. Parties from the mainland do not fight there so as to be able to distance themselves from its problems. To involve themselves too directly in Northern Ireland's affairs would be to risk taking sides on the issue of the border and alienating voters on the mainland. In every other part of the United Kingdom, by contrast, the major parties feel that they are unable to make any similar declaration of disinterest.

The success of the arrangements between the Conservatives and

Ulster Unionists resulted from a perfect compatibility of interest. Such a compatibility is more likely to be achieved if the parties co-operating in a pact have electorally distinctive constituencies, as, to a large extent, the Liberals and the LRC had in 1903. It is at least arguable that the Alliance between the Liberals and the SDP would have been more successful if the SDP had, from the beginning, sought to emphasize that it could tap electoral support which was spatially distinctive from that of the Liberal party, even at the cost of concentrating its efforts upon particular regions, rather than fighting across the whole country. This would have involved making an explicit appeal to the Labour electoral constituency in the north-east, from which a number of the Labour defectors came, and also in London, where the activities of the extreme Left were leading to widespread disaffection, to be tapped later in the 1980s by the Liberals. To have made such a strategic decision, the SDP would have had consciously to see itself as a predominantly regional party, as the early Labour party had done, and sought to fight intensively on a narrow front, rather than unsuccessfully on a wider front. Such a strategy would have avoided squabbles with the Liberals, since the two parties would no longer have been competing for the same electoral market; and, in retrospect, it might have offered a better chance of success than the strategy actually adopted, which was, in effect, to create a second Liberal party under another name.

VII

Developments in modern party politics—primarily the tightening of party organization and the nationalization of party politics—have made party lines in Britain more rigid, militating against both realignment and its concomitant phenomenon, the electoral pact. This is in many respects a pity. Until the Second World War, periodic realignments brought fluidity to the political system as new issues stimulated new political cleavages. Realignment proved the means by which the political system could adapt itself to new conditions. The 1903 Gladstone–MacDonald pact enabled politics to accommodate itself to the growth of the Labour interest and the politics of social reform. The Lloyd George coalition sought to overcome the sterile disputes of the pre-war period and to enable

Britain to adapt to fundamental structural change, both at home and on the international stage. Under the National government of 1931, the free trade–protection debate finally disappeared from British politics, and constitutional progress in India was achieved more easily than would have been possible under a purely Conservative government. In each of these cases, realignment proved a means of bringing new blood into governing parties, and putting new issues on to the political agenda.

Since 1945, by contrast, the British party system has become rigid and frozen, and the absence of any successful realigning movement has contributed to a remarkable loss of inelasticity in the party system. It is in large part because of this inelasticity that the call for reform of the electoral system and for constitutional reform has arisen. Yet, in all the questioning of our constitutional arrangements over the past two decades, the party system itself has largely escaped critical scrutiny. Few have been willing to ask whether the party system serves the common good as effectively as its beneficiaries would have us believe. This is a matter for some surprise, given that the major parties are, in effect, the custodians of the British Constitution. For this reason, any discussion of constitutional reform which fails to address the facts of party domination will be unrealistic.

Yet it is the inelasticity and rigidity of the party system which is, in the author's opinion, the prime source of Britain's failure to resolve its social and economic problems. The party system which, until 1939, proved, on the whole, a means of accommodating politics to social change has now become a barrier to such accommodation. That barrier is likely to remain until it is swept away by a reform of the electoral system.

Notes

I owe a great deal in the preparation of this chapter to Michael Steed, with whom I have enjoyed many stimulating discussions on electoral pacts. I am grateful also to Andrew Adonis for commenting on a first draft of the chapter. They are not, however, to be implicated in either my arguments or my conclusions.

1. This chapter does not deal with local pacts, nor with pacts in Northern Ireland.

References

Blewett, N. (1972), *The Peers, the Parties and the People: The General Elections of 1910* (London: Macmillan).

Bogdanor, V. (1983) (ed.), *Liberal Party Politics* (Oxford: Clarendon Press).

—— (1984), *What is Proportional Representation? A Guide to the Issues* (Oxford: Martin Robertson).

Bonar Law, A. (1918), Bonar Law MSS, House of Lords Record Office, 95/1, 5 Oct.

Butler, D. (1952), *The British General Election of 1951* (Macmillan).

—— (1963), *The Electoral System in Britain since 1918* (2nd edn., Oxford: Clarendon Press).

—— (1978)(ed.), *Coalitions in British Politics* (London: Macmillan).

—— and Butler, G. (1986), *British Political Facts, 1900–1985* (London: Macmillan).

—— and Ranney, A. (1979)(eds.), *Referendums* (Washington DC: American Enterprise Institute).

Chilston, 3rd Viscount (1961), *Chief Whip: The Political Life and Times of Aretas Akers-Douglas, 1st Viscount Chilston* (London: Routledge and Kegan Paul).

Craig, F. W. S. (1974), *British Parliamentary Election Results, 1885–1919* (London: Macmillan).

Edwards, Sir G. (1964), 'The Emergence of Majority Rule in English Parliamentary Elections', *Transactions of the Royal Historical Society*.

Grimond, J. (1979), *Memoirs* (London: Heinemann).

Hart, M. (1990), 'Electoral Pacts', *Contemporary Record*, 2/3, (Feb.).

Jones, A. (1972), *The Politics of Reform, 1884* (Cambridge: Cambridge University Press).

Josephs, J. (1983), *Inside the Alliance: An Inside Account of the Development and Prospects of the Liberal/SDP Alliance* (London: John Martin).

Macmillan, H. (1975), *The Past Masters* (London: Macmillan).

Poirier, P. (1958), *The Advent of the Labour Party* (London: Allen & Unwin).

Samuel, Sir H. (1931), Memorandum in Samuel MSS, House of Lords Record Office, A/77, 24 Aug.

Steed, M. (1987), 'How to Nobble the Thatcher Vote', *New Statesman*, 27 Nov.

Thorpe, A. (1991), *The British General Election of 1931* (Oxford: Clarendon Press).

Williams, P. (1964), *Crisis and Compromise: Politics and the Fourth Republic* (2nd edn., London: Longmans).

Wilson, T. (1970) (ed.), *The Political Diaries of C. P. Scott: 1911–1928* (London: Collins).

9

The British Electoral System: Fixture without Foundation

JOHN CURTICE

INTRODUCTION: WHY ARE ELECTIONS HELD?

Proponents of alternative electoral systems do not simply disagree about how the votes cast at elections should be counted. They also disagree about why elections should be held at all. Supporters of the continued use of the first-past-the-post (or single-member-plurality) system take one view of what British parliamentary elections should be about; those in favour of some form of proportional representation take another.

The differences between the two camps can be summarized under three broad headings, as shown in Table 9.1. The first and most important of these is a disagreement about what precisely is being elected (Schumpeter, 1976). Formally speaking, British general elections are about the election of 650 or so members of the House of Commons. But in everyday political discourse we talk about the Conservative or Labour party 'winning' an election—by which we mean winning enough seats to form the government. In theory British elections are simply legislative elections; in practice we have come to regard them as executive elections.

The elision of these two possible purposes of an election in everyday discourse has happened because one party has won an overall majority of seats in the House of Commons at all elections bar one since 1931. Under these conditions, it has been immediately apparent which party leader could command the confidence of the House and thus should be invited by the sovereign to form the next government. The lease to 10 Downing Street has effectively been granted directly by the electorate rather than indirectly through its representatives in the Commons. Indeed, the direct connection between electoral victory and executive power has been given

TABLE 9.1. *Purposes of elections*

First-past-the-post view	Proportional view
Choosing a government	Electing a representative assembly
Electing competent persons	Expressing policy preferences
Accountability and retrospective judgement	Prospective choice

symbolic expression by the practice which has developed of defeated prime ministers driving to Buckingham Palace, returning their seals of office, and making way for the erstwhile Leader of the Opposition to take up office within twenty-four hours of the closure of the polls.

But, of course, the ability of general elections to perform this role has rested heavily on the operation of the electoral system. No single party has won a majority of the votes cast in any post-war election. That the 'winning' party has nevertheless almost invariably secured a majority in the House of Commons has been a consequence of the tendency of the single-member-plurality electoral system to exaggerate the lead of the largest party over the second party, while at the same time discriminating against (some at least) third parties.

Thus defenders of the existing electoral system argue that its continued use is essential to ensuring that the most crucial power that an electorate can have—the ability to decide the political colour of the next government—remains in its hands. The system may be unfair to smaller parties, but this is less important than maintaining popular control of the executive. Putting the power to make and unmake governments in the hands of the legislature, it is argued, is but a recipe for unsavoury backroom deals that often put disproportionate power in the hands of smaller parties.

In contrast, advocates of proportional representation argue that elections should indeed be what they formally are—legislative elections. They argue that the aim of a general election is the election of a body which is representative of all the main shades of popular opinion—in short, a political microcosm of the nation (McLean 1991). They are happy to leave the decision as to who should form the executive to this representative legislature precisely because it is a faithful microcosm of the nation as a whole.

From this major disagreement between the two camps, two further differences follow. Formally, elections are held to select persons to hold office rather than to determine what they should do when in office. But if, as advocates of proportional representation prefer, elections are designed to select a representative microcosm of the nation, then it is essential that voters should have some idea of the policy preferences of the candidates. In other words, advocates of proportional representation tend to emphasize the role of elections as a mechanism for the electorate to express their policy preferences. Indeed, it is often argued that proportional representation encourages parties to magnify the ideological distance between themselves (Duverger 1964). Those favouring the existing system, in contrast, are more sceptical of the extent to which the electorate has clear policy preferences or of the suitability of elections for their effective expression. Rather, all that elections can be expected to achieve is an opportunity for voters to choose between alternative government teams, basing their judgements upon their likely competence in office rather than their ideological differences.

This leads automatically to the final difference between the two camps. Supporters of the single-member-plurality system argue that the principal purpose of elections is to ensure that the government is *accountable* to the electorate for its actions in office. The best guide to the current government's likely future competence in office is its previous performance to date. Thus, if the government has done well, it will be re-elected; if it has done badly, the electorate will vote to replace it with an alternative government. From this it follows that elections are primarily an opportunity for the electorate to make *retrospective* evaluations of government (and perhaps opposition) performance. In contrast, with its emphasis upon elections as an opportunity for the expression of policy preferences, the proportional school tends to regard elections as occasions when the electorate makes *prospective* evaluations of the parties.

So, the debate about electoral reform is far more complex than would at first appear. It cannot simply be resolved by examining the technical or mathematical merits of individual systems. It is not simply a debate about whether one electoral system is 'fairer' than another. Rather, the two camps differ fundamentally in what they think elections can and should achieve—and in consequence disagree about the criteria by which the merits of electoral systems should be evaluated.

This reasoning suggests that there is little point in asking how disproportional the existing electoral system is or whether it enables the electorate to express policy preferences. For these are not the objectives of the system. Rather, we should ask how successful it is in achieving the aims and objectives its proponents have established for it. Is the case made for the retention of the single-member-plurality electoral system sound on its own terms? This is the question this chapter seeks to address.

THE INTELLECTUAL FOUNDATIONS OF
FIRST-PAST-THE-POST

As already indicated, the ability of the single-member-plurality system to allow the electorate to choose between alternative governments rests on two crucial claims:

1. It discriminates against (and discourages the formation of) third parties by giving them few if any seats in the House of Commons.
2. It gives the winning party an electoral bonus. The gap between the winning party and the second party in seats is an exaggerated reflection of the gap between them in votes.

Much of the intellectual foundation for this case was laid down in the immediate aftermath of the Second World War—with the work of David Butler being particularly crucial. By the beginning of the 1950s the validity of the first proposition appeared self-evident. The rise of the Labour party in the inter-war period had apparently reached its inevitable conclusion with the collapse of the Liberal party to 2½ per cent of the vote in 1951. International comparison also attested to the coincidence of first-past-the-post and two-party systems, an association which was summarized by Duverger in the first half of his famous law, 'the simple majority single-ballot system favours the two-party system' (1964: 205).

But the basis of the second crucial proposition was not so clear. However, at the 1950 election David Butler announced his rediscovery of the 'cube law' (Butler 1951; see also Butler 1963). According to the law, if the votes for the two largest parties were cast in the ratio $a : b$, then, under the first-past-the-post electoral system, Commons seats would be divided between them in the ratio $a^3 : b^3$. In practical terms this meant that, at results close to 50 : 50, a 1 per cent switch of votes was worth a 3 per cent gain in seats. Thus, a party winning 51 per cent of the votes cast for the two main parties would win as many as 53 per cent of the seats. With few if any seats won by third parties, this meant that all but the very narrowest of voting leads would be sufficient to deliver the winning party an overall majority in the House of Commons.

Butler rediscovered the law in reading the evidence given by James Parker Smith in evidence to the Royal Commission on Electoral Systems in 1909. He attempted to apply the formula to recent British general election results and found that it seemed to work. His rediscovery meant that it could now be claimed that there was a clear systematic relationship between votes and seats under the British electoral system, and that the system could be successfully defended against the charge that it was a 'gamble'.

Butler's work was given crucial underpinning by Kendall and Stuart (1950). They demonstrated that the conformity of the first-past-the-post electoral system to the cube law rested upon the geographical distribution of Conservative and Labour support. The law would work only if this support were distributed in such a way that there were sufficient marginal constituencies which would change hands as a consequence of small shifts in the national popularity of the two major parties. Put simply, if a switch from 50 per cent to 51 per cent of the vote was to result in 3 per cent of seats changing hands, then in 3 per cent of the constituencies the gap between the two largest parties had to be less than 2 per cent. More broadly, this meant that three in ten of all constituencies had to be marginals—that is constituencies where the lead of the winning party locally would be less than 10 per cent when the two major parties were equal in support nationally.[1]

Kendall and Stuart found that these conditions were broadly met at the 1950 election. Further, it appeared that this was no accident, for the distribution of Democratic and Republican support in the United States outside the South also had the required characteristics. The cube law appeared to be an inherent characteristic of the first-past-the-post system.

So the case for the single-member-plurality system appeared secure. There was but one slight doubt, which was the existence of a slight bias against the Labour party in the way the system operated. The problem appeared not to be one of constituency size (despite the fact that the way in which the English Boundary Commission operated in the 1954 redistribution entailed the systematic creation of smaller constituencies in rural than in urban areas) but rather the fact that Labour's vote was distributed less efficiently than the Conservatives'; Labour wasted more votes piling up large majorities in safe constituencies than did the Conservatives. Indeed, this was one of the factors (the lack of contests in some safe Conservative and Unionist seats in Northern Ireland being the other) which enabled the Conservatives to win an overall majority in 1951 despite being nearly 1 per cent behind Labour in the popular vote.

THE FOUNDATIONS CRUMBLE

But how far have these two essential characteristics of the British electoral system operated in recent elections? On the surface all would appear to be well. All but one election since 1951 (February 1974) has delivered an overall majority for the winning party. The challenge of the Liberal–SDP Alliance proved unable to overcome the barrier presented by the electoral system: 26 per cent of the vote in 1983 produced just twenty-three Commons seats. But a closer and more systematic analysis of the evidence reveals that in fact neither characteristic is in operation.

This is not primarily because of what most concerned David Butler in the 1950s—electoral bias against the Labour party. Labour does indeed still waste more votes than the Conservatives in piling up votes in safe constituencies, a feature of its support which means that it currently has to win between 0.5 and 1 per cent of the vote extra to win a given number of seats than it otherwise would. But this has not proved to be a permanent feature of its support—in both February 1974 and in 1979 Labour's vote was more efficiently distributed than the Conservatives', helping it in February 1974 to edge four seats ahead of the Conservatives, despite being 0.75 per cent behind in votes. And, in any case, its impact has to a considerable degree been reduced by the fact that, from the 1960s onwards, Labour-held constituencies have tended to be smaller than Conservative-held ones, as the pattern of migration has seen a consistent drift of population from the cities to the suburbs and the countryside.

The change since the 1950s has been much more fundamental than this. The electoral system has failed to exclude third parties from the House of Commons, while the allocation of seats to the Conservatives and the Labour party no longer conforms to a cube law. The most crucial lesson of Kendall's and Stuart's piece has proved to be that the operation of the first-past-the-post electoral system is contingent upon electoral geography. And the existing electoral geography of electoral support means that the system is no longer capable of delivering either of its essential attributes.

Let us consider first of all the ability of the system to discriminate against third parties. When Duverger formulated his law, as many as five parties were represented in the House of Commons. But after the 1987 election there were eleven.[2] What is often not appreciated is that this meant that the British House of Commons contained representatives from more political parties than the majority of democratic legislatures in Western Europe, North America, and Australasia, including the majority of countries that elect their legislature by some form of proportional representation. Only Belgium, Israel, Italy, and Spain have more. Even the Dutch Tweede Kamer, elected by a national proportional system which guarantees a party a seat if it can win just 0.66 per cent of the vote, contains only nine political parties.

The ability of the single-member-plurality system to discriminate against third parties is wholly contingent upon the electoral geography of their support. The system does discriminate against parties whose support is geographically evenly spread—but does not discriminate against those third parties whose support is geographically concentrated. Two developments since the 1950s have brought about the rise of third parties whose support is geographically concentrated. One has been the divorce between the Northern Irish party system and the British party system (and within Northern Ireland the Unionist camp has demonstrated how an electoral pact can overcome the disincentives of first past the post against factionalism). In 1987 Northern Ireland (whose representation was increased from twelve to seventeen in 1979) supplied MPs from five different parties. The second development has been the growth of the Nationalist parties in Scotland and Wales, with

TABLE 9.2. *Seats and votes for third parties, 1987*

Parties	Seats	Seats (%)	Vote (%)
Liberal–SDP	22	3.4	22.6
Scottish National party	3	0.5	1.3
Plaid Cymru	3	0.5	0.4
Unionists	13	2.0	1.2
Republicans	4	0.6	0.7

Plaid Cymru's support also becoming significantly geographically concentrated in the Welsh-speaking part of north-west Wales.

Thus, as Table 9.2 shows, the electoral system now fails to discriminate against most third parties in the United Kingdom. Collectively, the three Unionist parties were actually overrepresented in the House of Commons in 1987, as also was Plaid Cymru. The only third parties who were disadvantaged by the electoral system in 1987 were the Scottish National party—whose support within Scotland is relatively evenly spread—and, most spectacularly, the Liberal–SDP Alliance.

What, of course, distinguished the former Liberal–SDP Alliance from all of the other political parties is that it alone fought elections in more than one of the component nations of the United Kingdom. The key to the failure of the single-member-plurality system to discriminate systematically against third parties appears then to lie in the fact that the United Kingdom is a multinational state. In such a state the potential for nationalist parties to gather support is always likely to be present. And support for such parties is always likely to be geographically concentrated. Thus, in such a state the single-member-plurality electoral system is likely to prove particularly ineffective as a barrier to the representation of third or small parties in the legislature. In contrast, some forms of proportional representation would actually be more effective; for example, a national-party-list system with a 2 per cent minimum threshold would have given representation in the Commons in 1987 to just four parties.[3]

What, then, of the second foundation of the single-member-plurality system, the cube law? A little simple mathematics can demonstrate that it did not operate in 1987. The Conservative party won 57.8 per cent of the votes cast for Conservative and

Labour combined. According to the cube law this should have secured it 72 per cent of the 605 seats won by either Conservative or Labour, that is, 435 seats. Its actual tally was 376 seats, or just 62 per cent of the total. The winner's bonus—4 per cent—was hardly greater than might occur under some proportional representation systems.

And this result is no freak. The exaggerative ability of the electoral system has been well below that which would be predicted by the cube law since the general election of February 1974. The cause has been a significant change in the electoral geography of Conservative and Labour support.

As indicated earlier, if the cube law is to operate, nearly one-third of all constituencies have to be marginal between Conservative and Labour. This implies that both parties' support is not unduly geographically concentrated. If their support were to become highly geographically concentrated, then, at the extreme, all constituencies would be either safe Conservative or safe Labour seats—and few if any constituencies would change hands as a consequence of a 1 per cent shift of votes at results close to national equality of support.

Yet, as has been widely demonstrated elsewhere (see, for example, Curtice and Steed 1986 and 1988), this is precisely what has happened. Since the mid-1950s support for the Conservative party has become increasingly concentrated in the south of England and the Midlands, while Labour has prospered in Scotland and the north of England and retained its former strength in Wales. At the same time, Labour's support has become concentrated in inner city and urban constituencies, the Conservatives' in rural and suburban ones. As a consequence, more and more constituencies have become either safe Conservative or safe Labour seats; the number of marginal constituencies has fallen to half what it was in the 1950s.

This is shown in Table 9.3, which shows the number of Conservative/Labour marginal seats at each election since 1955. In addition it also uses the standard-deviation statistic to measure the extent to which the Conservative and Labour ('two-party') vote is geographically concentrated—the larger the figure the more concentrated it is. The figures confirm Kendall's and Stuart's conclusion that in the 1950s the requirements of the cube law were largely met. The proportion of constituencies which were marginal

TABLE 9.3. *Marginal seats, 1955–1987*

Election	Marginal seats		Standard deviation of two-party vote
	No.	%	
1955	166	27.2	13.5
1959	157	25.7	13.8
1964	166	27.3	14.1
1966	155	25.6	13.8
1970	149	24.5	14.3
1974 (Feb.)	119	19.9	16.1
1974 (Oct.)	98	16.4	16.8
1979	108	17.8	16.9
1983	80	13.2	20.0
1987	87	14.4	21.4

was only just under the magic figure of 30 per cent. Now, with Conservative and Labour support much more geographically concentrated, the proportion has fallen to less than 15 per cent. If it is borne in mind that, if the proportion were to fall to 10 per cent, the electoral system would treat Conservative and Labour proportionately, we can see why the winner's bonus in 1987 was so low. The electoral system has all but lost its ability to exaggerate the lead of the largest party over the second party.

The ability of the single-member-plurality electoral system to facilitate choice between alternative governments has then come under pressure from two directions at once. On the one hand, the number of third-party MPs has risen—from eight in 1955 and seven in 1959 to forty-five in 1987. Thus, even if nothing else had changed, the electoral system would have had to have *increased* its ability to exaggerate the lead of the winning party over the second party simply to retain its ability to deliver an overall majority for the largest party in the event of a narrow result. But, in practice, the very opposite has happened. The probability of parliaments being elected in which no party has an overall majority—thereby endangering the direct link between the tenure of 10 Downing Street and electoral success—has increased considerably.

This can be seen if we simulate what the outcome in seats would be if we assume the geographical distribution of each party's electoral support were to be the same as it was in 1987, but then allow the overall popularity of the parties to vary. We can calculate for each possible outcome in votes the number of seats that each party would win in the House of Commons—and identify the lead in votes required by Conservative and Labour to win an overall majority of seats. First of all, we can examine what would happen if the Liberal Democrats were as popular as the Liberal–SDP Alliance was in 1987. On this assumption, the Conservatives need a lead of just under and Labour a lead of just over 4 per cent to secure an overall majority.[4] Even if we assume a lower level of Liberal Democrat support—say 15 per cent—these figures are little altered. Labour still requires a 4 per cent lead, although the Conservative target falls to 2 per cent. But that latter figure is highly dependent on the Conservatives' ability to make gains in seats from the Liberal Democrats' whose fortunes in the seats they are defending often fails to follow the national trend—without these gains the Conservative target again rises to 3 per cent. In short, the electoral system can no longer be expected to deliver an overall majority for either the Conservatives or Labour if their lead is at all narrow.

REASONS FOR CONTINUITY

The lesson of the last thirty years appears then to be that the ability of the first-past-the-post electoral system to deliver its proponents' objectives depends upon the electoral geography of electoral support. And, while the electoral geography of the 1950s did enable the system to facilitate electoral choice between alternative governments, the geography of the 1980s did not. Neither Duverger's law nor the cube law is a law at all—rather they are both accidents of geography.

Yet hung parliaments have not been a common feature of the last twenty years. True, no party had an overall majority in the brief parliament of February–October 1974 and the slim majority Labour did secure in October 1974 disappeared in 1976. But the Conservatives won the three elections between 1979 and 1987 with clear majorities. Does this not suggest that our analysis to date is irrelevant?

The explanation lies in the size of the Conservative victories. The Conservative lead over Labour ranged from 7 per cent in 1979 to

15 per cent in 1983. The Conservatives' success in these elections was not so much a reflection of the exaggerative power of the electoral system as a decline in the apparent competitiveness of the Labour party. Only at one other election between 1950 and October 1974—in 1966, when Labour secured a 7 per cent lead—did the lead of the winning party over the second party approach this scale.

The 1979–87 results thus do not provide any support for the position of the first-past-the-post camp. For these were elections when one of the major suppositions of the theory of elections as a choice between alternative governments—the existence of two close competitors for office—broke down. If the opposition party proves unable to make a credible challenge for power, the accountability of the government for its actions in office is, if anything, hindered rather than stimulated by the single-member-plurality system. What the system does is to guarantee the government party a hold on office, creating a 'dominant' rather than a competitive party system.[5]

Further, the unusual results of the 1983 and 1987 elections, at least when compared to previous post-war British experience, raise further difficulties for the case for the existing electoral system. It is debatable how far the system can still be defended on the grounds that it facilitates choice between alternative governments, when over a quarter of the electorate votes for other than the two main parties. Their votes do not have any opportunity to influence the political colour of the executive. The claim that the electoral system permits the electorate to choose inherently between alternative governments has a limited validity when that system does not contain any mechanism for ascertaining which of the two main contenders for power is the more popular amongst the whole electorate (for further discussion of this point, see Plant 1991).

Further, we might reasonably assume that, if the aim of the single-member-plurality system is to permit choice between alternative governments and to discriminate against third parties, then it would continue to exhibit these characteristics should a third party succeed in becoming a second party. That is, that it will always ensure that the party which is second in votes is also the second party in seats. Yet it is clear that the discrimination that the electoral system did operate against the Liberal–SDP Alliance in the 1980s would not have disappeared should it have succeeded—

rather than failing as it did by two percentage points—in overhauling the Labour party in 1983. If its support had been three points higher in the 1983 vote in all constituencies, and support for both Labour and the Conservatives one and half points lower—a switch sufficient to have put the Alliance two points ahead of Labour— the Alliance would have won just thirty-four seats, while Labour would have secured 206 seats. Indeed, on the 1983 electoral geography, the Alliance could have been first in votes yet still third in seats (Curtice and Steed 1984). The threshold that parties whose votes are geographically evenly concentrated have to pass before they are no longer discriminated against is in fact much higher than simply coming second.[6] Yet nothing in the intellectual foundations of the system would appear to justify this characteristic of its working.

A CODA: REPRESENTATION OF CONSTITUENCIES

It might seem, then, that we are ready to reach a clear conclusion— that the electoral system which we have come to regard as a fixture of our political system has lost its intellectual foundations. But there is one further argument that we have to consider before we can do so.

So far we have concentrated on the way in which the British electoral system produces aggregate outcomes of seats across the country as a whole. But defenders of the existing electoral system also make another argument in its favour. This is that the use of single-member constituencies ensures that all MPs are accountable to a clearly defined body of electors—their constituents. It is argued that this encourages them to foster the interests of their constituency by making themselves available to assist individual constituents with problems they may have with one or other department of government and by representing the interests of their constituency in Parliament. Thus, for example, Hain (1986) argues in his attack on proportional representation that 'Vital links between local communities and their elected MPs . . . would be undermined by both List and STV [single-transferable-vote] systems. The whole principle of democratic accountability would be weakened . . .' Here would appear to be an argument which our analysis so far has not challenged.

In practice, the argument contains three separate propositions, and it is worth examining each in turn. The first is that the single-member-constituency plurality system encourages members to provide services to constituents. Yet it is clear from comparative evidence that a high level of constituency service is not unique to those countries with single-member-plurality systems. One of the clearest examples is the Republic of Ireland, where elections are held using the single transferable vote in multi-member constituencies of between three and five members each. Under this system, candidates of the same party have to compete against each other as well as those of the Opposition to secure election—and one of the ways in which they can do so is in the provision of constituency service. Indeed 'choosing a candidate to look after the needs of the constituency' consistently emerges as the single most popular reason Irish voters give for the way that they vote (Farrell 1985: 247).

The second proposition entailed in the argument is that the electoral system encourages the representation of communities in Parliament. This argument draws upon a rich vein of British political culture. Before the nineteenth century, parliamentary constituencies were clear territorially defined historic communities of interest—that is boroughs or counties—which were defined with little or no reference to the size of their population. But in practice the maintenance of this tradition has been undermined since 1885 by demands for equality of representation. Although the Boundary Commissions tolerate a much wider variation in constituency size than would be considered acceptable in the United States, and indeed take into account arguments about which wards do or do not have a community of interest when drawing up their proposals, the principle of equal constituency size has come increasingly to supersede the principle of community of interest in the districting process (Steed 1985). In the most recent boundary review 83 per cent of constituencies were subject to more than a minor change, and outside London and some of the metropolitan counties local authority boundaries were regularly crossed. With the Boundary Commissions required to undertake a review of parliamentary constituencies once every ten to fifteen years, the 'vital link' between an MP and his constituents can in practice prove to be little more than a short-term lease.

Indeed a single-member electoral system is a particularly inappropriate system to use if one wishes to ensure both that constituencies should embody distinct communities and that the ratio of MPs to electors is approximately equal across constituencies. Under a single-member electoral system equality of representation can be achieved only by ensuring equality of constituency size—with an inevitable disruption to constituency boundaries if there are substantial population movements. A multi-member system, in contrast, makes it easier to draw and maintain constituency boundaries which coincide with distinct communities. Larger communities can simply be granted more MPs than smaller ones. And, if a constituency loses population, then equality of representation can be maintained by reducing the number of MPs it elects instead of redrawing its boundaries.

The last of the three propositions is that the single-member constituency ensures that MPs are accountable to a clearly defined body of voters. But, although there is some evidence that good constituency service can deliver MPs in marginal constituencies a vital personal vote (Curtice and Steed 1980; Cain *et al.* 1987), in practice most voters in the United Kingdom vote for the party rather than a candidate—and, as we have seen, do so increasingly in safe constituencies. Thus few MPs win or lose election because of their personal popularity. In practice, MPs are much more likely to be accountable to the electorate on the basis of their personal rather than their party's popularity in those countries which permit preferential voting in multi-member constituencies. For example, in the three Irish elections held in 1981–2, fifty-nine sitting deputies lost their seats—the equivalent of over one-third of the Dail— while a further twenty-six failed to defend their seats for a variety of reasons (Farrell 1985). More generally, in a review of the evidence of the impact of preferential voting systems, Marsh concludes that 'the security of incumbents is almost certainly less where preference voting is significant . . .' (1985: 376).

Thus even here it is by no means clear that the single-member-plurality electoral system is particularly effective at achieving the aims that have been set out for it. But, even if this were not the case, there would still be a problem. For there is an inherent contradiction between defending the electoral system on the grounds that it encourages a choice between alternative governments and the claim that it encourages MPs to be responsive to the interests of their constituents. For, in as much as the system succeeds in achieving the latter objective, it will be less successful at achieving the former. As Cain *et al* argue:

For single member simple plurality systems the problem is to achieve coherent national policy when individual members have little incentive to subordinate their personal activities to a larger end. These systems can fall prey to legislative parochialism. Single-member simple plurality systems can achieve the collective good of coherent policy only by reining in the natural inclinations of members through party control of legislative careers, minimal levels of member resources, and party domination of the policy agenda. These are important components of the modern British solution to the collective action problem. (1987: 227)

In short, British governments are only able to govern without undue restraint from Parliament and have clear responsibility for the successes and failures of public policy during their period of office because there are severe limitations upon the ability of British MPs to represent the interests of their constituents!

CONCLUSION

This chapter has demonstrated that the foundations of the intellectual case in favour of the use of the single-member-plurality electoral system have been seriously undermined since the 1950s. The claim that the system facilitates choice between alternative governments, thereby ensuring that the government is clearly accountable to the electorate, has been shown to be contingent upon the electoral geography of party support. And it has been demonstrated that the current geography of party support means that the electoral system has lost much of its ability to achieve its proponents' aims. Meanwhile it has been argued that the first-past-the-post system is not a particularly effective or unique means of ensuring that MPs are accountable to the electorate or represent communities of interest.

Meanwhile, the existing electoral system is actually more likely to bring about what its advocates consider to be some of the disadvantages of proportional representation. As noted earlier, it is argued that, by making it unlikely that any party will have an overall majority, proportional representation places disproportionate power in the hands of small parties in the process of government formation. Yet this is more likely to occur in the United Kingdom under the existing electoral system than under proportional representation.

For, as we have seen, the system has discriminated against the largest of the third parties, the Liberal–SDP Alliance, but has not discriminated against far smaller parties whose support is geographically concentrated. Thus, although quite a wide range of election outcomes would produce a parliament in which no party had an overall majority, in many cases this would not necessarily mean that the Liberal Democrats would hold the balance of power—that is be able to pass the 326 mark in tandem with either Labour or the Conservatives. The bargaining power of the far smaller Northern Irish Unionists, for example—or even of the Scottish and Welsh Nationalists—might be just as substantial.

Consider, for example, what might happen if both the Conservatives and Labour were to win 41 per cent of the vote while the Liberal Democrats secured 15 per cent. If the electoral geography of each party's vote remained as it was in 1987, this would give the Conservatives 313 seats, Labour 303, and the Liberal Democrats 11. The Liberal Democrats' total would not produce an overall majority in combination with either the Conservatives or Labour. Any government formed from such a legislature would require at least the tacit support of one party other than the Liberal Democrats—and indeed might well be able to survive without their support at all.[7]

None of this is to argue that the objectives of the advocates of the first-past-the-post system are invalid. Rather, what this chapter has demonstrated is that, in the context of the modern electoral geography of the United Kingdom, the single-member-plurality system is an inappropriate mechanism to achieve those objectives. If advocates of the existing system wish to ensure that British parliamentary elections continue to enable the electorate to choose between alternative governments, then they should no longer put their faith in the existing electoral system but rather come forward with proposals for an electoral system that would systematically exaggerate the lead of the largest party and discriminate against third parties, *irrespective of the electoral geography of their support*. At the same time the individual accountability of MPs to the electorate might well be improved by a switch to some form of preferential voting in multi-member constituencies. It would be perfectly possible to devise such an electoral system—as the experience of Greece before 1989 illustrates. That no such proposals have been forthcoming means that the intellectual scales in the electoral reform debate are currently heavily weighted in favour of the advocates of proportional representation.

Notes

1. More formally, Kendall and Stuart demonstrated that the frequency distribution of Conservative and Labour support across constituencies needed to approximate a normal distribution with a standard deviation of 13.7.
2. These were Conservative, Labour, Liberal, Social Democrat, Scottish Nationalist, Plaid Cymru, Official Unionist, Democratic Unionist, Popular Unionist, Social and Democratic Labour party, and Sinn Fein.
3. That is Conservative, Labour, Liberal, and Social Democrat.
4. The difference is a reflection of the electoral bias operating against Labour in 1987. All the calculations in this paragraph take into account the creation of a new (Conservative) constituency in Milton Keynes in 1992.
5. We should note also that the experience of the 1980s has also undermined the claim that the electoral system could be defended on the grounds that the time spent in office by Conservative and Labour since 1945 was proportionate to the vote that they had won over that period (see Taylor 1984). Labour won 48.7% of the votes cast between 1945 and 1987, but held office for only 37% of the period between 1945 and 1992. In any case, Taylor's own work has demonstrated that the single-member-plurality system has not produced 'proportional tenure' in any other country in which it operates (Taylor and Lijphart 1985).
6. We may note also that in October 1974 the Scottish National party remained the third party in Scotland in seats, although it overhauled the Conservatives by more than 5% in votes.
7. This, of course, is precisely what a minority Labour administration succeeded in doing between the autumn of 1978 and March 1979, following the conclusion of the Lib.–Lab. pact. That government only fell when the nationalist parties withdrew their support in the wake of the defeat of the devolution proposals in the Scottish and Welsh referendums.

References

Butler, D. (1951), 'An Examination of the Results', in H. G. Nicholas, *The British General Election of 1950* (London: Macmillan), 306–39.

—— (1963), *The Electoral System in Britain since 1918* (2nd edn., Oxford: Clarendon Press).

Cain, B., Ferejohn, J., and Fiorina, M. (1987), *The Personal Vote* (Cambridge, Mass. : Harvard University Press).

Curtice, J., and Steed, M. (1980), 'An Analysis of the Voting', in D. Butler and D. Kavanagh, *The British General Election of 1979* (London: Macmillan), 390–431.

—— (1984), 'Analysis', in D. Butler and D. Kavanagh, *The British General Election of 1983* (London: Macmillan), 333–73.

—— (1986), 'Proportionality and Exaggeration in the British Electoral System', *Electoral Studies*, 5: 209–28.

—— (1988), 'Analysis', in D. Butler and D. Kavanagh, *The British General Election of 1987* (London: Macmillan), 316–62).

Duverger, M. (1964), *Political Parties* (3rd edn., London: Methuen).

Farrell, B. (1985), 'Ireland: From Friends and Neighbours to Clients and Partisans', in V. Bogdanor (ed.), *Representatives of the People?* (Aldershot: Gower), 231–64.

Hain, P. (1986), *Proportional Misrepresentation* (London: Wildwood House).

Kendall, M. and Stuart, A. (1950), 'The Law of Cubic Proportions in Britain', *British Journal of Sociology*, 1: 183–96.

McLean, I. (1991), 'Forms of Representation and Systems of Voting', in D. Held (ed.), *Political Theory Today* (Cambridge: Polity Press).

Marsh, M. (1985), 'The Voters Decide?: Preferential Voting in European List Systems', *European Journal of Political Research*, 13: 365–78.

Plant, R. (1991), *The Plant Report: A Working Party on Electoral Reform* (London: *Guardian*).

Schumpeter, J. (1976), *Capitalism, Socialism and Democracy* (4th edn., London: Allen & Unwin).

Steed, M. (1985), 'The Constituency', in V. Bogdanor (ed.), *Representatives of the People?* (Aldershot: Gower), 267–85.

Taylor, P. (1984), 'The Case for Proportional Tenure: A Defense of the British Electoral System', in A. Lijphart and B. Grofman (eds.), *Choosing an Electoral System: Issues and Alternatives* (New York: Praeger).

—— and Lijphart, A. (1985), 'Proportional Tenure *vs* Proportional Representation: Introducing a New Debate', *European Journal of Political Research*, 13: 387–99.

10

Divided Party Control in the United States

AUSTIN RANNEY

Recent elections in the United States have continued a condition that is impossible in most democratic systems and rare in a few others, but seems to have become normal in America: namely, divided party control—a situation in which the President belongs to one party and the majority in one or both Houses of Congress belongs to the other party.[1]

Divided party control is possible only in those systems which directly elect both executives and legislators, with the voters casting separate votes for each. This makes it possible for voters to split their ballots between or among parties in voting for the two kinds of officials. Other systems in which this is possible are France under the Fifth Republic, Finland, and most Latin American nations (especially relevant for present purposes are those, such as Argentina, Brazil, Colombia, Costa Rica, Ecuador, and Venezuela, that now hold reasonably free elections).[2] If they maintain the courses on which they are now embarked, many republics of the former Soviet Union are likely to join the list (Lijphart 1984; Sartori 1987).[3]

Divided party control is rare but not unknown in presidential democracies other than the United States. The best-known instance in recent years was probably the period of 'co-habitation' in France from 1986 to 1988, when Socialist President François Mitterrand co-existed with a National Assembly controlled by the conservative Rassemblement pour la République party led by Prime Minister Jacques Chirac. The Latin American presidential systems provide a few other instances. For example, from 1969 to 1974, and again from 1979 to 1984, Venezuela's presidents were members of the Social Christian (COPEI) party, while the Congresses were controlled by the Accion Democratica (AD) party. From 1982 to 1986 Colombia's President was Conservative Beli-

TABLE 10.1. *Periods of unified and divided party control in the United States, 1832–1990*

Years	Total number of elections*	Type of control produced		
		Unified control	Divided control	Per cent divided
1832–40	5	5	0	0
1842–58	9	3	6	67
1860–72	7	7	0	0
1874–94	11	3	8	73
1896–1944	25	22	3	12
1946–90	23	9	14	61
TOTAL	80	49	31	39

Note:
   * Includes both presidential and mid-term elections, since each type can produce either unified or divided party control.

Sources: 1832–1970: Bureau of the Census (1975: pt. 2, p. 1083); 1972–1989: Bureau of the Census (1988: 242, Table 404); 1990: *Congressional Quarterly*.

sario Betancur Cuartas, while both Houses of Congress were controlled by the Liberal party. In Guatemala in 1991 the voters elected Jorge Serrano Elias of the Solidarity Action Movement (MAS) party as President, but gave control of the Congress to the National Centrist Union (UCN) party. However, such episodes have been so frequent at both the national and state levels in the United States and so brief and scattered elsewhere that we can say it is a largely US phenomenon.

THE INCIDENCE OF DIVIDED PARTY CONTROL

In the National Government

Table 10.1 shows the main periods of unified and divided party control in the national government of the United States since popular election of the President was fully established in 1832. As Table 10.1 indicates, from 1832 to 1990 there was a total of eighty national elections. Forty of them were held in 'presidential years', in which the President, all the members of the House of Representatives, and one-third of the members of the Senate were elected.[4]

The other forty were 'mid-term elections', in which there was no presidential election and all the members of the House and one-third of the members of the Senate were elected. Thus, from 1832 to 1990 US voters had eighty opportunities to give control of both the Presidency and the Congress to one party or to divide control of the two branches between the two major parties. As Table 10.1 shows, some periods had mainly unified control, while others had mainly divided control. What were the main characteristics of the latter?

The first period of divided control (1842–58) was marked by deep divisions over the issues of slavery and secession that ultimately led to the Civil War (1861–5). Not surprisingly, it featured great turmoil in the party system, as manifested by the dissolution of the Whig party and the emergence of several new parties (the Free Soil party, the American or 'Know-Nothing' party, and the Republican party). The second period of divided control (1874–94) featured the closest two-party competition in history for control of both the Presidency and Congress, and it was also the heyday of third parties, with the Greenbackers, the Grangers, and the Populists each winning a number of seats in Congress as well as controlling some state legislatures and governorships.

However, Table 10.1 shows that the most recent period has seen the greatest incidence of divided party control in US history. It began in 1946, and, with two short breaks (1948–54 and 1976–80), has persisted through the mid-term election of 1990. Most observers expect it to continue through the election of 1992 and beyond, probably well into the twenty-first century.

As Morris Fiorina points out, the current period differs from the two earlier periods in at least one major respect. In the nineteenth century, divided control was almost always the result of the loss of congressional seats incurred by the party holding the White House in the mid-term elections following the elections in which the presidential party had won control of both branches. Between 1832 and 1952 only three of the eighteen elections that resulted in divided control occurred in presidential years, and each resulted from unusual circumstances: the three-way presidential race of 1848, the disputed election of 1876, and the extremely narrow Democratic victory of 1884. Fiorina concludes: 'Before Eisenhower's re-election in 1956, winners of two-way presidential races had *always* carried the House, and only in 1884 had one failed to carry the Senate' (Fiorina 1992:12; emphasis in the original).

In the modern period, however, winning the Presidency has been no guarantee that a party would also win control of Congress. For instance, in 1956 Republican President Dwight Eisenhower won re-election by a large margin, but the Democrats retained control of both Houses of Congress. In 1968 Republican Richard Nixon narrowly won the Presidency, but the Democrats continued to control Congress. In 1972 Nixon was re-elected by a landslide, but the Democrats still controlled the Congress. In 1980 Republican Ronald Reagan won the Presidency from incumbent Democrat Jimmy Carter, and the Republicans also won control of the Senate for the first time since 1954. Even so, the Democrats held on to the House in 1980, 1982, and 1984, when Reagan was winning re-election with another landslide. Then the Democrats regained control of the Senate in the mid-term election of 1986, and in 1988 Republican George Bush was elected President while the Democrats retained control of Congress, as they did in the mid-term election of 1990.

At the time of writing, most observers are convinced that divided party control, featuring Republican presidents and Democratic congresses, has become a semi-permanent feature of the US political landscape, likely to last well into the twenty-first century, and not a passing aberration resulting from unusual or short-term circumstances.

In the Congressional Districts

The proximate cause of divided party control is the fact that a number of congressional districts and states are carried by one party for the Presidency and the other party for Representative or Senator. In the mid-1960s Milton Cummings, jun., pioneered scholarly research on divided party control. He surveyed the district-by-district results of presidential and House elections from 1920 to 1964, and found that the proportion of split districts had risen steadily from 3 per cent in 1920 to 33 per cent in 1964, with the sharpest increase coming in the Eisenhower election of 1956 (Cummings 1966: 10, Table 1.1). His data for the period 1972–88 have been updated, and the results are shown by region in Table 10.2.

TABLE 10.2   *Straight and split districts by regions, 1972–1988 (%)*

	East	South	Border	Mid-west	Mountain	Pacific
Dem. Pres, Dem. House	31	23	29	23	6	28
Dem. Pres, Rep. House	3	3	5	2	0	3
Rep. Pres, Dem. House	29	44	43	29	34	32
Rep. Pres, Rep. House	36	29	21	46	60	35
Other	1	1	2	0	0	2
	100	100	100	100	100	100

Sources: 1972: Barone, Ujifusa, and Matthews (1972); 1976: Barone, Ujifusa, and Matthews (1977); 1980: Barone and Ujifusa (1981); 1984: Barone and Ujifusa (1985); 1988: Duncan (1989); 1990: *Congressional Quarterly*

The data in Table 10.2 show that the number of split districts since 1972 has stayed at the high level Cummings observed in the 1960s. The two middle rows of the table show, as we would expect, that most of the split decisions have chosen Republican presidents and Democratic representatives rather than Democratic presidents and Republican representatives, and that the highest incidence of split districts has occurred in the southern and border states. It is worth noting in passing, however, that a few districts have consistently gone the other way. One notable example of these mavericks was the First District of Massachusetts, which was repeatedly won by liberal Republican Silvio Conte (on one occasion the defeated Democratic candidate was the eminent political scientist James MacGregor Burns), despite the fact that Democratic presidential candidates just as repeatedly carried the district. Other well-known examples have been New York's Fifteenth ('Silk Stocking') District, held for many years by Republican William Green while Democratic presidential candidates were carrying the district; and Rhode Island's Second District, held by Republican Claudine Schneider throughout the 1980s despite Democratic presidential victories in the district in 1980, 1984, and 1988 (she left the seat for an unsuccessful Senate race in 1990).

TABLE 10.3. *Two-year periods of united and divided party control in the US states, 1946–1988*

Type	All states		Non-southern states		Southern states	
	No.	%	No.	%	No.	%
Unified control	610	58.0	396	49.1	214	87.0
Divided control	420	40.0	389	48.3	31	12.6
Other*	22	2.0	21	2.6	1	0.4
TOTALS	1,052	100	806	100	246	100

Notes: Excludes states with non-partisan legislatures: Nebraska throughout, and Minnesota, 1959–1970.

  * Governor and one House controlled by one party; other House even.

Sources: for governors and legislatures, 1954–88: Bureau of the Census (1992); for legislatures, 1946–63: Council of State Governments (1948–90); for governors, 1946–62: Scammon (1948–64).

In the States

Divided party control is as common in the state governments as in the national government, as is shown by the data in Table 10.3. This table shows that the states, like the national government, have had divided party control about 40 per cent of the time since 1972, and in the states outside the South they have had it almost half the time. The table also displays the recent sharp decline of Democratic dominance of gubernatorial elections in the southern states: from 1946 to 1964, the Democrats consistently controlled the governorships and huge majorities in both houses of the legislatures in all eleven southern states.[5] The first breakthrough for the Republicans came in 1966, when Arkansas and Georgia elected Republican governors. Since then divided party control has become more and more common in the South. In both 1986 and 1988 only six southern states had unified party control, while five (Alabama, Florida, North Carolina, South Carolina, and Texas) had Republican governors and Democratic legislatures (see Petrocik 1987).

The Exception or the Rule?

The increasing frequency of divided party control at both the national and state levels has caught the attention of a number of

US political analysts in recent years. Some believe and/or hope that it is only a temporary lapse, which will be corrected when the Democratic presidential party returns to its senses and once again nominates appealing candidates (only a handful of Republican partisans suggest that unified party control will return as the result of new Republican dominance of the Congress). Others believe that there has been a sea-change in the US system, and that divided party control has become the rule, not the exception. However that may be, an increasing number of scholars of both persuasions are trying to explain the causes of divided party control and identify its consequences for the capacity of the national and state governments to deal effectively with the problems they face. I turn next to some of the leading explanations that have been offered.

CAUSES OF DIVIDED PARTY CONTROL

Structural Causes of Split Districts

Gerrymandering. Some analysts—especially those associated with the Republican party—suggest that divided party control is mainly the result of 'gerrymandering'.[6] They contend that the Democrats have been able to retain control of the House of Representatives ever since 1954, despite the Republicans' dominance of presidential elections, mainly because they have used their control of state governments to gerrymander congressional district boundaries so as to translate the number of Democratic voters into the maximum number of districts winnable by Democratic candidates.

However, most political scientists find convincing the argument of Gary C. Jacobson, the leading scholar of US congressional elections, that gerrymandering does not account for the Democrats' success in House elections. His multi-variate analysis of a number of possible structural explanations for the Democratic dominance of House elections concludes that

in reality . . . Republican difficulties have little to do with gerrymandering. . . . When the previous Democratic vote in the district, the national swing, and incumbency status are taken into account, whether or not district lines were redrawn had no substantively or statistically significant effect on the outcome' (Jacobson 1990: 98–9)

Incumbency. Some analysts contend that continued Democratic control of the House, despite the Republicans' superiority in presidential elections, is simply the result of the incumbency advantage. They point to the fact that since 1950 an average of 92.6 per cent of the incumbent members of the House of Representatives running for re-election have been successful (Ornstein, Mann, and Malbin 1990: 56, Table 2–7).[7] They conclude that, since the Democrats begin with substantially more incumbents than the Republicans, and since over 90 per cent of all incumbents are re-elected, the perpetuation of Democratic control is inevitable.

But *why* are so many House incumbents re-elected? The answers usually given are these. Most state legislatures are controlled by the Democrats, and they draw congressional district lines to protect Democratic incumbents. Incumbents perform many services for their constituents and make sure their benefactions are well publicized, and are thus much better known than their challengers. Incumbents have many campaigning advantages over their challengers. They get the nearly free use of expensive radio- and television-producing facilities maintained by the House. Their mail to their constituents is postage-free. To cap it all, even though challengers can hope to overcome the incumbents' advantages by mounting much more vigorous, and therefore more expensive, campaigns, incumbents almost always raise much more campaign money than their challengers because even business political action committees want to contribute to winners, not losers, and would much rather have access to Democratic incumbents than the moral satisfaction of supporting ideologically sympathetic but losing Republican challengers.

Jacobson, however, rejects the incumbency explanation. If Democratic incumbents win solely or mainly because they are incumbents, he argues, then Republican candidates in open seats—that is, in districts in which neither candidate is an incumbent—ought to do substantially better than Republican challengers of Democratic incumbents. But they do not. Jacobson's study of House elections since 1946 shows that Democrats have won significantly more of even the open seats than Republicans. Moreover, victories by Republican presidential candidates and Democratic House candidates are almost as common in the open seats as in the seats with Democratic incumbents. Why? Fundamentally, Jacobson says, because the Democrats usually put up better candi-

TABLE 10.4. *Straight- and split-ticket voters, 1968–1988* (%)

Year	Dem. Pres. Dem. House (DD)	Dem. Pres. Rep. House (DR)	Rep. Pres. Dem. House (RD)	Rep. Pres. Rep. House (RR)	Total splitters
1968	42	7	10	41	17
1972	30	5	25	40	30
1976	41	9	16	34	25
1980	34	8	20	38	28
1984	36	5	20	39	25
1988	41	7	18	34	25

Source: National Election Studies data.

dates, especially in that many more of their non-incumbent candidates than the Republicans' have had extensive previous experience
in state and local government, and that is a great asset for
congressional candidates (Jacobson 1990: ch. 3). He concludes
that neither gerrymandering nor incumbency explains the Democrats' continuing dominance of the House, and suggests looking at
the voters' attitudes for better explanations of divided party
control.

Attitudinal Sources of Ticket-Splitting

Patterns of ticket-splitting. A second category of explanations
suggests that divided party control is mainly the product of
attitudes of many US voters, inclining them to split their tickets.
To investigate such explanations, I extracted from the National
Election Studies (NES)[8] all the respondents in the presidential-year
studies from 1952 to 1988 who reported voting for the presidential
candidate of one party and a House candidate of the other party.
The distribution of straight-ticket and split-ticket voters are displayed in Table 10.4. This table shows that a sharp increase in
ticket-splitting took place in 1972, when it jumped from 17 per
cent to 30 per cent, mainly because a large number of voters voted
for Nixon (or against McGovern) but also for Democratic candidates for the House. In subsequent elections the proportion of
ticket-splitters has hovered around 25 per cent, and, as we would
expect, the number who have voted for Republican presidential

TABLE 10.5.   *Ticket-splitting and party identification, 1952–1988* (%)

Voting pattern	Strong Dem.	Weak Dem.	Indep. Dem.	Indep.	Indep. Rep.	Weak Rep.	Strong Rep.
Dem. Pres. Dem. Rep.	83	59	61	27	7	8	2
Dem. Pres. Rep. House	5	8	11	7	3	5	1
Rep. Pres. Dem. House	8	20	14	25	21	16	9
Rep. Pres. Rep. House	4	13	14	41	69	71	88
	100	100	100	100	100	100	100

Note: Total No. is 9,054. Excluded are the 22,463 voters in mid-term elections, and voters in presidential elections whose votes for President or the House were not ascertained.
Source: National Election Studies data.

candidates and Democratic House candidates (coded RD) exceeds the number who have voted for Democratic presidential candidates and Republican House candidates (coded DR), by margins ranging from 7 per cent to 15 per cent. These ticket-splitters, especially those in the RD category, have produced divided party control. Who are they, how do they resemble and differ from the straight-ticket voters (coded DD and RR), and why do they split their tickets?

Weak partisanship.   We would expect that people who identify with a particular party would be less likely to split their tickets than those whose party identification is weaker. Table 10.5 shows that this is indeed the case. With one exception, Table 10.5 supports the hypothesized relationship between strength of party identification and ticket-splitting. The strong Democrats (13 per cent) and strong Republicans (10 per cent) have the smallest proportions of ticket-splitters, while the Independent–Independents (32 per cent) have the largest proportion. The Independent Democrats keep the relationship from steady linearity, for they have had almost as few splitters (25 per cent) as the strong Democrats and many fewer than the weak Democrats (28 per cent).

This finding is consistent with the conclusion of Raymond Wolfinger and his colleagues that, in general, 'independent leaners' are considerably more partisan in their behaviour than weak identifiers (Keith *et al.*, 1992). It also supports the conclusion of Martin Wattenberg (1986, 1991) that split-ticket voting has been one of the chief products of the much-discussed decline in the intensity of party identifications since the 1960s and, for many voters, the consequent decline in the importance of candidates' party affiliations as reasons for choosing one over another.

Parties are less important for ticket-splitters than straight-ticket voters in several other respects. Ticket-splitters are less likely to see important differences in what the two major parties stand for (18–24 per cent). They are less likely to believe that parties help make the government pay attention to what ordinary people think (22–26 per cent), and they are less likely to care strongly about which candidate wins the presidential election (18–28 per cent). Consequently, favouring a presidential candidate of one party and a House candidate of the other party is less likely to cause the weaker partisans the kind of *angst* that might deter strong Democrats or strong Republicans.

Levels of motivation.   The first major survey-based study of straight- and split-ticket voting was published by Angus Campbell and Warren E. Miller in 1957 (Campbell and Miller 1957; see also de Vries and Tarrance 1972). They reported finding two kinds of ticket-splitters. The voters in one group were weakly motivated, little interested in either the parties or the candidates, cared little about which party won, and split their tickets by voting for candidates whose names suggested the right ethnic affiliations or whom friends urged them to support. Those in the other group were highly motivated people, who put aside their partisan loyalties and split their tickets at both the national and state levels in order to support candidates for executive and legislative offices whose positions on issues were most like their own.

Campbell and Miller found that in the 1952 and 1956 elections there were more weakly motivated than highly motivated ticket-splitters. My findings show the same pattern in recent elections. For example, ticket-splitters in recent years are less likely than

TABLE 10.6. *Public opinion on divided control of the federal Government, 1981 and 1989* (%)

Preference	'Do you think it is better for the country to have a president who comes from the same political party that controls Congress, or do you think it is better to have a president from one political party and Congress controlled by the other?'	
	November 1981	September 1989
Same party	47	35
Different parties	34	45
Don't know	19	20

Source: *New York Times*/CBS News Poll, quoted in Jacobson (1990: 119).

straight-ticket voters to care a lot about who wins the presidential election (18–28 per cent). They are less likely to follow politics closely (19–24 per cent). And they are less likely to participate in politics in ways other than voting (12–22 per cent). In short, now as then, most people who split their tickets do so, not because that is the best way to promote their policy preferences, but because they are not much concerned with the party affiliations of either presidential or House candidates.

Hedging bets. It is possible that voters who split their tickets do so because they, in the spirit of James Madison, believe that it is dangerous to give control of the entire government to one political party and that the best way to prevent government from becoming too powerful and oppressive is to vote for one party's candidate for the Presidency and the other party's candidates for Congress. Some analysts consider this possibility remote, for, they contend, such voting requires far more sophisticated understanding of and deep concern for the principles of separation of powers, and checks and balances than most voters possess. That certainly accords with the finding that most ticket-splitters are relatively uninterested in politics. Yet, it is worth noting that, when, in 1981 and again in 1989, national samples were asked directly whether they prefer unified or divided party control, they showed an increasing preference for divided control. Their answers are shown in Table 10.6.

The answers in the table probably do not stem from the respondents' sophisticated cost-benefit analyses of separation of powers and its consequences. Yet, four-fifths of them understood the question well enough to state a preference, and the preference of the majority is not merely consistent with split-ticket voting but accords with the view widely purveyed by high school civics teachers and textbooks, that the conscientious citizen 'votes for the person, not the party'.

Different votes for different ends. To understand the current period of divided government we need to explain not only why a quarter of the voters split their tickets but also why most of them split in favour of Republican presidential candidates and Democratic House candidates. Some analysts contend that most voters have split their votes thus, not because of their commitment to the abstract principle of checks and balances, but because Republican candidates seem more likely to provide what they want in a president, while Democratic candidates seem more likely to provide the quite different things they want in their Members of Congress.

These analysts suggest that many US voters want their President to be one who, in foreign affairs, promotes a powerful defence and pursues a strong foreign policy advancing the United States' national interests, and who, in domestic affairs, holds the line against welfare spending, high taxes, and inflation. In the recent presidential choices that the parties have put before the voters, the Republican candidates (especially Nixon, Reagan, and Bush) have seemed much more likely to be such presidents than their Democratic opponents (especially McGovern, Mondale and Dukakis).

On the other hand, they also want a Congress that will preserve the government spending programmes, tax breaks, and social security payments that put money in their pockets—and individual Representatives who will fight hard to defend the interests of their districts. Democrats are generally regarded as more likely than Republicans to protect domestic welfare programmes and distribute their benefits fairly. Thus, it makes sense for people who want these different things in their President and their Member of Congress to vote for Republican presidential candidates and Democratic congressional candidates (Jacobson 1989).

*

Those are the main structural and attitudinal explanations presently offered for the prevalence of divided party control in the United States. In my view, none of them—nor all of them together—offers a completely satisfying account, and scholars still have a lot of work to do to develop better explanations.

But is it worth the trouble? Is divided party control only a technical variation from the patterns in other democratic systems that is interesting to scholars but not of much consequence for anything else? Or does it have important consequences for how well or badly the US system operates? That is my final concern.

CONSEQUENCES OF DIVIDED PARTY CONTROL

For Congressional Party Unity

In his seminal book *The Congressional Party* David B. Truman (1959) observed that in two significant respects each congressional party behaves differently when it has a fellow partisan in the White House than when it does not. For one thing, congressional parties support the President more when they are the in-party than when they are the out-party.[9] For another, the congressional in-party, whether it is in the majority or the minority in its chamber, tends to be more united than the out-party.

Most of the data in Truman's book were drawn from periods prior to the great increase in divided party control that began in 1954. To test the validity of his generalizations for recent years, I have used data on party unity and opposition scores from *Congressional Quarterly*'s weekly reports and yearly almanacs. The scores for each party's unity in recent years are shown in Tables 10.7 and 10.8.

The figures in Table 10.7 show that Truman's thesis holds very well for congressional Democrats in recent years. In the nine years from 1964 to 1988 in which they were the in-party the Democratic congressional parties had a mean party unity score of 44, while in the sixteen years in which they were the out-party they had a score of 39. The difference is not enormous, but it lies in the direction that Truman's generalization would lead us to expect.

However, the data in Table 10.8 show that his thesis does not hold for the Republicans in recent years. In the sixteen years from

TABLE 10.7. *Democratic congressional party unity and opposition scores*

As the in-party				As the out-party			
Year	Unity score	Opposition score	Net score*	Year	Unity score	Opposition score	Net score*
1964	67	18	49	1969	62	n.a.	n.a.
1965	65	18	47	1970	57	n.a.	n.a.
1966	61	18	43	1971	62	24	38
1967	66	20	46	1972	57	24	33
1968	57	22	35	1973	68	22	46
				1974	63	24	39
1977	67	24	43	1975	69	22	47
1978	64	25	39	1976	65	22	43
1979	69	23	46				
1980	68	24	44	1981	69	23	46
				1982	72	20	52
MEAN	65	21	44	1983	76	17	59
				1984	74	17	57
				1985	79	14	65
				1986	78	14	64
				1987	81	14	67
				1988	78	14	64
				MEAN	69	20	39

Notes: n.a. = not available.
* net score = opposition score subtracted from support score.
Source: *Congressional Quarterly*, weekly reports.

1964 to 1988 in which they were the in-party the Republican congressional parties had a mean party unity score of 46, while in the nine years in which they were the out-party they had a mean score of 49—a small difference, but one that lies in the opposite direction from what Truman's thesis would predict. Accordingly, while congressional Democrats seem to have been somewhat more united under Democratic presidents than under Republican presidents, congressional Republicans have been slightly *less* united in support of Republican presidents than in opposition to Democratic presidents.

The two tables also show that the congressional Democrats were more united in their opposition to Reagan than in their

TABLE 10.8 *Republican congressional party unity and opposition scores*

As the in-party				As the out-party			
Year	Unity score	Opposition score	Net score*	Year	Unity score	Opposition score	Net score*
1969	62	25	37	1964	69	18	51
1970	59	n.a.	n.a.	1965	69	26	43
1971	66	21	45	1966	67	15	52
1972	64	21	43	1967	71	17	54
1973	68	24	44	1968	63	21	42
1974	62	26	36	1977	70	21	49
1975	65	25	40	1978	67	23	44
1976	66	23	43	1979	72	20	52
				1980	70	20	50
1981	76	18	58				
1982	71	21	50	MEAN	69	20	49
1983	74	20	54				
1984	72	21	51				
1985	75	19	56				
1986	71	22	49				
1987	74	21	53				
1988	68	24	44				
MEAN	68	22	46				

Note: n.a. = not available.
   * Net score = opposition score subtracted from unity score.
Source: *Congressional Quarterly*, weekly reports.

oppostion to Nixon (their unity scores rose from 40 to 52 in Reagan's first two years to 67 and 64 in his last two years). On the other hand, the tables show that Republican Members of Congress were more united in support of Reagan than in support of Nixon or Ford, but less united in Reagan's second term than his first. Both parties were less united in the early years of an opposition president's first term than in the later years of that term and in all of his second term—no doubt as they increasingly focused on impending presidential elections and their chances of recapturing the White House. But most important for our present purpose is the fact that each congressional party has behaved somewhat differently in conditions of divided control than in conditions of unified control.

For Presidential Support

American advocates of the doctrine of responsible party government, from Woodrow Wilson and A. Lawrence Lowell to E. E. Schattschneider and James L. Sundquist, have assumed that a president's programme is more likely to be enacted by a Congress controlled by his own party than by a Congress partly or wholly controlled by the other party (Ranney 1954; Schattschneider 1942; Sundquist 1988–9). This is the case partly because the President's party wants him to succeed and the opposition party wants him to fail, and partly because the members of the congressional in-party are more likely than those of the out-party to agree with the merits of the President's proposals. But whatever the reason, the advocates of responsible party government are convinced that the government operates more efficiently and effectively under unified party control than under divided control.

The proposition is easily, though perhaps not definitively, tested. *Congressional Quarterly* has reported 'presidential support scores'[10] for each President, beginning with Eisenhower in 1953. A summary of their scores for Republican presidents both with Republican-controlled and Democratic-controlled Congresses is set forth in Table 10.9.

The data in the table generally support the responsible-parties assumption. Republican presidents had a mean congressional support score of 86 in the brief two years (1953–4) in which they enjoyed Republican control of both Houses of Congress, and a mean support score of only 64 when they faced a Congress with one or both Houses controlled by the Democrats.

An additional pattern is worth noting: Ronald Reagan was the only President during the period who, during part of his administration, faced a Congress in which his party controlled the Senate and the opposition controlled the House. The responsible-parties view would lead us to expect that Reagan's support scores would be significantly higher when his party controlled one chamber than when it controlled neither chamber, and that was indeed the case: Reagan's mean support score was 67 during the six years in which he dealt with a Republican Senate and a Democratic House

TABLE 10.9. *Presidential support scores of Republican presidents, 1953–1988* (%)

Year	Republican control of Congress	Democratic control of Congress
1953	89	
1954	83 (86)	
1955		75
1956		70
1957		68
1958		76
1959		52
1960		65 (68)
1969		74
1970		77
1971		75
1972		66
1973		51 (69)
1974		60
1975		61
1976		54 (58)
1981		83
1982		72
1983		67
1984		66
1985		60
1986		56 (67)
1987		43
1988		47 (45)
MEAN	86	64

Note
Figures in parentheses are mean support scores for particular presidencies or periods of a single presidency.
Source: *Congressional Quarterly*, almanacs.

(1981–6), but declined precipitously to a mean of 45 in the two years (1987–8) in which he dealt with a Democratic Senate as well as a Democratic House.

In short, if high party-unity and high presidential-support scores are good indicators of efficient and effective government, and low scores are symptoms of systemic malaise, then divided party control indeed has the bad consequences that the responsible-parties school deplore. But such scores, by themselves, show only how united the parties are and how much Congress supports presidential recommendations; they tell us little about differences in the substance or quality of legislation under divided or unified party control. For that more critical matter we need to look at other indicators.

For Congressional Outputs

In my opinion, the most careful and convincing study yet made of the consequences of divided party control for congressional outputs is that by David R. Mayhew (1991). He acknowledges Sundquist's argument that divided party control means escalated war between the President and Congress, usually resulting in the kind of deadlock exemplified by the failure of Republican presidents and Democratic Congresses to do something about budget deficits throughout the 1980s (Sundquist 1988–9). Mayhew tests that argument by asking whether there have been any significant differences in congressional outputs between the periods of unified and divided party control from 1946 to 1990.

Congressional investigations of the executive. The first output Mayhew studies is high-publicity congressional investigations of wrongdoing in the executive branch, which he hypothesizes will be significantly more frequent when Democratic Congresses face Republican presidents than when both branches are controlled by the same party. In fact, however, he finds no such relationship. He identifies thirty instances of such investigations, exactly half of which occurred in periods of divided control and half in periods of unified control (Mayhew 1991: ch. 2). To underline his point, he notes that some of the most bitter and divisive investigations during the period were unrelated to the existence of unified or divided party control. The Watergate hearings of the early 1970s and the Iran-Contra hearings of the late 1980s were both investigations of Republican executives by Democratic Congresses—but the congressional hunts for Communists in the executive led by the House Un-American Activities Committee and by Senator Joseph

McCarthy took place under unified Democratic control (1948–53) and unified Republican control (1953–54). He concludes that such congressional attacks on the executive are not caused or even exacerbated by divided party control.

Major legislation.   The second output that concerns Mayhew is major legislation. To compile a consensual list of the major Acts of Congress from 1946 to 1990, he began by examining many end-of-the-congressional-year wrap-ups written by journalists and academics, and compiled a list of all the legislative enactments they identified as especially significant. This 'first sweep' produced a total of 211 enactments. Mayhew then canvassed the main recent long-range retrospective analyses to see what enactments are still generally regarded as especially significant without regard to when they were adopted. Putting the two lists together yielded a total of 267 major enactments.

Mayhew then asked whether there was any significant difference in the rate of production of these enactments between the nine two-year segments of unified party control and the thirteen two-year segments of divided party control. The answer, he found, was: very little. The unified-control segments produced an average of 12.8 enactments each, while the divided-control segments produced an average of 11.7 enactments. The result lies in the hypothesized direction, but the difference is too small to be significant (Mayhew 1991: chs. 3–9).

Mayhew concludes that, in at least these two categories of congressional outputs, 'it does not seem to make all that much difference whether party control of the American government happens to be unified or divided', and his regression analysis shows that other factors (e.g. events, the public mood, issue cleavages, the quality of presidential and congressional leadership) explain much more of the variance (Mayhew 1991: ch. 7).

CONCLUSION

The main academic commentators on divided party control today are Morris Fiorina, David Mayhew, and James Sundquist. They agree that the persistence of divided party control is a major new feature of the US political system, but they disagree about its causes and even more about its probable consequences.

Sundquist, for one, argues that the people have made no deliberate decision to abandon unified party control for divided control; it is, he says, simply an accident of the electoral system, which permits people to split their tickets and thus to vote one way for executives and another way for legislators. Accordingly, he says, the nation needs only to change the electoral system to make ticket-splitting impossible. After all, ticket-splitting between candidates for President and Vice-President is already illegal in most states, and the United States could, by constitutional amendment, extend the principle to elections for the House and Senate. Or we could require a party's candidates for Congress to be also its candidate for the electoral college, and thus a voter could cast a vote for a party's presidential candidate only by casting votes for its congressional candidates. Sundquist recognizes that such constitutional changes are unlikely, and so he challenges political scientists to develop a new theory of how effective government can be achieved under conditions of divided party control. He emphasizes that *something* needs to be done, because, as things now stand, continued divided party control guarantees that the congressional Democrats will always have a stake in blocking the policy proposals of Republican presidents, and the presidents will always blame Congress for the government's failures. So long as that continues to be the case, promising solutions for the nation's mounting problems will be contaminated or blocked by partisan squabbling and buck-passing between the two branches, and neither branch nor party can effectively be held responsible for the sorry state of affairs (Sundquist 1988–9: 631–4).

Benjamin Ginsberg and Martin Shefter (1990) add that the parties' sham fights and the government's partisan gridlock have made elections insignificant for resolving conflicts and making public policy, and have transferred the real policy-making process to such arenas as congressional investigations, media revelations, and litigation.

The data presented in this chapter show that divided party control indeed has some effect on how the national government operates, especially with respect to the unity of the congressional parties and congressional support of presidential legislative proposals. On the other hand, David Mayhew argues convincingly that, in at least two measurable respects, government outputs in periods of divided control differ very little from those in periods of unified control, and he makes a powerful case for disputing Sundquist's claim that divided party control cripples the government's ability to act.

Writing in 1992, Fiorina recalls that in 1980 he published an article deploring the decline of party responsibility in the Carter administration, which, he notes, was the most recent instance of unified party control. 'The point', he writes in 1992, 'was not that party responsiblity was the ideal, but that the alternative was irresponsibility, not some other form of responsibility.' He concludes that,

if responsibility was problematic in American politics even when government was unified, the problem is compounded when government is divided. Presidents blame Congress for obstructing carefully crafted solutions, while members of Congress attack the president for a lack of leadership. Citizens genuinely cannot tell who is to blame, and the meaning of election outcomes becomes increasingly confused. (Fiorina 1992: 109–10)

It seems to me that the argument of Sundquist, Fiorina, and Ginsberg–Shefter that divided party control deadlocks the government rests on the assumption that the Democrats in Congress and the Republicans in the executive place partisan interests first, believe that those interests require united party action against the other party, and act together cohesively to accomplish their partisan goals. In fact, however, everything we know about US politics tells us that neither the Democrats nor the Republicans are united on anything, whether it be questions of public policy or the relative importance of clinging to party programmes or winning elections. If US parties were as unified as the parties in most other democracies, then divided party control would surely produce deadlock, and unified control would just as surely produce efficient government. But they are not, and I believe that is the basic explanation for Mayhew's finding that the ability of government to act is about the same under divided control as under unified control.

Indeed, the more I ruminate about the causes and consequences of divided party control, the more I am convinced that it is entirely compatible with, even a logical extension of, such other features of the US system as separation of powers, checks and balances, and the election of presidents and members of each House of Congress by different constituencies in different ways and for different terms.

Similarly, the more I read the discussions of the consequences and desirability of divided party control, the more they seem to me to constitute a new version of an old debate among US political scientists—the debate over whether the values of responsiveness, majority rule, and coherent programmes are superior to the values of compromise, consensus, and protecting minority rights. If the majoritarian position is correct, then clearly presidential democracy is greatly inferior to parliamentary democracy, and the growing frequency of divided party control is simply the most recent, and perhaps one of the most egregious, symptoms of the system's basic malaise.

If the majoritarian position is wrong, however, then divided party control is another check and balance among several. How does one choose between the two positions? It depends, I suppose, on what one thinks the United States needs most from its governing system. Sundquist and Fiorina apparently believe that the nation's greatest need is for efficient majoritarian institutions that will once and for all achieve undiluted victories for majority policy preferences. What preferences would those be in the 1990s? Public opinion polls give us useful clues. They show that strong popular majorities favour, among other policies, free abortions, non-discrimination but no preferential treatment for African–Americans and other minorities, and getting tough with crime even if it dilutes the rights of persons accused of crime.

Those policies would probably be the winners in a system that guaranteed unified control for disciplined parties responsive to strong majority preferences. Yet, there is no doubt that millions of Americans are deeply committed to outlawing abortions; others are passionately convinced that government-mandated affirmative action is the only way women, African–Americans, Hispanics, and native Americans can be compensated for the centuries of injustice they have suffered; and still others feel deeply that making sure the guilty are punished does not justify risking oppression of the innocent. Would they peacefully accept no-compromise defeats of their most cherished political ideals? The nation's history suggests that they would not. Whatever else can be said about checks and balances, fragmented political parties, and separation of powers, they have served historically as the principal agencies keeping political issues in the United States from being structured as Armageddons of total victory or unconditional surrender.

However one evaluates the historic and future role of divided party control, it is clear that it poses no imminent crisis. The United States has lived with it quite comfortably for two-fifths of its history since 1832 and well over half the time since 1946. There is every reason to believe that it will continue to do so during most of the 1990s and beyond.

Notes

1. A situation in which the President and majorities in both Houses of Congress belong to the same party is generally called 'unified party control'.
2. Uruguay's election laws require voters to vote for the same party for legislative and executive positions in a particular election; hence divided party control is impossible.
3. Several nations, such as Austria, Iceland, Ireland, and Portugal, also directly elect their presidents. Those officers, however, have little power and are more like elected constitutional monarchs than heads of government, and will not be considered here.
4. Some of the members of the Senate were indirectly elected by the legislatures of their states until the adoption of the Seventeenth Amendment to the US Constitution in 1913.
5. The term 'southern states' is usually reserved for the eleven states that formed the Confederacy from 1861 to 1865: Alabama, Arkansas, Florida, Georgia, Louisiana, Mississippi, North Carolina, South Carolina, Tennessee, Texas, and Virginia.
6. That is, the drawing of legislative district boundary lines so as to advantage a particular political party or interest group.
7. The percentages of House incumbents re-elected in the Reagan–Bush years (1980–1990) were: 90.7, 90.1, 95.4, 90.0, 98.5, and 98.8. Senate incumbents have been more vulnerable: their average rate of re-election from 1950 to 1988 was 77.0 % (Ornstein, Mann, and Malbin 1990: 57, Table 2.8).
8. The National Election Studies consist of personal interviews with national samples of adult Americans taken in the course of every presidential and mid-term election since 1952 by the Center for Political and Social Studies of the University of Michigan, funded in recent years by the National Science Foundation. Their data are

available to all scholars, and I have used them through the services of the State Data Program and the Computer-Assisted Survey Methods Program of the University of California, Berkeley.

9. As I am using the terms, a congressional 'in-party' is one that also holds the Presidency regardless of whether it is the majority or minority party in Congress; and an 'out-party' is one that does not hold the White House. Thus, in 1991, the Republicans were the in-party and also the minority party in both Houses of Congress, while the Democrats were the out-party and also the majority party in both Houses.

10. The score is derived by identifying all congressional votes on which the president has taken a stand and calculating the percentage of those votes in which majorities have voted in favour of the president's stand.

References

Baker, R. K. (1989), The Congressional Elections', in Baker (ed.), *The Election of 1988: Reports and Interpretations* (Chatham, NJ: Chatham House), 153–76.

Barone, M., and Ujifusa, G. (1981), *The Almanac of American Politics 1982* (Washington, DC: Barone).

—— —— (1985), *The Almanac of American Politics, 1986* (Washington, DC: National Journal).

—— —— and Matthews, D. (1972), *The Almanac of American Politics, 1972* (New York: Gambit).

—— —— —— (1977), *The Almanac of American Politics, 1978* (New York: Dutton).

Beck, P. A. (1984), 'The Dealignment Era in America', in R. J. Dalton, S. C. Flanagan, and P. A. Beck (eds.), *Electoral Change in Advanced Industrial Democracies* (Princeton, NJ: Princeton University Press), 240–66.

Brady, D. W. (1985), 'A Re-evaluation of Realignments in American Politics: Evidence from the House of Representatives', *American Political Science Review*, 79: 28–49.

Bureau of the Census (1975), *Historical Statistics of the United States from Colonial Times to the Present* (Washington, DC: Bureau of the Census).

—— (1988), *Statistical Abstract of the United States, 1988* (Washington, DC: Bureau of the Census).

—— (1992), *Statistical Abstract of the United States, 1991* (Washington, DC: Bureau of the Census).

Burnham, W. D. (1970), *Critical Elections and the Mainsprings of American Politics* (New York: W. W. Norton).

Campbell, A. and Miller, W. E. (1957), 'The Motivational Basis of Straight and Split Ticket Voting', *American Political Science Review*, 51: 293–312.

—— Converse, P. E., Miller, W. E., and Stokes, D. E. (1960), *The American Voter* (New York: John Wiley).

Campbell, B. A. (1979), *The American Electorate: Attitudes and Acts* (New York: Holt, Rinehart, & Winston).

Clubb, J. M., Flanigan, W. H. and Zingale, N. H. (1980), *Partisan Realignment: Voters, Parties, and Government in American History* (Beverley Hills, Calif.: Sage Publications).

Cook, R. (1989), 'Key to Survival for Democrats lies in Split-Ticket Voting', *Congressional Quarterly Weekly Report*, 8 July (1989), 1710–16.

Council of State Governments (1948–90), *The Book of the States* (Lexington, Ky.: Council of State Governments).

Cox, G. W., and Kernell, S. (1991) (eds.), *The Politics of Divided Government* (Boulder, Colo: Westview Press).

Cummings, M. C., jun. (1966), *Congressmen and the Electorate: Elections for the House and the President, 1928–1964* (New York: The Free Press).

De Vries, W., and Tarrance, L. (jun.), (1972), *The Ticket-Splitter: A New Force in American Politics* (Grand Rapids, Mich.: Eerdmans Publishing Co.).

Duncan, P. (1989) (ed.), *Politics in America, 1990* (Washington, DC: Congressional Quarterly).

Epstein, L. D. (1986), *Political Parties in the American Mold* (Madison, Wis.: University of Wisconsin Press).

Evans, Eldon Cobb (1917), *A History of the Australian Ballot System in the United States* (Chicago: University of Chicago Press).

Fiorina, M. P. (1992), *Divided Government* (New York, Macmillan).

Ginsberg, B. and Shefter, M. (1990), *Politics by Other Means: The Declining Importance of Elections in America* (New York: Basic Books).

Jacobson, G. C. (1989), 'Meager Patrimony: Republican Representation in Congress after Reagan', in L. Berman (ed.), *The Reagan Imprint* (Baltimore, Md.: Johns Hopkins University Press).

—— (1990), *The Electoral Origins of Divided Government, 1946–1988* (Boulder, Colo.: Westview Press).

Keith, B. E., Magleby, D. B., Nelson, C. J., Orr, E., Westlye, M. C., and

Wolfinger R. E. (1992), *The Myth of the Independent Voter* (Berkeley, Calif.: University of California Press).

Lijphart, A. (1984), *Democracies* (New Haven, Conn.: Yale University Press).

Mayhew, D. R. (1991), *Divided We Govern: Party Control, Lawmaking, and Investigations, 1946–1990* (New Haven, Conn: Yale University Press).

Ornstein, N. J., Mann, T. E., and Malbin, M. J. (1990), (eds.), *Vital Statistics on Congress, 1989–1990* (Washington, DC: Congressional Quarterly).

Petrocik, J. R. (1987), 'Realignment: New Party Coalitions and the Nationalization of the South', *Journal of Politics*, 49: 347–76.

Pomper, G. M. (1989), 'The Presidential Election', In Pomper (ed.), *The Election of 1988: Reports and Interpretations* (Chatham, NJ: Chatham House), 129–52.

Ranney, A. (1954), *The Doctrine of Responsible Party Government* (Urbana, Ill.: University of Illinois Press).

Rusk, J. G. (1970), 'The Effects of the Australian Ballot Reform on Split Ticket Voting: 1876–1908, *American Political Science Review*, 64: 1220–38.

Sartori, G. (1987), *The Theory of Democracy Revisited* (Chatham, NJ: Chatham House).

Scammon, R. (1948–64) (ed.), *American Votes* (Pittsburgh, Pa.: University of Pittsburgh Press).

Schattschneider, E. E. (1942), *Party Government* (New York: Rinehart & Co.).

Schlesinger, J. A. (1985), 'The New American Political Party', *American Political Science Review*, 79: 1152–69.

Sundquist, J. L. (1988–9), 'The New Era of Coalition Government in the United States', *Political Science Quarterly*, 103: 613–35.

Truman, D. B. (1959), *The Congressional Party* (New York: John Wiley).

Wattenberg, M. P. (1986), *The Decline of American Political Parties, 1952–1984* (Cambridge, Mass.: Harvard University Press).

—— (1991), *The Rise of Candidate Centered Politics: Presidential Elections of the 1980s* (Cambridge, Mass.: Harvard University Press).

11

The Electoral Systems Researcher as Detective: Probing Rae's Suspect 'Differential Proposition' on List Proportional Representation

ARE N D   L I J P H A R T

The purpose of this chapter is to solve an intriguing mystery in Douglas W. Rae's (1967) celebrated book *The Political Consequences of Electoral Laws*: his 'differential proposition' on list proportional-representation formulas is based on a weak, logically flawed, hypothesis—but is nevertheless clearly confirmed by his empirical evidence. I shall show that this mystery can be satisfactorily solved, but only after a great deal of careful and persistent sleuthing and the sorting-out of a large number of promising but insufficient clues.

Rae formulates his findings in a large number of what he calls 'differential' and 'similarity' propositions that state, respectively, how electoral rules differ in some but are alike in other respects. Two of Rae's three main conclusions concerning the effect of the electoral formula on the election outcome are that no formula produces perfectly proportional results (a similarity proposition) but that plurality and majority formulas are less proportional than proportional representation (a differential proposition). These conclusions are undoubtedly valid and, while not particularly surprising, Rae's great contribution was to confirm their validity by means of a broadly comparative analysis and systematic empirical evidence. Rae's (1967: 104–7) third proposition is that there are substantial differences within the family of proportional representation systems and that, in particular, highest-averages formulas yield less proportional results than largest-remainders formulas.

DIFFERENCES AMONG PROPORTIONAL-REPRESENTATION FORMULAS

The distinction between these two types of list proportional-representation formulas, which are also often referred to as divisor methods and quota methods respectively, is indeed an important one—but mainly as far as the practical procedures are concerned that election officials have to use to allocate seats to party lists. In quota systems, the first step is to calculate a quota of votes that entitles parties to a seat; a party gets as many seats as it has quotas of votes; any unallocated seats are then given to those parties having the largest numbers of unused votes (remainders). In divisor systems, seats are awarded sequentially to parties having the highest 'average' numbers of votes per seat until all seats are allocated; each time a party receives a seat, its 'average' goes down; these 'averages' are not averages as normally defined but depend on the given set of divisors that a particular divisor system prescribes.

However, the two groups of methods should *not* be expected to differ with regard to the proportionality they produce. The degree of proportionality logically depends on the particular quota or divisor that is used. This means that differences with regard to proportionality should occur *within* each group instead of *between* them. Among the highest averages (divisor) methods, the d'Hondt formula (which uses the divisor series 1, 2, 3, 4, etc.) is the least proportional and systematically favours the larger parties. It contrasts with the Sainte-Laguë formula, which, in the original form proposed by its inventor (using the odd-integer divisor series 1, 3, 5, 7, etc.), approximates proportionality very closely and treats large and small parties in a perfectly even-handed way. In practice, the Sainte-Laguë method is more often used in a modified form which uses 1.4 instead of 1 as the first divisor, thereby making it harder for small parties to gain their first seats—and hence, reducing the proportionality of the election result to some extent. According to their logical properties, therefore, the three highest-averages methods can be placed on the following scale from the most to the least proportional: pure Sainte-Laguë, modified Sainte-Laguë, and d'Hondt.

Similar differences occur within largest-remainders (quota) systems. The oldest and best-known of these simply uses as its quota the total number of valid votes cast in a district divided by the district magnitude (m, the total number of seats available in the district). This quota, usually referred to as the Hare quota, is impartial as between small and large parties and tends to yield closely proportional results. Less proportional outcomes are produced by the Droop quota (substantially the same as what in continental Europe is often called the Hagenbach–Bischoff quota), which divides the votes by $m + 1$ instead of m, and the Imperiali quota, used in Italy, which normally uses $m + 2$ as the denominator. The use of these lower quotas means that there will be fewer remaining seats to be allocated—and hence also more wastage of remaining votes, which is especially harmful to the smaller parties and results in a decrease in proportionality.

A small mystery within the main mystery I want to solve is why Rae overlooked the above differences within quota and divisor systems. Of course, his book was published in 1967, before the more detailed analyses of all the different proportional-representation formulas had appeared (see Balinski and Young 1982: 60–6; Lijphart 1986: 172–5). But he did have access to—and he explicitly cites—Stein Rokkan's analysis of electoral systems in draft form, subsequently published in the *International Encyclopedia of the Social Sciences* in 1968 and in Rokkan's book *Citizens, Elections, Parties* in 1970. He also cites George van den Bergh's 1955 study *Unity in Diversity*, which includes a clear discussion of the pattern of decreasing proportionality as the quota is lowered. Van den Bergh also shows that, when the quota is lowered even further than the Droop and Imperiali quotas, to the extent that there will not be any remaining seats, the outcome becomes exactly the same as that of the D'Hondt formula—suggesting that d'Hondt is the least proportional among the principal quota and divisor methods (van den Bergh 1955: 68–72).

Rae (1967: 33–4) does not discuss the pure Sainte-Laguë method at all, and he mistakenly suggests that the modified Sainte-Laguë and d'Hondt formulas have similar overall results, since, as he argues, modified Sainte-Laguë is less favourable to the largest parties but also discriminates against the smallest as a result of its higher initial divisor. He cites Rokkan (1970: 159–61) as his authority but misinterprets Rokkan's argument: what Rokkan says about the treatment of the smallest parties refers to the contrast between pure and modified Sainte-Laguë, not to the contrast between modified Sainte-Languë and d'Hondt.

Rae does not mention the Droop method as a variant of largest remainders (LR), and he gives mixed signals about what he believes to be the effects of LR–Hare and LR–Imperiali.[1] He states, correctly, that, unless the Imperiali quota is used, 'the largest remainders formula [i.e. LR–Hare] is likely to produce . . . nearly proportional results', but he exaggerates the disproportionality of LR–Imperiali when he argues that it 'is likely to be the least proportional' even compared with systems using the d'Hondt method (Rae 1967: 35, 41 n.) He exaggerates in the other direction when he states that LR–Imperiali has the effect of 'helping weak parties' (Rae 1967: 34); on the contrary, its disproportionality results from the tendency of *hurting* the smaller parties. Probably because of this confusion, he ends up placing the LR methods in a single category.

Rae's book is one of the major and most authoritative works on electoral systems—it received the 1989 George H. Hallett Award of the American Political Science Association's Representation and Electoral Systems section—and its conclusions have been and continue to be widely cited, including his differential proposition on list proportional representation. For instance, Douglas Wertman writes: 'The largest-remainder formula, according to a study by Douglas Rae, is the most proportionate of the proportional-representation formulas [and] the variant used in Italy, the *imperiali* largest-remainder system, is especially designed to help small parties . . .' (1977: 45). If this appears to be wrong on logical grounds, as I have argued, it is also important to demonstrate that it is empirically wrong and to explain why Rae mistakenly concluded it to be correct.

SEVEN POTENTIAL EXPLANATIONS

In spite of the logical weakness of Rae's hypothesis, it is confirmed by his empirical data. Rae (1967: 106) reports that there is a substantial difference in the average deviation of the parties' vote and seat shares, in the direction he hypothesizes, between largest-remainders and highest-averages systems: 1.22 and 1.78 per cent respectively. Seven potential explanations of this unexpected result come to mind.

First of all, Rae's findings must be checked for possible errors in his empirical analysis. Rae's (1967: 104–7) method is to contrast the twelve elections in three largest-remainders systems (Italy, Luxemburg, and Israel since 1951) with thirty elections in seven countries using highest-averages formulas (Israel in 1949, Austria, Belgium, Finland, Sweden, Norway, and Switzerland), and to exclude list proportional representation systems based on a combination of the two types of formula.[2] This is a perfectly acceptable and appropriate procedure, but Rae makes an astounding number of mistakes in classifying his cases: (1) Luxemburg used the d'Hondt formula, and the three Luxemburg elections should therefore be moved from the largest-remainders to the highest-averages category. (2) Austria and Belgium used two-tier districting systems with different formulas applied to each tier—LR–Droop and d'Hondt in the Austrian case and LR–Hare and d'Hondt in Belgium—and the five and six elections that were held in these two countries respectively should, therefore, be excluded instead of being grouped with the highest-averages systems. (3) Rae fails to include fourteen elections in four countries which should all be classified as highest-averages systems. Six elections in the Netherlands and two in France, in 1945 and June 1946, are straightforward d'Hondt cases; two elections in Iceland, in 1959 and 1963, used the d'Hondt formula at both tiers of districts; and the four Danish elections from 1945 to April 1953 used a combination of d'Hondt and pure Sainte-Laguë, which are both highest-averages systems. The remaining twenty-eight elections are correctly classified by Rae, but an exactly equal number are misclassified.

These errors obviously call for a reanalysis based on a corrected classification.[3] The first two rows of Table 11.1 present Rae's original percentages and the new percentages based on a correct classification of the elections under the two types of formula. The corrected figures are considerably lower than Rae's, but the difference in the degree of disproportionality between largest-remainders and highest-averages formulas remain. If anything, the difference looks even more impressive: the disproportionality under highest

TABLE 11.1. *Average degrees of disproportionality of largest-remainders and highest-averages formulas, 1945–64 and 1945–85* (%)

Measure	1945–64		1945–85	
	Largest remainders	Highest averages	Largest remainders	Highest averages
As reported by Rae (I)	1.22 (12)	1.78 (30)	—	—
After correction of misclassifications	0.65 (9)	1.27 (36)	—	—
Using complete data	0.65 (9)	1.22 (43)	0.68 (16)	1.14 (87)
Using electoral systems instead of elections as cases	0.61 (2)	1.40 (12)	0.60 (2)	1.36 (13)
Using D instead of Rae's I as measure of disproportionality	3.62 (2)	4.68 (12)	3.60 (2)	4.86 (13)
Controlling for district magnitude (large-district cases only)	3.62 (2)	4.12 (4)	3.60 (2)	4.42 (4)

Note: The numbers of cases on which the percentages are based are in parentheses.
Source: Based on data in Rae (1967: 106), Mackie and Rose (1982, 1983, 1984), Mackie (1985, 1986), and Service Central de la Statistique, Grand-Duché de Luxembourg (1984: 120–1).

averages (1.27 per cent) is now almost twice that of largest-remainders systems (0.65 per cent). The mystery remains unsolved.

My next two steps will be to test whether Rae's hypothesis still holds when more complete data are used: *all* elections in the 1945–64 period in the twenty countries, including those not analysed by Rae, and these same elections plus the ones held from 1965 to 1985. The first of these is not likely to change the findings. Rae (1967: 157–60) already uses a virtually complete set of data; the only exceptions are the November 1946 election in France, the first two post-war elections in Luxemburg, and six elections on which he reports that parts of the data are missing (Australia in 1955, Austria in 1945, and the four elections from 1951 to 1963 in Switzerland).[4] Except for Australia, these are all list proportional-representation systems, and seven of the eight proportional-representation systems use the d'Hondt formula. When these seven are added to the thirty-six highest-averages cases considered earlier, the percentage of disproportionality decreases but only very slightly: from 1.27 to 1.22 per cent. When the analysis is extended through 1985—almost doubling the number of cases—the difference between the two types of formula narrows a bit more: 0.68 and 1.14 per cent (see the third row of Table 11.1). But the gap is obviously still substantial.

The fourth possible explanation concerns Rae's units of analysis: each election represents a different case in his comparative study. This has two undesirable consequences. One is that it artificially and deceptively inflates the total weight of the evidence because the elections are not really independent cases; for instance, the nine largest-remainders elections are really only repeated operations of two electoral systems. The other problem is that it entails an artificial weighting of the evidence. For instance, because France held only three d'Hondt elections in the 1945–64 period (all of them in 1945 and 1946) while the Netherlands had six, the Dutch evidence is counted double compared with the French evidence.[5] Another example is the five elections in Israel during the same period: four used LR–Hare and one used d'Hondt, which means that the Israel LR–Hare experience is given four times the weight of its experience under d'Hondt. There is no good theoretical reason for doing any weighting. Instead, it makes much more sense to define the cases in such a way that they are as independent as possible, that is, in terms of electoral systems—each electoral system being defined as one or more elections held under basically the same or closely similar rules—rather than elections. To use the above examples again, instead of having fourteen Dutch, French, and Israeli cases (elections), this approach defines four cases: Israel in 1949, Israel in 1951–61, France in 1945–6, and the Netherlands in 1948–63.

As Table 11.1 shows, my deliberately unweighted approach does not weaken Rae's hypothesis. On the contrary, the differences in the degree of proportionality between largest-remainders and highest-averages formulas is larger than ever both for 1945–64 and for the longer 1945–85 period: 0.61 versus 1.40 per cent and 0.60 versus 1.36 per cent respectively.

My fifth line of enquiry finally yields some progress towards the solution of the mystery. It is suggested by a closer look at the two cases of largest remainders: Israel (1951–61) and Italy. They are among the extreme multi-party systems, and both are characterized by an unusually large number of small parties. As Richard S. Katz points out, Rae's index of disproportionality, which he calls I and which he defines as the mean difference between the parties' vote and seat shares, 'has the problem of *giving too much weight to small parties*; at the extreme, if the infinite number of (hypothetical) parties that receive no votes and obtain no seats is included, every electoral system would appear perfectly proportional (1980: 140, emphasis added). Rae (1967: 84) tries to avoid this problem by disregarding parties with less than 0.5 per cent of the vote, but this arbitrary cut-off point is still quite low; the presence of several parties with just over 0.5 per cent of the votes will depress I even if these parties fail to win any seats.

An index that avoids this problem is John Loosemore's and Victor J. Hanby's (1971) measure D. It has become the most widely used index of disproportionality (see, e.g., Mackie and Rose 1982: 411–12; Taagepera and Shugart 1989: 104–11). D is the total percentage by which the overrepresented parties are overrepresented—which is, of course, the same as the total percentage of underrepresentation. In order to calculate D, the absolute values of all vote–seat share differences are added, as for Rae's I, but then divided by 2, instead of Rae's division by the number of parties. Hence, except in the hypothetical case of a pure two-party system, D will always yield higher values than I. Table 11.1 shows that, when the more satisfactory index D instead of Rae's I is used, the percentage-point difference between largest remainders and highest averages is still in evidence, but in relative terms the difference narrows considerably: 3.62 versus 4.68 per cent in 1945–64 and 3.60 versus 4.86 per cent in the longer period.

My sixth potential explanation is also prompted by a closer look at the Israeli and Italian cases: in addition to using largest-remainders formulas, they both use high-magnitude districts—which tend to yield more proportional results than small districts. This means that, in order to measure the difference between electoral formulas correctly, district magnitude must be controlled for. Rae (1967: 105) comes close to perceiving the necessity of this when he states, in a 'word of caution', that the Israeli system of 'at-large election, producing a district magnitude of 120 seats' (that is, the entire country forms a single electoral district), exerts a further proportional effect.[6] But he does not follow up the suggestion that this cautionary comment implies. Because of the existence of two tiers of districts in many electoral systems, district magnitude is difficult to define and measure, but the necessary control can be conveniently introduced by focusing on what Rae (1967: 41) himself calls 'large-district PR' systems: three with an average magnitude above thirteen seats (the Finnish, Italian, and Luxemburg cases) and the three at-large cases with a magnitude of over one hundred seats (the highest-averages and largest-remainders Israeli cases plus the Netherlands).[7] As expected, the difference in disproportionality between the formulas is reduced: by about half in 1945–64 and by about a third in 1945–85. But, as the last row of Table 11.1 also shows, the difference has by no means disappeared completely.

In order to try to explain this last bit of the stubborn mystery, the other set of cases must be examined more closely: those using highest-averages formulas. In particular, it is important to ask which *type* of highest averages they use. The answer is that, instead of a more-or-less even distribution among the three types—d'Hondt and pure and modified Sainte-Laguë—the most prevalent type is d'Hondt. Of the twelve highest-averages cases in 1945–64 (thirteen cases in 1945–85), nine used d'Hondt and one, Denmark during 1945–53, is a case of combined d'Hondt plus pure Sainte-Laguë. Only two use modified Sainte-Laguë during the 1945–64 period and three when the subsequent two decades are included: Norway since 1953, Sweden from 1952 to 1968, and Sweden from 1970 on. Of the four large-district highest-averages cases examined in the previous paragraph, *all* use d'Hondt. Since, as I have argued earlier, D'Hondt tends to be the least proportional of the proportional-representation formulas, it is now clear why Rae's weak hypothesis still appears to be supported: it is a fortuitous result produced by the fact that d'Hondt happens to be the most frequently used highest-averages formula.

EPILOGUE

Having disproved Rae's differential proposition on list proportional representation, and having solved the mystery of how Rae was able to claim empirical validation of his flawed hypothesis, I have accomplished what I set out to do in this chapter. The only task that remains is to comment briefly on what happens when my alternative hypothesis is subjected to an empirical test. My hypothesis, based on the discussion of differences within quota and divisor formulas in the beginning of this chapter, uses a threefold classification: (1) pure Sainte-Laguë and LR–Hare are likely to be the most proportional; (2) modified Sainte-Laguë, LR–Droop, and LR–Imperiali should be less proportional; and (3) d'Hondt is likely to be the least proportional of the proportional-representation formulas.

This hypothesis is amply confirmed. Using the same data and methods and almost the same cases as in the fifth row of Table 11.1 (the exceptions are Denmark in 1945–53, which used a combination of d'Hondt and pure Sainte-Laguë, and Italy, which uses both LR–Hare and LR–Imperiali—formulas that respectively fit the same category for Rae but are in separate categories for me), the percentage of disproportionality increases monotonically from the LR–Hare and pure Sainte-Laguë category to d'Hondt both in the period 1945–64 (2.62, 4.10, and 5.06 per cent) and in 1945–85 (2.53, 4.29, and 5.32 per cent). Moreover, the differences between my high and low categories are much greater than between Rae's two categories: the percentage-point differences are roughly 2.5 per cent compared with only slightly more than 1.0 per cent for Rae, and the percentages in my high category are about twice those in the low category, compared with only about a one-third increase for Rae. And, as I have reported elsewhere (Lijphart 1990), these results are not affected by two further improvements in the analysis: sorting out the problematic two-tier districting cases, so that they can also be included in testing the differences among proportional-representation formulas, and introducing district magnitude as a control variable: the latter reduces the association between proportional-representation formulas and disproportionality, but only slightly, and the former strengthens it.

Notes

This chapter is a revision of part of a long paper presented at the XIVth World Congress of the International Political Science Association in Washington DC, 1988. I should like to express my gratitude to the collaborators in the comparative project of which this chapter is a product:

Don Aitkin, Asher Arian, Thomas C. Bruneau, Ivor Crewe, Wilfried Dewachter, A.-P. Frognier, William P. Irvine, W. K. Jackson, Gary C. Jacobson, Markku Laakso, Rafael López Pintor, Thomas T. Mackie, George Th. Mavrogordatos, Sten S. Nilson, Dieter Nohlen, Cornelius O'Leary, Jean-Luc Parodi, Mogens N. Pedersen, Anton Pelinka, Bo Särlvik, Yasunori Sone, Alberto Spreafico, Björn S. Stefánsson, Jürg Steiner, and Jan Verhoef. I also want to thank the German Marshall Fund of the United States and the Guggenheim Foundation for their financial support.

1. Rae (1967: 36–7) does discuss the Droop quota as a feature of the single transferable vote (STV).

2. He also excludes the Irish single-transferable-vote system, since it is not a list proportional-representation formula. Instead of twelve largest-remainders elections, Rae (1967, 106) actually reports eleven such elections in the table in which he presents his results. However, since he does not indicate any missing data for the five Italian, three Luxemburg, and four Israeli (since 1951) elections he analyses (Rae 1967: 159), I assume that this is a typographical error. Another confusing misprint in this table is that the numbers of elections are placed in the wrong columns.

3. For the purpose of this reanalysis, I relied mainly on the election data in Thomas T. Mackie's and Richard Rose's (1982) standard handbook. Rae was so kind as to make his original data for 1945–64 available to me, but I decided that it was preferable to use the Mackie–Rose data in order to facilitate replication by other researchers and because I also used the latter data for the 1965–85 period. Moreover, where there are slight discrepancies between the two data sets, Mackie–Rose is likely to be more reliable. The Mackie–Rose handbook includes the elections held through 1981. For the 1982–5 elections I turned to the annual updates in the *European Journal of Political Research* by Mackie and Rose (1983, 1984), and Mackie (1985, 1986). Since the Luxemburg voting figures reported by Mackie and Rose fail to adjust for the unequal numbers of votes that voters have in different districts, I used the official statistics published by Luxemburg's Service Central de la Statistique (1984).

4. Rae (1967: 157) also states that his 1949 Austrian election data do not include 'minor elective parties', but this problem was apparently so slight that he was still able to use this election in most of his analysis. The two Luxemburg elections, not covered by Rae, were held in 1945 and, in the form of two staggered elections of half of the legislature (which may be treated as one regular election), in 1948 and 1951.

5. In 1951 and 1956 France also used d'Hondt, but with majoritarian features added to and not in all districts; the Paris districts used straight

LR–Hare. Rae's (1967: 36, 42) description mistakenly reverses the formulas for the Paris and provincial districts.

6. Rae (1967: 105) makes two additional cautionary remarks that are less pertinent. One is that in the Italian case the smaller parties—and hence proportionality—are also helped by the LR–Imperiali formula, as compared with LR–Hare. However, as discussed earlier, the former must be regarded as less instead of more proportional and favourable to small parties than the latter. Secondly, Rae states that the ordinal ballot in Luxemburg, which allows each voter to vote for more than one party, may benefit the smaller parties. But he later rejects this explanation himself (Rae 1967: 126–9), and, of course, Luxemburg is not a largest-remainders system in the first place.

7. One minor qualification must be stated: Rae (1967: 41, 45) places Luxemburg in the special category of 'ordinal PR' because voters can divide their votes among two or more parties, unlike in the other 'categorical' large-district proportional-representation countries. However, apart from this feature, which is not relevant here, Luxemburg fits the large-district category perfectly.

References

Balinski, M. L., and Young, H. P. (1982), *Fair Representation: Meeting the Ideal of One Man, One Vote* (New Haven, Conn.: Yale University Press).

Katz, R. S., (1980), *A Theory of Parties and Electoral Systems* (Baltimore, Md.: Johns Hopkins University Press).

Lijphart, A., (1986), 'Degrees of Proportionality of Proportional Representation Formulas', in B. Grofman and A. Lijphart (eds.), *Electoral Laws and their Political Consequences* (New York: Agathon Press).

—— (1990), 'The Political Consequences of Electoral Laws, 1945–85, *American Political Science Review*, 84: 481–96.

Loosemore, J., and Hanby, V. J. (1971), 'The Theoretical Limits of Maximum Distortion: Some Analytic Expressions for Electoral Systems', *British Journal of Political Science*, 1: 467–77.

Mackie, T. T. (1985), 'General Elections in Western Nations during 1984', *European Journal of Political Research*, 13: 335–39.

—— (1986), 'General Elections in Western Nations during 1985', *European Journal of Political Research*, 14: 695–7.

—— and Rose, R. (1982), *The International Almanac of Electoral History* (2nd edn., New York: Facts on File).

—— —— (1983), 'General Elections in Western Nations during 1982', *European Journal of Political Research*, 11: 345–9.

—— —— (1984), 'General Elections in Western Nations during 1983', *European Journal of Political Research*, 12: 335–42.

Rae, D. W. (1967), *The Political Consequences of Electoral Laws* (New Haven, Conn.: Yale University Press).

Rokkan, S. (1970), *Citizens, Elections, Parties: Approaches to the Comparative Study of the Processes of Development* (Oslo: Universitetsforlaget).

Service Central de la Statistique, Grand-Duché de Luxembourg (1984), 'Les Élections législatives de 1945 à 1984', *Bulletin du Statec*, 30: 119–31.

Taagepera, R., and Shugart, M. S. (1989), *Seats and Votes: The Effects and Determinants of Electoral Systems*. (New Haven, Conn.: Yale University Press).

Van den Bergh, G. (1955), *Unity in Diversity: A Systematic Critical Analysis of All Electoral Systems* (London: Batsford).

Wertman, D. (1977), 'The Italian Electoral Process: The Elections of June 1976', in H. R. Penniman (ed.), *Italy at the Polls: The Parliamentary Elections of 1976* (Washington, DC: American Enterprise Institute).

Erratum

Since I have been critical of Rae's errors, it only serves me right that I now have to confess an error of my own. Professor Jørgen Elklit of Aarhus University recently proved to me that, contrary to several authoritative pronouncements in the literature on electoral systems, Denmark used LR–Hare—*not* pure Sainte-Laguë—for its higher-tier district from 1945 to 1953. This means that Rae erred on only twenty-four instead of twenty-eight elections in his classification of fifty-six proportional-representation systems. It also affects some of the details, but not the overall thrust, of my reanalysis of Rae. And my counter-hypothesis remains confirmed, because the Danish 1945–53 case is not included in the empirical evidence on which it is based.

12

Northern Ireland, 1921–1929:
A Failed Consociational Experiment

CORNELIUS O'LEARY

I

In the second decade of this century the British Liberal government was faced with an apparently intractable problem in Ireland—the fact that the Unionist majority in the province of Ulster seemed determined to carry opposition to the modest measure of Home Rule Parliament demanded by the overwhelming majority of the rest of Ireland to the point of civil war; so it searched desperately for what would nowadays be called a consociational formula. Various devices to conciliate the minority were considered—a qualified veto on legislation and additional members nominated by the government—but the device most widely supported was the Hare method of proportional representation, the single transferable vote (STV). This was canvassed by an influential pressure group, the Proportional Representation Society, first in submissions to the Royal Commission on Electoral Systems (1910) and then specifically in relation to the all-Ireland legislature envisaged in the Home Rule Bills of 1910, 1911, and 1912. An Irish Proportional Representation Society was established in 1911 and secured qualified support from the dominant Nationalist party and enthusiastic support from the new, more advanced, nationalist, Sinn Fein party as 'the one just system of election under democratic government' (Griffith 1911). When the third Home Rule Bill was going through the Commons, a Unionist member secured the passing of amendments, introducing STV for nine urban constituencies in the proposed Irish House of Commons, electing three or more members.

The Home Rule Act of 1914 was stillborn, but the Asquith government showed that, whatever its misgivings regarding STV for a homogeneous country like Great Britain, it regarded it as appropriate for a country like Ireland with its dual-minority problem. The prospect of large constituencies also appealed to the southern Unionists, a small but influential minority who, even under the existing system, were able to secure the occasional return of a member for Dublin, but with STV could expect more seats in the capital and also in Cork and some rural areas.

However, the Ulster Unionists expressed strong opposition to STV ('un-British, too complicated, unworkable' (Royal Commission on Electoral Systems, (ed. 5163/1910: 499–505)) from the time when Sir James Craig gave evidence to the Royal Commission on Electoral Systems.

The subject re-emerged in the proceedings of the Irish Convention, a body summoned by Lloyd George in the aftermath of the Easter Rising as a last desperate effort to find consensus between Unionist and Nationalist Ireland. Boycotted by Sinn Fein, the convention predictably divided into Nationalist and Unionist blocs, the latter steadfastly opposing any suggestion of Home Rule. However, the Chairman, Sir Horace Plunkett, insisted on the production of a report, which was carried by a majority of Nationalists and a few southern Unionists, the Ulster Unionists voting *en bloc* against (Lyons 1971: 385–6).

The Convention is derided by Irish historians as a failure, but it provided the occasion of a formal government commitment to STV in any future Irish legislature. The majority report proposed an all-Ireland legislature of 160 members, in constituencies of varying size, with STV as the electoral formula in constituencies returning three or more members. (It also proposed that the Lord-Lieutenant be empowered to appoint additional members to represent the Unionists of the three southern provinces.) The report was issued on 8 April 1918, but previously, in a letter to Plunkett (25 February 1918) thanking the members for their labours, Lloyd George had pointed out that, while issues on which there was an acute difference of opinion must be held over for determination after the war, it was the government's view that the solution lay in a single Irish legislature with adequate safeguards for the interests of Ulster and the southern Unionists. (CAB 23/47, 351)

II

The matter came to the forefront of the Cabinet agenda on 16 April 1918 in a discussion on ways of mollifying Irish public opinion over the highly unpopular issue of conscription. The Cabinet, somewhat surprisingly, came to the conclusion that there was a probability that 'a large number of Unionists' would regard it as their duty to support the Government in passing a measure of Home Rule, provided that some substantial agreement could be found between the various sections of the Nationalist party (CAB 23/7, 392).

An attempt was made to draw up a bill, based on the Convention report, by a Cabinet committee in the summer of 1918, but its activities were cut short by the debates on the Representation of the People Bill and the redistribution of seats, which led to the election of December 1918 and the Sinn Fein landslide—seventy-three out of 105 Irish members returned by a greatly expanded electorate. The only other significant group was the twenty-six Ulster Unionists. Sinn Fein members refused to take their seats and formed a separate parliament in Dublin, the first Dail, with the object of complete independence from Britain.

The next initiative from Westminster was the Local Government Act 1919, introduced in the Commons on 11 March, prescribing STV for all local authorities, urban and rural, in elections to be held during the following year. The aim was to blunt the edge of the Sinn Fein success in the southern provinces and Unionist success in Ulster. The bill passed the Commons with scarcely any discussion, the only opposition coming from one or two Ulster Unionists.

In an intemperate speech Carson said: 'I really regard the whole of this bill with the greatest contempt. It is the most wretched miserable bill and nobody wants it' (*Proc. Deb. HC*, 116 (27 May 1919), 1968). It is true that the few Nationalists left in the House expressed no enthusiasm for the bill, but they were far more satisfied with the outcome of the ensuing elections than the Unionists. In spite of pleas from politicians and newspapers to vote the 'straight party ticket', the Unionists lost control of two county councils, Fermanagh and Tyrone, to Nationalists and Sinn Fein. Derry city council was evenly divided and in Belfast a Unionist block of fifty-two councillors was reduced to twenty-nine, the largest alternative group being the Belfast Labour party with ten councillors. The pro-Nationalist *Irish News* prematurely rejoiced at the 'death-blow to the Unionist clique' (19 January 1920).

The local elections took place in January 1920, but already the drafting of the measure that became the Government of Ireland Act 1920 was well under way by a committee chaired by the Colonial Secretary, Walter Long. The draft bill accepted by the Cabinet on 2 December 1919 provided for two Irish bicameral parliaments, the popular House in each case to be elected by STV. The parliaments were to have powers over most internal matters, but certain 'imperial' services were reserved to Westminster. The Bill provided for a Council of Ireland, comprising an equal number of members of both parliaments to discuss matters of common concern and prepare the way for reunification of the country which an Explanatory Memorandum attached to the bill stated to be its ultimate objective.[1]

With little opposition the Government of Ireland Bill passed into law on 20 December 1920. It is interesting that the minister chiefly responsible for drafting the measure should have been the Colonial Secretary, Walter Long, who had served for a time as a Unionist MP for Dublin County and had actually been leader of the Irish Unionists before Carson. Yet Long clearly envisaged an ultimate all-Ireland solution and produced an essentially consociational formula, designed to provide both parts of the country with institutions satisfactory to the majority with adequate safeguards for the minority (STV), and 'to afford every facility'[2] for eventual reunion.

The Act provided for constituencies to return from three to eight members—the boundaries to be established by commissioners—for each House of Commons. (The second chambers were of different composition.) In his magisterial history, *Ireland, 1912–1985*, Professor J. J. Lee asserts that the Ulster constituencies 'were naturally arranged to maximise Unionist seats' at the following general election (1989: 59). This criticism is unjust. The commissioners took the existing counties, Fermanagh being joined with Tyrone as for Westminster elections, and Belfast was similarly divided into four four-seat divisions. The other constituencies ranged from four seats (Armagh) to eight seats (Down).

TABLE 12.1. *Election, 1921: The high point for Unionism*

Party	% of vote	Seats	% of seats	Index
Unionist	66.9	36 (+4)*	75	112
Nationalist	11.8	6	12.5	106
Sinn Fein	20.5	6	12.5	61
Labour	0.6	0	0	—
Independent	0.2	0	0	—

Notes: The index of proportionality is calculated by dividing a party's percentage of seats by its percentage of first preference votes.

 * The 4 Queen's University seats are excluded, because the relationship between university seats and votes is disproportionate.

III

In the following election, in May 1921, the Unionists—led by Sir James Craig, since Carson had become a Lord of Appeal in January 1921, secured forty out of fifty-two seats—their highest score in the entire history of the Parliament. Every constituency was contested and the turn-out was 89.2 per cent, the highest ever in any general election in the United Kingdom (Table 12.1).

The enormous Unionist success was facilitated by the fact that it was the only party organized to contest the election and that it chose to make it a plebiscite on the issue of devolution. (Knight and Baxter-Moore, 1972: 14). The Nationalists and Sinn Fein parties fought on an abstentionist policy as a protest against partition, and competed against each other. Perhaps most important was the fact that the Belfast Labour party, which had won 14 per cent of the votes and ten seats in the local elections of the previous year, was largely intimidated from putting up candidates—three stood, all losing their deposits—and the generally disturbed state of the country, with the IRA fighting the British forces in the three provinces and making occasional forays into Ulster, also helped the Unionist cause. A feature of the election was the success of four Sinn Fein leaders (Eamon de Valera (Down), Arthur Griffith (Fermanagh–Tyrone), Michael Collins (Armagh), and Eoin MacNeill (Londonderry)), none of whom had the slightest intention of taking his seat. The anti-Unionist vote was badly fractionalized, with few transfers going from Nationalist to Sinn Fein. It was also notable that Joe Devlin, the Nationalist leader who had been active in Belfast politics since 1897, came only second in the West Belfast constituency, which he had represented at Westminster since 1906.

The election result, combined with Nationalist and Sinn Fein abstentionism, helped the new Unionist Cabinet headed by Craig quickly to establish the machinery of government—a civil service, legal system, and police service all of unquestionable loyalty. But it was soon faced with a constitutional problem. The Anglo-Irish Treaty (6 December 1921) established the whole of Ireland as a dominion (the Irish Free State) but allowed Northern Ireland to opt out within a month. That right was duly exercised by the all-Unionist Parliament. But in the same month the county councils of Tyrone and Fermanagh decided by majority vote to join the Irish Free State, and Londonderry City Council also decided to do so by the casting vote of the Nationalist Mayor.

Since county option was the theoretical basis for the Government of Ireland Act, the British government might have been expected to take cognizance of these decisions, but it made no move. Seizing its opportunity, Craig's government introduced a bill abolishing STV for local elections and promising a commission to draw up fresh electoral areas under the first-past-the-post system.

This bill quickly passed through the Parliament but then met an unexpected obstacle. In 1922, in the interim between the departure of the old administration from Dublin and the enactment of the Constitution of the Irish Free State, Irish affairs came within the responsibility of the Colonial Secretary (Winston Churchill), who informed Craig that he was withholding the Royal Assent, on the ground, as Craig reported to the Cabinet, that to change the electoral system for counties was 'a matter affecting the whole of Ireland'. The Cabinet resolved to resign *en bloc* unless Churchill could be persuaded that such interference by London would create a disastrous precedent for the new legislature. Craig was later able to inform the Cabinet that Churchill had adopted 'a more reasonable attitude' (NI CAB 4/50/1 (27 July 1922)) and the Royal Assent was duly given by 12 September. Sir Dawson Bates, the Minister of Home Affairs, then pressed for a commission to devise new electoral areas, as the existing ones were 'very anomalous' (NI CAB 4/51/3 (9 Aug. 1922)). The Commissioners, with the help of Bates's department, performed their task so efficiently that, at the next set of county and borough council elections, Derry City and

Fermanagh and Tyrone County Councils went firmly Unionist, as they were to remain until 1972, and the Nationalists controlled a mere seven out of sixty-six local authorities.

The abolition of proportional representation for local elections was a clear breach of the spirit of the 1920 Act, but the Unionists succeeded. They were also successful in frustrating the activities of the Boundary Commission (whose report was suppressed in 1925) and in securing a ruling from a complaisant Speaker (1922) that matters within the jurisdiction of the Northern Ireland Parliament should not be the subject of parliamentary questions at Westminster.

IV

However, the second STV election in May 1925 provided a serious setback. By then the province was peaceful, and the Southern government quiescent. So several parties emerged to contest the election, most notably the Northern Ireland Labour party (NILP, founded in 1923), and small groups—Town Tenants, Unbought Tenants—as well as a cluster of independent Unionists also appeared. On the other side the Nationalists were clearly the dominant group. Sinn Fein, which had split after the Treaty, put up no candidates, but two 'Republicans' (including de Valera) contested the election. Devlin, the Nationalist leader, had by then realized the futility of abstentionism and promised to bring his party into the House of Commons soon after the election.

In the election the turn-out dropped to 67.6 per cent. The results were deeply disappointing to Craig. His party lost eight seats, including those of two junior ministers. The gainers were Labour (3), Unbought Tenants (1), and Independent Unionists (4). Incidentally, no government candidate headed the poll in any of the four Belfast constituencies, and in West Belfast Devlin headed the poll with a substantial lead. The eight-seat constituency of Down was uncontested, its members including Craig and de Valera. The Queen's University constituency was also uncontested (4 Unionists) (Table 12.2).

In the aftermath of the 1925 election occurred a brief interlude of voluntary consociationalism—strangely ignored by historians, except for Buckland (1981: 57–8)—during which the Nationalist

TABLE 12.2. *Election, 1925: Reversal for Unionism*

Party	% vote	Seats won	% seats	Index
Unionist	55.0	22[+10]*	55	100
Nationalist	23.8	9[+1]	22.5	94.5
Ind. Unionist	9.0	4	10	111
NILP	4.7	3	7.5	160
Republican	5.4	1[+1]	2.5	46
Independent	2.1	1	2.5	119

Notes: The index is calculated as in Table 12.1.
  * Results from two uncontested constituencies excluded.

minority appeared ready to work the new political system. Devlin persuaded all his colleagues—the last in 1927—to take their seats in the Northern Ireland House of Commons, and in his speech on the debate on the address in 1926 adopted a distinctly conciliatory tone:

We are all Ulstermen and proud to be Ulstermen [Hon. Members: Hear, Hear]. We want to further the welfare of our Province. We are all Irishmen and want to see North and South working harmoniously together. The causes that divided them have largely disappeared. We rejoice at that, because we do not believe that unity can ever spring out of conflict. (*NI HC Deb.*, 7 (9 Mar, 1926), 38)

Devlin was as good as his word. In the sessions of 1926 and 1927 his party, together with the Labour party, led by Sam Kyle, provided a constructive Opposition and the volume of debates for those years swelled to two thousand pages. Devlin's belief that politics should be about economic and social issues anticipated Gerry Fitt by some forty years. He also established a mass organization for his party, with the usual machinery of local branches, an annual conference, and an elected council. For the following election he prepared a socially progressive manifesto calling for an end to unemployment, public works, higher pensions, and slum clearance.

If ever an opportunity existed for voluntary consociationalism in Northern Ireland, it was during these years, when the Catholic representatives were working the political system and the new forces of law and order had established peace. But with a degree of myopic selfishness, which in retrospect seems incredible, the Unionist government threw away the opportunity. It was afraid that the next election might further erode its majority (of twelve seats) and even that an alternative leftist, Nationalist–Labour coalition might take its place. So in July 1927 Lord Craigavon (ennobled in that year) announced that the government would introduce a bill to abolish STV for parliamentary as for local elections. The bill duly appeared in 1929. The Government of Ireland Act allowed both Parliaments to change the electoral system after three years, but the Unionists had found it prudent to await the report of the Boundary Commission (November 1925). The government's argument in 1929 was that proportional representation served as a 'distraction' from the all-important constitutional issue. Craigavon in a speech in 1927 had frankly admitted that there was room in the province for only two parties, the corollary being that the Unionists would always be the majority party and Nationalists in permanent Opposition (*NI HC Deb.*, 8 (25 Oct. 1927), 2271–3). The entire Opposition argued that proportional representation was a safeguard for all minorities and that the government's majority was not seriously threatened. Towards the close of the debates the Labour members entreated the Home Secretary to prevent this further dilution of the 1921 settlement, but Sir William Joynson-Hicks gave them no encouragement and the bill passed into law.

The election of 1929 under the first-past-the-post system inaugurated a period of sustained Unionist hegemony which lasted until 1969. Unionist parliamentary strength went up to thirty-seven seats, while Labour was reduced to one seat and the Independent Unionists to three. The Nationalists lost just one seat, but after 1929 they appear to have lost heart. They rarely attended the Parliament and left many seats uncontested while Devlin concentrated on his Westminster role. (He died in 1934.)

Craigavon had succeeded—but at a price. As his most recent biographer has written:

His avowed aim was always to maintain Northern Ireland as a bulwark against a united Ireland, but he tried to achieve this in ways which ultimately led to the collapse of Stormont. Instead of making a sustained attempt to win over the minority by assuaging their fears and suspicions, he preferred to concentrate on maximising his party's support and sustaining Unionist control in the North. (Buckland 1980: 109–10)

A contributory factor to the failure of consociation in the 1920s was the surprising indifference of successive British governments as to the success or failure of an experiment into the construction of which they had put so much effort. Unlike the Free State, Northern Ireland remained part of the United Kingdom, and Westminster's supreme authority was proclaimed by Section 75 of the Government of Ireland Act. But this authority was never exercised in the 1920s. Instead, the Unionists had a remarkable run of good luck. They were allowed to abolish STV for local elections and to gerrymander the new electoral areas; the Boundary Commission report recommended only minor territorial changes and was suppressed at the request of the Dublin government; the Council of Ireland never met and was abolished in the Tripartite Agreement of 1925 (Belfast–Dublin–London) following the Boundary Commission. So by the end of 1925 any serious external threat to the new system had disappeared and favourable financial arrangements with Whitehall were in train. Yet it was at this very time, after a modest improvement in their representation in the Ulster Parliament, that the Nationalists made their overture which, with Unionist encouragement, might have legitimized the new regime in the eyes of the Catholic population generally, who had seen their representatives lose control of two counties, one county borough, and many smaller authorities over the previous two years.

Why did the Baldwin government not try to preserve the last remnant of the consociational settlement of 1921—the Parliament elected by STV? The answer seems to be that it had lost interest in Irish affairs. Once the Treaty and civil war were out of the way, Conservative, Labour, and Liberal politicians alike were content to let both Dublin and Belfast governments manage their own problems as best they could. Their successors of half a century later were to reap the bitter harvest of this neglect. From 1929 to 1965 inclusive the electoral pattern remained roughly the same—continuous substantial Unionist majorities and sometimes up to half the seats uncontested. But one further Stormont election deserves attention, because it shows an attempt to break out of the strait-jacket of the past.

V

In 1965 Captain Terence O'Neill became the fourth Unionist Premier. Unlike his predecessors, he saw that a polity from which one-third of the electorate was alienated was inherently unstable.

TABLE 12.3. *Election, 1969: The fragmentation of Unionism*

Party	% votes	Seats	% seats
Pro-O'Neill Unionist	46.6	22	48.9
Anti-O'Neill Unionist	15.6	11	24.4
Protestant Unionist	4.7		
NILP	8.4	2	4.4
Nationalist	8.6	5	11.1
Civil Rights	7.6	3	6.6
National Democrat	4.8	0	
Republican Labour	2.4	2	4.4
Others	1.3	0	
TOTAL	100	45	100

Unopposed: 7 (6 Unionists (5 Pro-O'Neill); (1 Nationalist)
Turn-out: 59.3%
Source: C. O'Leary, (1969: 123–36).

He deliberately tried to change the adversarial climate by cultivat-
ing good relations with the Catholic minority. The Nationalist
politicians responded; their leader assumed (for the first time) the
role of Leader of the Opposition and, like Devlin, was prepared to
play the parliamentary game. But O'Neill soon faced opposition
from two quarters—his own hardline followers, who preferred the
old confrontations, and a new movement of young Catholics
demanding specific reforms, especially concerning the local government franchise (which excluded one-third of the parliamentary
electorate), the gerrymandering of Derry, and certain repressive
statutes.[3] The autumn of 1968 was marked by marches and
counter-marches, and then a back-bench revolt threatened to
unseat O'Neill. He then played the last card available to him—a
general election campaign. During the campaign O'Neill refused to
endorse those outgoing Unionists who had opposed him, and in
every such constituency an 'independent pro-O'Neill Unionist'
stood. In some constituencies the Nationalists were opposed by
new civil rights candidates—the most prominent being John Hume.
On the eve of polling O'Neill warned the electorate that it had a
choice between voting for 'an Ulster in which all its people would
have a part to play and a desire to play it, and voting to put the
clock back' (C. O'Leary 1969: 132).

It is clear from these results that O'Neill 'nearly made it', even under the constraints of the first-past-the-post system. The losses by Nationalists and NILP are striking. When it is remembered that, of all the parties contesting the election, only the Anti-O'Neill Unionists and Protestant Unionists were opposed to the O'Neill policies, it is obvious that with lower preference votes under STV he would have secured a comfortable overall majority of seats; and his 'programme to enlist the people' would probably have been saved. Instead the hardliners managed to force O'Neill out of office. Within two months two of the dubious O'Neillites joined the anti-group and, rather than risk the ignominy of being voted out of office, O'Neill resigned.

That was the beginning of the end of the Stormont system. O'Neill's successors proved unable to prevent the unrest from deteriorating into terrorism. The IRA rapidly revived and, together with its loyalist counterparts, so destabilized the province that in March 1972 the Heath government suspended the operation of the Government of Ireland Act and replaced the Ulster Government and Parliament by a Secretary of State aided by a variable number of junior ministers, directly responsible to Westminster.

The first Secretary of State, William Whitelaw, immediately announced his intention to restore devolved government as soon as possible, and a Green Paper of October 1972 listed the conditions necessary to avoid the mistakes of the past. They recommended that any new institutions must 'seek a much wider consensus than has hitherto existed' and assure minority groups of 'an effective voice and a real interest' (HMSO 1972: 35). Five months later the government published firm proposals in a White Paper. This was quickly followed by legislation establishing one Assembly of seventy-eight members, elected by STV from constituencies returning five to eight members apiece.

This White Paper expressed the hope that the reintroduction of STV would produce an assembly that 'should reflect the wishes of the Community as accurately as possible' (HMSO 1973: 11), and that from it the Secretary of State would construct an executive that would command widespread support within the Assembly and community—the power-sharing concept. With the reintroduction of STV, existing parties fragmented and new ones appeared. The Official Unionists split into two groups—one led by Brian Faulkner (the last Stormont Premier), who pledged to support the principles

TABLE 12.4. *Assembly election, 1973*
(78 seats, all contested)

Party	% vote	Seats	% seats	Index
Official Unionist	29.3	24	30.8	105
Unpledged Unionist	8.5	8	10.3	121
Democratic Unionist	10.8	8	10.3	95
Vanguard Unionist	10.5	7	9.0	86
West Belfast Loyalist Coalition	2.3	3	3.7	160
Other Loyalists	0.5			
Alliance	9.2	8	10.3	112
NILP	2.6	1	1.3	50
SDLP	22.1	19	24.3	110
Republican Labour	0.2			
Republican Clubs	1.8			
Nationalist	1.2			
Communist	0.0			
Liberal	0.1			
Independent	0.9			
	100.0	78		

Source: Lawrence, Elliot, and Laver (1973).

of the White Paper, the other (anti-White Paper) led by Harry West. Two new Unionist parties appeared—Democratic Unionists led by Revd Ian Paisley, and Vanguard Unionists led by William Craig[4]— while the old Nationalists were faced by a rival party, the Social Democratic and Labour party (SDLP) led by Gerry Fitt (founded 1970). The Alliance party was a new middle-class, middle-of-the-road group. The 210 candidates far exceeded the maximum number for any Stormont election—eighty-eight in 1945.

The results in terms of seats were remarkably close to the first preference totals—so the British government's desire for a 'mirror-image' assembly was entirely met. Within six months the 'Whitelaw miracle'—the power-sharing executive, incorporating the Official Unionists, SDLP, and Alliance, with the tacit support of the single NILP member, was established, with Brian Faulkner as Chief Executive and Gerry Fitt as his deputy. It seemed that consensual government had arrived at last.

But appearances were deceptive. Although the coalition had a clear parliamentary majority, representing 61 per cent of the electorate, its support was religiously asymmetrical; for the 61 per cent comprised the entire Catholic representation, while the four opposition Unionist parties (Unpledged (UUP), Democratic Unionists (DUP), Vanguard Unionists (VUP), and the West Belfast Loyalist Coalition (WBLC)) commanded a majority of the Protestant voters (32.1 per cent). That was the fundamental flaw in the 1974 'power-sharing' arrangement—that it was never truly consociational. The decision of Edward Heath to call a general election in February 1974 in wich the 'Loyalist Coalition' secured over 50 per cent of the votes de-legitimized the executive just four months before the general strike organized by the Ulster Workers' Council gave it the *coup de grace*.

VI

For the past sixteen years successive British governments have tried to revive the power-sharing regime by various devices—a constitutional convention (1975–6), a second assembly (1982–6)—ending with the Brooke talks in 1991. All have failed because the present leaders of the major parties, James Molyneaux (UUP), Ian Paisley (DUP), and John Hume (SDLP) are insufficiently motivated to embrace consociationalism. Direct rule allows them the dual advantage of disclaiming any responsibility for governing the province and of blaming the British government for all the atrocities in the low-intensity civil war which has endured since 1971.

Direct rule has manifestly failed to cope with terrorism and, as a scholar has recently written, 'There are only two ways to stabilize the province: through consociation or through another partition' (B. O'Leary 1989: 588). To the present writer the latter would be no solution at all, because, however the boundary is redrawn, half the Catholics (those living in the Belfast conurbation) would be left on the wrong side. So, as British politicians of varying parties try hard to persuade the present Ulster groups to accept a new consociational formula, they might profitably reflect on the manner in which the earlier consociational experiment was frustrated, as recounted in this chapter.

Notes

1. Government of Ireland Act, 1920, Explanatory Memorandum.
2. Ibid.
3. Especially the Special Powers Act 1922, which authorized detention without trial at the fiat of the Minister of Home Affairs.
4. William Craig, the hardline Minister of Home Affairs, having been dismissed from his post by Terence O'Neill in December 1968, founded his own splinter group from the Unionist party in 1972. Its policies were similar to those of Paisley's Democratic Unionists.

References

Buckland, P. (1980), *James Craig, Lord Craigavon* (Dublin: Gill and Macmillan).

—— (1981), *A History of Northern Ireland* (Dublin: Gill and Macmillan).

Griffith, A. (1911), *Sinn Fein*, 25 Feb.

HMSO (1972), *The Future of Northern Ireland: A Paper for Discussion* (London).

HMSO (1973), *Northern Ireland Constitutional Proposals* (London: HMSO; Cmnd 5259).

Knight, J., and Baxter-Moore, N. (1972), *Northern Ireland: The Elections of the Twenties* (London: Arthur McDougall Fund).

Lawrence, R. J., Elliott, S. and Laver, M. J. (1973), *The Northern Ireland General Elections of 1973* (London: HMSO; Cmnd 5851).

Lee, J. J. (1989), *Ireland 1912–1985: Politics and Society* (Cambridge: Cambridge University Press).

Lyons, F. S. L. (1971), *Ireland since the Famine* (London: Weidenfeld and Nicolson).

O'Leary, B. (1989), 'The Limits to Coercive Consociationalism in Northern Ireland', *Political Studies*, 37. 562–88.

O'Leary, C. (1969), 'The Northern Ireland General Election of 1969', *Verfassung und Verfassung swirklichkeit* (Cologne), 123–36.

Contributors

HUGH BERRINGTON is Professor of Politics at the University of New-castle upon Tyne and a one-time party activist. He has written numerous books and articles on political parties and Parliament. He is at present writing a book for Oxford University Press on the British party system.

VERNON BOGDANOR is Reader in Government, Oxford University, and Fellow of Brasenose College. His books include *Devolution* (1979), *The People and the Party System* (1981), *Multi-Party Politics and the Constitution* (1983). Over the last few years he has helped David Butler conduct the Oxford Seminar on British Politics, at which politicians contrast the textbook picture of British politics with the reality, and has co-edited books with David.

JOHN CURTICE is Senior Lecturer in Politics at the University of Strathclyde, having previously been both a Student and a Research Fellow at Nuffield College, Oxford. He has been co-director of the British Election Study since 1983 and is co-author with Anthony Heath and others of *How Britain Votes* (1985) and *Understanding Political Change* (1991). He has also been co-author with Michael Steed of the statistical appendices to the Nuffield election studies since 1979.

DENNIS KAVANAGH has been Professor of Politics at Nottingham University since 1982. He has taught at the University of Manchester, Stanford, and the University of California, San Diego, and Florence. He is the author of numerous books, including (with David Butler) all Nuffield general election studies since 1974, *Thatcherism and British Politics,* and *Politics and Personalities.*

ANTHONY KING has been Professor of Government at Essex University since 1969. He wrote the 1964 and 1966 Nuffield election studies with David Butler and is now preparing a book-length study of the British prime ministership.

AREND LIJPHART is Professor of Political Science at the University of California, San Diego. He has also taught at the University of Leiden and at the University of California, Berkeley. He has published *Democracy in Plural Societies* (Yale University Press, 1977), *Democracies* (Yale University Press, 1984), *Power-Sharing in South Africa* (Institute of International Studies, Berkeley, 1985), *Parliamentary versus Presidential Government* (Oxford University Press, 1992), and other books and articles.

IAN MCALLISTER is Professor of Politics at the University of New South Wales, Duntroon. He has made contributions on voting behaviour to *American Political Science Review, American Sociological Review, British Journal of Political Science*, etc. He is co-author of four books with Richard Rose, most recently, *Loyalties of Voters*, and editor of *Australian Journal of Political Science*.

DAVID MCKIE is an assistant editor and leader-writer for the *Guardian*. He was formerly a political reporter and parliamentary columnist.

CORNELIUS O'LEARY has been Professor of Political Science at the Queen's University of Belfast since 1979. He is author of several books on British and Irish Politics, most recently *The Northern Ireland Assembly, 1982–86* (with S. Elliott and R. A. Wilford). He was David Butler's first D. Phil. student at Nuffield College.

AUSTIN RANNEY is Emeritus Professor of Political Science at the University of California, Berkeley, and a former President of the American Political Science Association. He has collaborated with David Butler in co-editing two books, *Referendums: A Study in Practice and Theory* (1978) and *Democracy at the Polls* (1981), and they are currently co-editing a third volume on the changing techniques and impact of electioneering practices in modern large democracies, to be published by the Oxford University Press in 1992.

RICHARD ROSE is Director of the Centre for the Study of Public Policy, University of Strathclyde. He has been visiting Professor at Wissenschaftszentrum, Berlin, European University Institute, and Stanford University and Visiting Fellow at American Enterprise Institute, Brookings Institution, and International Monetary Fund, Washington DC. He is author or editor of more than three dozen books on comparative politics and public policy, including *Do Parties Make a Difference?, The Problem of Party Government, Electoral Behaviour*, and *The International Almanac of Electoral History*. He is editor of *Journal of Public Policy*, and co-author with David Butler of *The British General Election of 1959*.

COLIN SEYMOUR-URE is Professor of Government at the University of Kent at Canterbury. His many books on the press and politics include *The Political Impact of the Mass Media, The American President: Power and Communications*, and *The British Press and Broadcasting since 1945*, and he has regularly contributed chapters on the press in the Nuffield election studies.

DONALD STOKES is University Professor of Politics and Public Affairs and Dean of the Woodrow Wilson School of Princeton University. He is author or co-author of various works on voting behaviour and represent-ative government in the English-speaking world, including (with David Butler) *Political Change in Britain*. His current research is on the politics of science policy.

Index